The Politics of the
British Cameroons Plebiscites

SPEARS STUDIES IN AFRICAN AND AFRICAN DIASPORA HISTORY

Editors

Womai I. Song, *History & African & African American Studies, Earlham College, Indiana*

Walter Nkwi, *History, Leiden University*

Editorial Board

George Njung, *History, Baylor University*

Bridget Teboh, *History, UMass Dartmouth*

Francis Dube, *History, Morgan State University*

George Kintiba, *History, University of Maryland, College Park*

The series is interested in a variety of titles that range from single monographs to edited volumes insofar as they engage with issues of African history and the diaspora. Area specializations that may be considered by the board include but are not limited to economic, political and social history. It is particularly interested in historical accounts that focus on changes in daily life, including music, dance, marriage, architecture, family life, fashion, and technology, to reveal patterns of continuity and change in the African experience. It aims to shed light on the often-neglected ordinary people who are pivotal to understanding transformative moments in the history of continental and diasporan Africans.

1. *Basel Mission Education in Cameroon: 1886-1968* by Mathew B. Gwanfogbe
2. *In Search of Harmony: A History of Bali Nyonga* by Fondi Ndifontah Nyamndi
3. *The Politics of the British Cameroons Plebiscites: Expectations, Calculations and Strategies* by Fondi Ndifontah Nyamndi

The Politics of the British Cameroons Plebiscites

Expectations, Calculations and Strategies

Fondi Ndifontah Nyamndi

SPEARS BOOKS

Denver, Colorado

SPEARS BOOKS
AN IMPRINT OF SPEARS MEDIA PRESS LLC
7830 W. Alameda Ave, Suite 103-247
Denver, CO 80226
United States of America

First Published in the United States of America in 2025 by Spears Books
www.spearsbooks.org
info@spearsmedia.com
Information on this title: www.spearsbooks.org/
the-politics-of-the-british-cameroons-plebiscites

Library of Congress Control Number: 2025934136
ISBN: 9781957296494 (Paperback)
ISBN: 9781957296500 (eBook)

Spears Media Press has no responsibility for the persistence or accuracy of urls for external or third-party internet websites referred to in this publication, and does not guarantee that any content on such websites is, or will remain, accurate or appropriate.

Designed and typeset by Spears Media Press LLC
Cover design: D. Kambem

Distributed globally by African Books Collective (ABC)
www.africanbookscollective.com

Contents

ILLUSTRATIONS

TABLES

Preface

During the decade of African awakening, many colonies sought the right to become masters of their destinies. The negotiations with colonial masters were painstaking and sometimes acrimonious, but all ended in the attainment of independence as well as an understanding on the nature of their post-independence relations.

When it came to the Trust Territories, the negotiations were multilateral rather than bilateral, given that the Territories were under the collective tutelage of the United Nations, with the Administering Authorities acting as mere surrogates. In that multilateral setting, however, the Trust Territories were not active participants, since they were not members of the United Nations where the negotiations took place.

Such was the fate of the British Cameroons. As that fate unraveled, the United Nations took two decisions that would shape the history of the Territory: Firstly, that the British Cameroons was not economically viable to be completely independent and that its independence should be perceived in terms of union with one of its neighbors. The size of the Territory thus became a determinant of its future. Secondly, the United Nations decided to organize plebiscites in the Territory in 1959 and 1961 to enable the people to choose which neighbor they would join upon becoming independent. Each plebiscite was a game of options, entailing calculated choices by those involved. The organization and conduct of the plebiscites were subject to conflicting interests and influences in the Territory and within the international community.

Those plebiscites marked a turning point in the lives of the people of the British Cameroons. Yet their story was never adequately told. Aspects of it have been erased, blurred or distorted. But as Ahmadou Ahidjo once said, "No one has the right to erase the history of a people, for a people without history are a people without a soul." This is a history of the British Cameroons, with emphasis on what transpired between 1959 and 1961. How? And with what consequences?

Now in a revised form, it was first presented as a PhD thesis in the International Relations Department of the London School of Economics and Political Science. I am grateful to Professor James Mayall for supervising the initial project, to Professors Lovet Elango, Verkijika Fanso and George Nyamndi for editing the revised script, and to my wife, Nashua, and our children, whose devoted support made the rigors of research and writing somewhat bearable.

FNN
Yaounde, 2025

Abbreviations

AG	Action Group
CAMDEV	Cameroons Development Corporation
CDC	Colonial/Commonwealth Development Corporation
CNF	Cameroons National Federation
CPNC	Cameroon Peoples National Convention
CYL	Cameroons Youth League
EEC	European Economic Community
ICJ	International Court of Justice
KNC	Kamerun National Congress
KNDP	Kamerun National Democratic Party
KPP	Kamerun Peoples Party
KSC	Kamerun Socialist Congress
KUNC	Kamerun United National Congress
NCNC	National Council of Nigeria and the Cameroons
NEPU	Northern Elements Progressive Union
NKDP	Northern Kamerun Democratic Party
NPC	Northern Peoples Congress
OAU	Organization of African Unity
UC	Union Camerounaise
UK	United Kingdom
UMBC	United Middle-Belt Congress
UN	United Nations
UPC	Union des Populations du Cameroun

Introduction

The fate of the West African Territory of the British Cameroons was the subject of vigorous debates at the United Nations between 1959 and 1961, in culmination of a process of claim and counterclaim of the Territory that had begun with the colonial era itself.

That fate raised pertinent questions of nationalism, self-determination, decolonization and independence. As part of a former German protectorate, the British Cameroons was one of the territories over which the international regimes of mandate and trusteeship applied. It thus became an international dependency in which decolonization or, more appropriately, the termination of trusteeship, was not the responsibility of a single colonial power but of the international community.

Unlike most other Trust Territories, the British Cameroons was a very small territory indeed, only a narrow strip of land in fact, with a total area of less than 35,000 square miles and a population of less than two million in 1960. This smallness, which was one of its distinguishing characteristics, was to have a dual impact on the Territory. On the one hand, it greatly increased international interest in its affairs, as the world community was constantly on the lookout that no one should take undue advantage of so small a colonial state. On the other hand, the smallness of the British Cameroons led to its being very closely linked with its two neighbors, the French-administered Trust Territory of Cameroun,[1] with which it had formed the German protectorate of Kamerun before the First World War, and the British protectorate of Nigeria with which it was in administrative union after that War. From its very origins, therefore, the British Cameroons never existed as a political entity by itself, and its fate was seldom considered without association with the fate of its larger neighbors. So it came as no surprise that the UN debate on its future

---

1   Some people called it the "French Cameroons." But we shall stick to the French appellation "Cameroun."

1

coincided with the attainment of independence by these two neighbors.

As that future unfolded, the UN, without consulting the people concerned, decided that the prosperity of the Territory lay in union with one of its neighbors. And the international body selected the plebiscite -- at which the inhabitants of the Territory were asked to state their preference between Nigeria and Cameroun -- as the framework for determining that future. Three plebiscites were held for that purpose, an inconclusive exercise in the northern part of the Territory in 1959 and one final ballot in the northern and southern parts in 1961.

The results of the 1961 plebiscites caused a major row within the UN. Some Members accused others of corrupting portions of the exercise and called for the cancellation of the corrupt parts. So bitter was the disagreement that some States refused to take further part in the debate, while some later referred the matter to the International Court of Justice.

Those developments raised a number of questions about the British Cameroons: were the plebiscites an appropriate means of determining the wishes of the people with regard to their future? Why would they be corrupted? What were the stakes involved? What were the views and preferences of Member States of the UN on the matter? How were those views and preferences advanced? With what consequences on the territory, its neighbors, the African continent, and the world at large?

These are some of the questions that inform this study. We are not concerned with passing value judgments on the choices made by the States involved and the people of the Territory, but in identifying the underlying motivations of those choices and analyzing their impact on those affected.

The question of the British Cameroons was partly a theoretical question: a question of trusteeship, of decolonization and of sovereignty.

In the long history of mankind, few issues have engendered greater emotional reaction than colonialism. Initially regarded as an indispensable framework for a so-called "manifest destiny" towards "uncivilized" peoples, colonialism later came to be denounced as an indefensible form of exploitation by "civilized" peoples. Either way, it has been at the center of world history for centuries. The notion was frequently re-defined to suit the needs and moods of the ages. Hence colony, protectorate, dependency, territory, dominion, overseas province, *et cetera,* have all been used to describe a situation whereby a people are placed, or place themselves, under the tutelage of a foreign country.

With the coming of international organizations after the First World War, a new form appeared, which saw some colonies placed under international supervision. This new form of colonial administration also undertook a process of redefinition, from conventional zones through mandates to trusteeships. It became fashionable when, upon realizing that colonies were a source of added strength, the victorious Powers decided to further weaken the vanquished nations by seizing all their colonies, the ensuing booty being shared mainly between Britain and France and administered under the League of Nations as mandated territories. The League insisted that tutelage over such peoples constituted a temporary trust, held by the Administering Powers in the name of humanity.

However, there were no specific criteria for the distribution of mandates between Britain and France. Some territories, like Togoland and Kamerun, were partitioned between them, sowing the seeds of later controversies.

The United Nations Organization [UN], which replaced the League of Nations after the Second World War, also replaced the mandate system with the trusteeship system, for the administration and supervision of "such Territories as may be placed thereunder by subsequent individual agreements."[2] The individual Trusteeship Agreements constituted the legal basis of the Trusteeship System. Those agreements designated the Administering Authorities and established the general principles governing the administration of the Trust Territories. The Territories included those then held under mandate, those that might be detached from enemy States as a result of the Second World War, and all others voluntarily placed under the system by the administering country.

That appeal did not incite colonial powers to volunteer their colonies for trusteeship, nor were Territories then held under mandate automatically placed under trusteeship. The transition from mandate to trusteeship, far from being a legal obligation, was seen as a political discretion on the part of the Administering Powers. A long-standing victim of that discretion was Namibia which the Union of South Africa refused

2   *Charter of the United Nations*, Article 75.

to place under trusteeship, thereby creating one of the most complicated colonial problems in history.

The Trusteeship Council exercised responsibility for the trusteeship functions of the United Nations on behalf of the General Assembly. Unlike the League Mandates Commission, which had been composed of independent experts, the Trusteeship Council consisted of representatives of Member States drawn from three categories: the Administering Authorities, the other members of the Security Council, and other members of the General Assembly elected to ensure a balance between Administering and non-Administering Members. The Council carried out the basic functions of Trusteeship, namely, to consider the annual reports of the Administering Authorities, examine petitions on the Trust Territories, and organize periodic visits to those Territories.

The importance of those functions depended on the nature and location of the Trust Territories. They played an increasing role in the political relations of States by dint of the power, strategic position and control over resources that they conferred upon the Administering Authorities. It was thus of consequence to the UN, and more particularly to the great powers, what the Administering Authorities did with the Territories under their control. No wonder, many an eyebrow was raised by the practice of administrative union of Trust Territories with the adjacent colonies of the Administering Authorities. As a matter of fact, the question of administrative union, its operation and termination, was one of the root causes of the British Cameroons controversy.

Whatever guarantees that the General Assembly sought from the Administering Authorities, the termination of trusteeship, as indeed the termination of other forms of colonization, was always going to be a thorny problem. Colonial powers were generally edgy over the seemingly interminable debates on decolonization. Those debates, fanned by the communist countries who saw the colonies as the Achilles' heel of their capitalist adversaries, were usually very acrimonious. They often forced the colonial powers into defensive corners, and their attitudes, apologetic and defiant by turns, gave the debates even sharper relief. Sir Winston Churchill foretold the latter stance when he vowed at the Yalta Conference never to consent to "the fumbling fingers of forty or fifty nations prying into the life's existence of the British Empire."[3]

Churchill's determination, notwithstanding, the feeling eventually gained ground, even among the colonial powers, that once a certain stage of development was attained, colonial peoples would no longer accept colonial government, however good, as a substitute for self-government. In short, decolonization was inevitable.

It was effected in one of two ways: by the attainment of independence or by union with an already independent country. With the first alternative, sovereignty was either painstakingly negotiated and transferred in an orderly manner, or it was unilaterally seized in rebellion. Whichever way, it was assumed that the newly independent country would constitute a viable unit in the world of nations.

Relative size and location, population and economic resources, became the criteria of sovereignty. Weakness in any of those areas enhanced the option of sovereignty by union with another country.

Those requirements were also true of trusteeship, which was understood to be temporary and to cease whenever its purposes had been attained. The UN seemed particularly concerned with the future of small Trust Territories, a lot more so than it was with the fate of larger ones. It was in relation to such Territories that the level of economic viability, as a prerequisite for independence, gained currency.

But the UN did not apply the same standards to ordinary colonies, otherwise many would not have gained independence in their current form; and it did not venture to unite small colonies with other countries. As a matter of fact, the British Cameroons was bigger than many countries in West Africa. Indications are that the requirement of economic viability was peculiar to the Trust Territories, and to the British Cameroons in particular. The British who pushed the idea did not apply it to their colonies: they granted independence to Gambia, which was so much smaller than the British Cameroons, without seeking to unite it with neighboring Senegal.

The future of the small Trust Territories, although based on material considerations, was generally thought to require popular approval. Thus,

3   Cf. Sir Alan Burns. *In Defence of Colonies,* (London: Allen and Unwin, 1957) p. 102.

unlike in ordinary colonies or large Trust Territories where independence was discussed mainly between the colonial power and the elected or delegated leaders of the Territory, the UN took the added precaution in small Trust Territories to consult the people on their future. The mechanism chosen for that sort of consultation was the plebiscite.

The notion of the plebiscite has its roots in ancient Rome when the word *plebiscitum,* from which it is derived, entered political vocabulary as representing a resolution with the force of law adopted by an assembly of plebeians.

Its meaning evolved with time. In the 18th and 19th centuries, it became the device through which conquerors ratified their conquests by giving them a semblance of popular approval. Recently, it has departed from such cynical use to become an electoral concept approved and promoted by the United Nations as a democratic process through which to determine the future of a people in doubt. It is commonly used to determine the wishes of a population caught in a situation where different groups or regions are pulling in different directions. Plebiscites typically occur in times and places of discord and among peoples without a long tradition of competitive politics, which would have enabled them to sharpen their positions about their own future. Such was the case with the plebiscites of Schleswig in 1920, the Saar in 1935, British Togoland in 1956, and the British Cameroons in 1959 and 1961. In each of those cases the future of the Territory in question was thought to lie with one of its neighbors, so an internationally supervised plebiscite was organized to enable the people decide which neighbor that would be.

As an electoral mechanism, the plebiscite has been criticized as untrustworthy because a vote on a single issue, taken hurriedly without free and full discussion may not represent the true feelings of the people. For political unions, it contains a further shortcoming in that the people with whom the union is sought do not also express themselves on the question; and without mutual consent, the exercise might lead to an unsolicited union. Still, its essential validity as a democratic process remains beyond doubt.

CHAPTER ONE

Creation and Development of the British Cameroons

The British Cameroons question was not merely a theoretical question; it was also a historical question, which grew out of developments and circumstances peculiar to the Territory, its nature, and its environment. It ripened with time, bearing at all stages the imprint of the men who made it.

The Idea of the British Cameroons

The nineteenth-century "scramble for Africa" brought waves of Europeans to the continent. They came as traders and explorers, and ended up claiming colonies and protectorates for their governments, some many times the size of their home countries.

The Germans were late to the party, but still helped themselves to hefty chunks of the pickings. On 12 July 1884, two German trading firms Woermann, and Jantzen and Thormaelen, signed a treaty of protection with Kings Bell and Akwa of the coastal town of Douala in present-day Cameroon. The Douala area was declared a German protectorate on 17 August 1884 by the explorer Gustav Nachtigal, acting on behalf of the German government, who had instructed him to conclude treaties with native rulers in order to acquire sovereign rights over the territory. He signed treaties with the Kings of Douala, Bimbia and Batanga, which became the legal basis for German claims. From Douala the Germans extended their control inland, sometimes peacefully but often forcefully, establishing themselves over the vast area in-between the British protectorates of Nigeria and French possessions in Equatorial Africa. The German Kamerun, as the protectorate was called from 1901, covered an area of 495,000 square kilometres, with Buea and then Yaounde as its capital. That area was significantly enlarged on 4 November 1911 when France ceded part of French Equatorial Africa to Germany in exchange for German recognition of a French protectorate in Morocco, as part of the resolution of the Agadir crisis. The additional area, which the Germans called "Neukamerun", increased the size of the protectorate to 790,000 square kilometres. In the settlement, Germany also ceded to France the eastern flank of the Logone River in northern Kamerun, in an area known as the "Bec de canard."

The German Kamerun was one of the casualties of the First World War. As the War progressed, Germany was attacked both in Europe and in her overseas possessions. In Kamerun, the German resistance began to crumble when a joint Anglo-French expeditionary force led by Major General Dobell captured the town of Douala in 1916. The conquest of Kamerun was surprisingly easy, with minimum involvement of the population. The protectorate had not developed a personality or acquired a political culture with which the people could identify. No sense of belonging to it had emerged, especially in the hinterland where it had mostly been imposed by force.[1] The Germans were associated with the brutality of those early encounters, which made it easy for the population to embrace the newcomers during the War. In the end, the conquest of Kamerun was not resisted by the indigenes. Neither was the eventual partition of the territory.

The fall of Douala necessitated an interim administration over the liberated areas while the war effort was being pursued in the hinterland. And on the proposal of the British Foreign Office, the French government accepted that the administration of those areas be placed in the hands of General Dobell and his staff, subject to reinforcement in personnel from neighboring British and French colonial authorities.[2] General Dobell was given full latitude to manage the affairs of the region, ensuring that there was no conflict of interest between the two Powers.

1   In later years, there developed in hindsight a mythical attachment to the German Kamerun that had not existed while it lasted. The protectorate had been resisted by many indigenes who did not identify with the brutal methods used to establish it.
2   Message from the Secretary of State for the Colonies to General Dobell, London, September 21, 1915. Cf. Adamou Ndam Njoya, *Le Cameroun dans les Relations Internationales* (Paris: Librairie Générale de Droit et de Jurisprudence, 1976) p. 85.

But the French soon accused the General of favoring his compatriots in the administration of the occupied territory. To restore equity, they proposed a "carefully balanced" Franco-British condominium over the Territory until the conclusion of peace.[3]

The British rejected the idea of a condominium, arguing that it would distract from the war effort, and create unnecessary friction between the two countries.[4] They were instead of the opinion that the Allied Governments should work towards an equitable division of administrative spheres, to be brought into force as soon as the Germans capitulated.[5] The British Secretary of State for the Colonies, Sir Edward Grey, felt that the interest of both parties would be better served by an agreement for the provisional division of the protectorate into two administrative spheres under their respective Governments.[6] And so was born the idea of the partition of Kamerun— a British counter-proposal to the condominium advocated by France. Prior to the partition, however, France recuperated all the areas of the "Neukamerun" that she had ceded to Germany in 1911 and incorporated them back into French Equatorial Africa where they later formed parts of Chad, Central African Republic, Congo and Gabon. She took back what she had given to Germany in 1911, without giving back what she had received in the same settlement.

The French welcomed the idea of partitioning what was left of the German Kamerun, insisting that their administrative sphere must include Douala, the chief port of the Territory. In discussions at the British Foreign Office on February 24, 1916, the French delegate, Georges Picot, made it clear that as the only outlet for French Equatorial Africa, his government was adamant on the issue of Douala. He produced a map showing that the whole of Kamerun was desired by France, with the exception of a tiny strip of land along the eastern border of Nigeria, south of Yola,[7] and called for the British response to the offer. The notion of balance and equity that had underpinned the proposal for a condominium vanished when it came to actual negotiations.

---

3   British Foreign Office Records, F.0./7086.Sec., 6 February 1915.

4   F.0./3577, 22 January 1916.

5   F.0./9886, 13 March 1915.

6   F.0./7533, 16 February 1916.

7   British Colonial Office Records, Letter No. 35941/16 of 24 February 1916.

After consultations with the War Committee, the British Government surprised even the French by accepting the proposals, demanding only that the northwestern tip of Kamerun, which constituted part of the Borno empire of Nigeria, should be included in the British sector.[8] Concerning Douala, the British accepted the French proposal on condition that their merchant vessels and warships would continue to use the port during the war.[9] At any rate, the lines shown on the French map were regarded as only roughly indicating the actual division, liable to modifications needed to avoid the partition of villages, tribal lands and plantations.[10]

The deal was concluded on March 3, 1916,[11] marking the formal partition of the German Kamerun. It was said to be provisional, pending a definite settlement at the end of the war. But the arrangements of 1916 had all the trappings of permanency. The partition was formalized by the Franco-British Declaration of July 10, 1919, signed in London by the British Secretary of State for the Colonies, Viscount Milner, and the French Minister for the Colonies, Henry Simon, putting an official seal to the partition, and describing in outline the frontier between both spheres. That frontier was still rather fluid, linking with vague and often confusing lines the few prominent natural features available. The Declaration left the delicate task of actual demarcation to expert boundary commissioners from both sides. A period of six months was allowed after the exercise for any persons who wished to migrate across the frontier to join portions of their families or lands.[12]

The British-administered sector was called the British Cameroons. It consisted of two mountainous strips of land to the east of Nigeria -- the eastern part of the Borno Caliphate and the southern area originally offered by the French. Geographically, it was divided into two sections by a protrusion of Nigerian territory for some 45 miles around the river Benue. It was 700 miles long and on the average about 65 miles wide, with a total area of 34,081 square miles. By comparison with the French-administered eastern sector, the British Cameroons was one-sixth of the

8   F.O./9154/16 of 26 February 1916.
9   Colonial Office Records, C.O. No. 39073/16 of 24 February 1916.
10   F.O./9154/16 of 26 February 1916.
11   C.O. No. W.39493/16 of 4 March 1916.
12   Franco-British Declaration on the Cameroons, Art. 2.

area of the defunct Kamerun, with one quarter of its population.

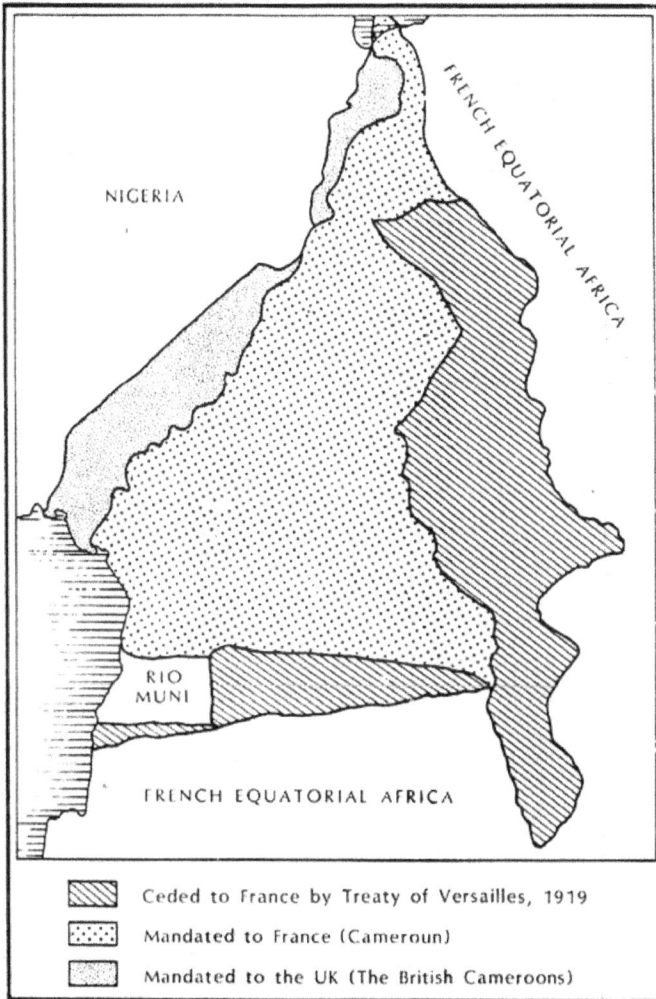

Figure 1.1. Breakup of the German Kamerun and the birth of the British Cameroons

It is curious that the British accepted such a small share of the "booty", after commanding the campaign and administering the liberated areas prior to the partition. But the Secretary of State for the Colonies pointed out that the British approach to the partition was based on considerations affecting global British relations with the French rather than as recompense for the respective parts played in the conquest of Kamerun.[13] From its very origins, therefore, the British Cameroons was both a product and a tool of international relations, a quality that would be significant throughout its history.

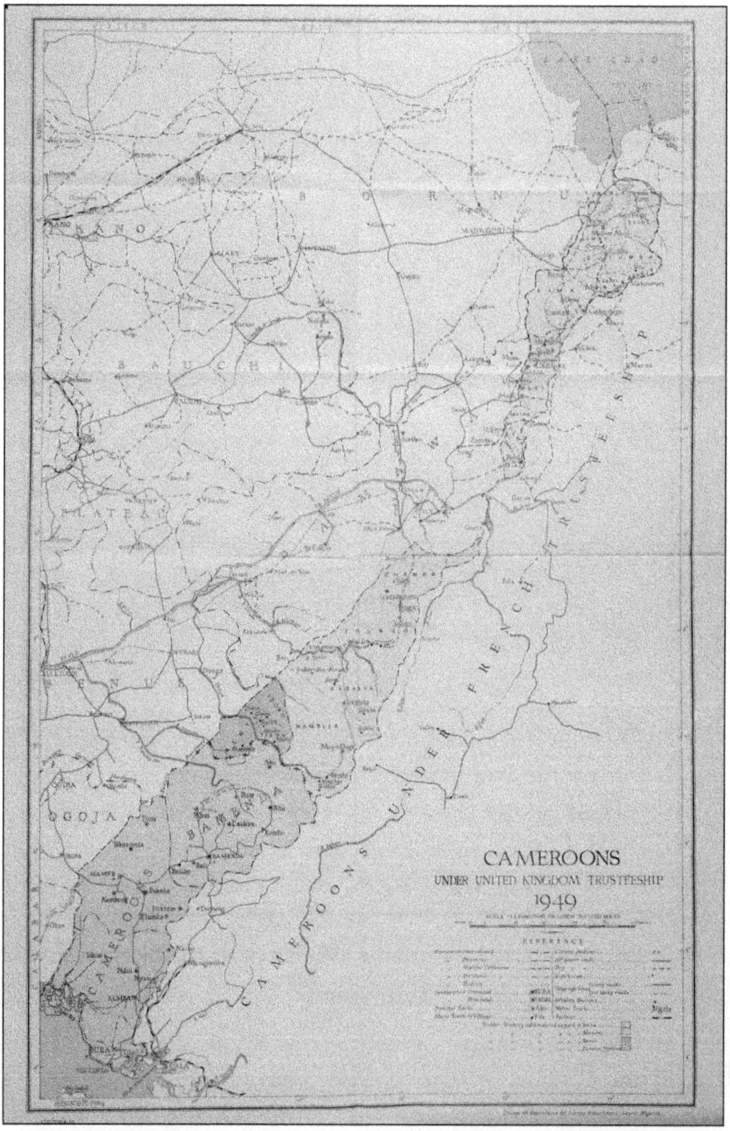

Figure 1.2. Cameroons under UK Administration

13   Telegram to the Governor-General of Nigeria, in F.0./9999/16 of 1 March 1916.

International Status of the British Cameroons

By Article 119 of the Treaty of Versailles signed on June 28, 1919, Germany renounced all her rights over her overseas possessions in favor of the Principal Allied and Associated Powers. The Supreme Council of the Allied Powers, meeting on May 7, 1919, had fixed the general conditions under which the administration of the former German colonies would be carried out, and divided to Great Britain and France, League of Nations mandates over former German colonies in the Pacific, Asia and Africa –with the exception of Togoland and Kamerun.

For those two, the Council decided that the British and French Governments should agree among themselves as to the partition of the territories and the administrative regime to be applied thereto,[14] and submit to the Supreme Council for approval a joint recommendation on the dispositions upon which they would have reached agreement.

The two Governments reached agreement on the partition, as sanctioned by the Franco-British Declaration of July 10, 1919. They also agreed that the spheres under their control could usefully be brought into customs, fiscal and administrative union with their neighboring possessions.[15] But they disagreed on the definite status of the partitioned territories.

The British held that the arrangements of 1919 were strictly temporary and had to be replaced by a permanent settlement under the League of Nations. They suggested that the Cameroons and Togoland should be placed under class "B" mandates, identical to that adopted for East Africa.[16]

The French disagreed, arguing that the decision of the Supreme Council to omit both territories from its list of mandates while calling for a joint recommendation by the Governments of Britain and France meant that.

> *dans l'esprit et dans la lettre, le Togo et le Cameroun doivent*
> *être considérés non pas comme des pays à mandat, mais comme*
> *des colonies françaises et anglaises, sous réserve de la " joint*

14   F.O./173606/W/18 of 2 February 1920.
15   French Embassy Note to the Foreign Office, 3 November 1919; enclosed in ibid.
16   Foreign Office Memorandum of 23 January 1920; enclosed in F.O./173606/ W18 of 2 February 1920.

recommendation" qui a été prévue.[17]

That position made the liberation of the German Kamerun look like a simple annexation. But the French were not ruffled by that: *La Dépêche Coloniale* of 17 July, 1919, affirmed that *"Le Cameroun sera une précieuse annexe de notre Congo français."*

The French position was out of tune with the spirit of the League of Nations to hold the former German colonies as a "sacred trust of civilization." Immense pressure was brought to bear on France by the other Allied Powers and eventually the Paris Government reluctantly accepted the idea of a mandate for Togoland and the Cameroons. As its Ambassador in London, Paul Cambon, pointed out, *"le Gouvernement français estime qu'il fait à la Puissance alliée et amie* [Great Britain] *une concession considérable en se ralliant à l'idée du mandat."*[18]

That was enough to enable the signing of a joint Anglo-French recommendation to the Council of the League of Nations, suggesting that in accordance with Article 22 of the Covenant, mandates to administer the Cameroons and Togoland be granted to them.

The document conferring a mandate upon the British Monarch to administer the British Cameroons was signed in London on July 20, 1922. Formulated by the British Government, it endorsed the partition of 1919, allowing for slight boundary modifications by mutual agreement with the French in order to correct any inaccuracies on the original map or satisfy local needs.

The administrative obligations of Britain in the British Cameroons were few and vague. Britain assumed responsibility for the "peace, order and good government" of the Territory as well as the promotion of the material and moral well-being and social progress of its inhabitants.[19]

17   French Government Memorandum of 8 July 1920; enclosed in F.O./C.2368/154/18 of 11 August 1920. Translated as follows: "in the spirit as in the letter, Togo and Cameroun should be regarded not as mandated territories but as French and British colonies, subject to the 'Joint Declaration' provided for."

18   Letter to the Foreign Office, 20 November 1920: enclosed in F.O./C.12031/154/18 of 25 November 1920. Translated as follows: *"the French government considers that it is making a considerable concession to the Allied and friendly Power by coming round to the idea of the mandate."*

19   Mandate Document. Art. 2.

Even though the Cameroons had been won in war, Britain assumed no military responsibility in the British Cameroons: the mandate Instrument, loyal to the spirit of the times, strictly prohibited the establishment of military bases in the Territory. The Instrument was more anxious to amend humanitarian deficiencies there. Britain undertook to suppress slavery and abolish forced labor, which the Allies claimed had been rampant in German colonies. She further undertook to make an annual report to the Council on the administration of the mandate and seek its consent for any modification of the Instrument.

After roughly thirty years as part of the German Kamerun and following a general war in which Germany was branded as the atrocious villain, the British Cameroons was born into the "orphanage" of the League of Nations, with the United Kingdom as foster parent.

The history of the British Cameroons as a political unit begins with the Franco-British Declaration of 1919. The first three years of that history were somewhat uncertain. But with the League of Nations, and upon further agreement between Britain and France, the British Cameroons emerged from its temporary state as an occupied war zone into a more permanent status as a mandated Territory. That international involvement would become a key factor in the Territory's development. From the beginning, the British Cameroons showed two distinct international characteristics. Firstly, the fate of the Territory was generally decided outside it, by foreigners, and sometimes for motives far from the well-being of its inhabitants. Secondly, that fate became closely linked with the destiny of the international system.

The post-war international system seemed doomed from the start. It had so many loopholes that it was easily the victim of its own intrinsic weaknesses.[20] Its failure was epitomized by its inability to prevent another war. For, however much the First World War was regretted, and whatever frantic efforts were made to avert another major war, the Second World War broke out still, witnessing devastation on a scale never seen before. One of its very first casualties was the international system of the day.

As the dust of the War settled, a new system emerged with much the

---

20   F. S. Northedge and M. J. Grieve, *A Hundred Years of International Relations* (London: Duckworth, 1971) pp. 161-163.

same goals as its predecessor, but with a wider membership and more complex structures. The headquarters of that new system moved from the Old World to the New [from Geneva to New York], indicating that its epicenter was different.

The United Nations Organization, around which the new system was built, inherited most of the responsibilities of the defunct League of Nations. Among these was supervision of the administration of the mandated territories. It was for that responsibility that the United Nations created the Trusteeship System, under which Administering Authorities voluntarily placed their mandated territories.

As had been the case with the establishment of the British Cameroons mandate, its transformation into trusteeship was the subject of discussions between France and Britain. At a meeting in London on December 18, 1945, both sides agreed to place their mandated territories in Africa under UN trusteeship.[21] The British Colonial Secretary, O.F.G. Stanley, had noted the previous year that "I do not think there can be any serious question of our not placing these Territories under trusteeship. Any other course would be unacceptable internationally."[22]

Subsequently, Britain circulated the draft Trusteeship Agreement for the Cameroons to the "states directly concerned" for their comments: France, on grounds of regional interest; Belgium, on a reciprocal basis; and the Union of South Africa, on strategic grounds.[23] The Agreement was approved by the General Assembly on December 13, 1946. It was based on the existing mandate, modified to take into account the new features of the Trusteeship System as well as improvements gained from past experience.

The supervisory role of the United Nations was greatly enhanced in the British Cameroons. The bulk of the Trusteeship Agreement was predicated upon consistency with the basic objectives of the International Trusteeship System, and the administration of the Territory had to be carried out primarily for that purpose. Britain undertook to collaborate fully with the UN in the discharge of its trusteeship functions, as well as

21　F.O./371/57131 of 1 January 1946.
22　Ibid. of 17 December 1945.
23　British Colonial Office Memorandum of 4 January 1946, Annex IV, p. 24.

to facilitate the activities of UN Visiting Missions to the Territory.[24] The review of the annual reports of the Administering Authority enabled the UN to keep an eye on the British Cameroons and ensure that the interests of the people of the Territory were adequately protected.

The participation of the peoples of the Cameroons in running their own affairs was one sensible improvement upon the practice of the Mandate System. The League of Nations had held the view that the inhabitants of the mandated territories were not "able to stand by themselves under the strenuous conditions of the modern world."[25] By contrast, the Trusteeship System felt that the opinion of the peoples of the trust territories had to be genuinely taken into account in pursuing the objectives of the system. Given the political nature of those objectives, Britain undertook to promote the development of free political institutions in the Territory and, progressively, involve its inhabitants in the administration and legislation of the Territory.[26] The Agreement also gave the people a say in framing laws relating to land and natural resources.[27]

Britain retained more power over the Cameroons than it had exercised during the mandate. It still assumed routine responsibilities for peace, order, and the good government of the Territory, but its scope widened to include defense. The British Cameroons, like any other Trust Territory had a role to play in the maintenance of international peace and security. So, Britain was entitled to establish naval, military and air bases in the Territory, erect fortifications, station and employ its own troops and, in case of need, recruit volunteer forces from the Territory.[28]

The Trusteeship Agreement strengthened Britain's hand in the economic and commercial sectors. During the mandate, the British Cameroons had been open to indiscriminate international economic activity under the guise of the "open door" policy. Britain argued that the policy had not always operated to the advantage of the mandated territories,[29]

---

24   Trusteeship Agreement for the Territory of the Cameroons under British Administration, Art. 3.
25   Covenant, Art. 22.
26   Trusteeship Agreement, Art. 6.
27   Ibid. Art.   8.
28   Ibid. Art. 4 (b) and Art. 5 (c).
29   Colonial Office Memorandum, 4 January 1946.

and sought its limitation in order to protect the economic advancement of the inhabitants of the Territory.[30] The administering authority assumed the power to limit the economic activities of other countries if it judged that those activities were detrimental to the advancement of the interests of the people of the British Cameroons.

It is superfluous to talk of the Trusteeship Agreement tightening the grip of Britain over the British Cameroons when the Territory was in a comprehensive administrative union with Nigeria.[31] The British Cameroons plebiscites were mainly about that relationship.

Administrative Union with Nigeria

The idea first appeared in 1916. On March 23 of that year, while the First World War was going on, the British Monarch signed a Commission to the Acting Governor of Nigeria, Sir Donald Charles Cameron, empowering him "to administer such parts of the Cameroons as may from time to time be occupied by British forces."[32] That was the legal precedent of the future administrative union. It arose from a contingency of war, to relieve soldiers of the burdens of administration, so that they may concentrate on the war effort. But the British King failed to specify the duration of the Commission, with the result that the makeshift arrangement crystallized into a long-term union.

By the time of the Franco-British discussions on Kamerun, the idea of bringing their eventual spheres of the territory into administrative unions with neighboring possessions was already an accepted principle on both sides. They were even of the opinion that:

> The administrative union would enable certain indigenous communities, artificially separated in the past by arbitrary frontiers, to form ethnic and political units that would facilitate their development within their natural boundaries.[33]

The League of Nations endorsed the idea by approving mandate

30   Trusteeship Agreement, Art. 10.
31   Ibid, Art. 5 (b).
32   *The Nigerian Gazette*, 24 May 1924, p. 278.
33   F.O./173606/W/18 of 2 February 1920.

agreements which provided for such unions. Article 9 of the Agreement for the British Cameroons authorized Britain to bring the Territory into administrative union with an adjacent territory under its control, an obvious reference to Nigeria. The effective union constitutionally derived from the British Cameroons Order-in-Council of June 23, 1923, which provided for various parts of the Trust Territory to be administered as parts of the Provinces of the Protectorate of Nigeria.

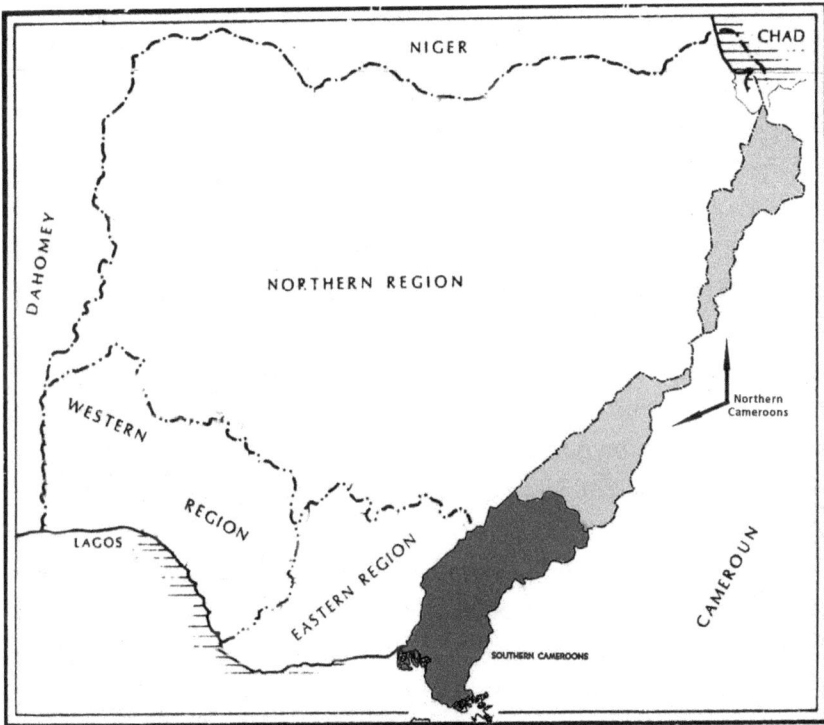

Figure 1.3. The Administrative Union with Nigeria

However, the endorsement of the League was far from enthusiastic. The new ideas on administrative union met with suspicion from countries like the USA which feared for their missionary activities and other interests in the Territories concerned.

The British Government argued that the administrative union of the British Cameroons was motivated by the fragmentary nature of the Territory, the configuration of the land and the affinities of its peoples with those of neighboring Nigeria; in addition to the fact that separate administrative, judicial and technical departments would impose an unjustifiable burden on the limited resources of the Territory.[34] Some have suggested that administrative union with Nigeria was the only way to administer the British Cameroons, given that it was not self-contained in a geographical, ethnic or economic sense.[35]

But these arguments did little to allay general suspicions of annexation. Some of those suspicions were aroused by the British themselves: the Governor of Nigeria declared that the northern part of the British Cameroons was geographically, politically and ethnologically a part of Borno;[36] David Gardinier argued that the Southern Cameroons was ethnologically part of the Eastern Region of Nigeria;[37] and Edwin Ardener concluded that the acquisition of the British Cameroons was "mainly an exercise of 'infilling' on the Nigerian border."[38]

The 1923 British Cameroons Order-in-Council was the constitutional basis of the administrative union and the legal framework for the effective administration of the Territory. It partitioned the British Cameroons into two areas, each of which had to be administered as part of the coterminous Provinces of Nigeria. Hence the Northern Cameroons designated the portion of the Territory administered as part of the Northern Provinces of Nigeria, and the Southern Cameroons referred to the portion administered as part of the Southern Provinces of Nigeria.

However, although the mandated Territory consisted of two geographically distinct strips, separated by a 45-mile gap of Nigerian territory, the partition did not follow that existing division. Instead, an arbitrary line was drawn around the middle of the southern strip of the Territory, so that the boundary between the Northern and Southern Cameroons coincided with the boundary between Northern and Southern Nigeria.

34   GAOR. 5th Session, Supplement No. 4, Annex, p. 191.
35   Tambi Eyongetah and Robert Brain, *A History of the Cameroon*, (London: Longman, 1974) p. 99.
36   C.0./657/19 of December 1920. p. 208.
37   David E. Gardinier, The British in the Cameroons, 1919-1933"; P. Gifford and W. R. Louis (eds.), *Britain and Germany in Africa: Imperial Rivalry and Colonial Rule*, (New Haven: Yale University Press, 1967) p. 51.
38   Edwin Ardener, "The Political History of the Cameroons" in *The World Today*, Col. 18, August 1962 (London: OUP, 1962), p. 343.

The partition of the British Cameroons, which would have such serious incidence on the future of the Territory, was not motivated by any geographical or economic considerations within the Territory itself, but rather for the sole purpose of fitting into the existing regional structure of Nigeria. And the authorities went to great lengths to maintain that separation. V.E. Mukete reports that the UN Visiting Mission recommended a road link between the Northern Cameroons and the Southern Cameroons, but the Premier of the Northern Region vehemently opposed the idea to discourage contact between the peoples of the two sections of the Trust Territory.[39]

Both sections of the Territory were further sub-divided into smaller units. The Southern Cameroons was divided into two Provinces - Bamenda and Cameroons Provinces respectively. The Northern Cameroons on its part was divided into three areas -- the Tigon-Ndoro-Kentu enclave, which was administered as part of the Benue Province, the middle areas physically separated by Nigerian territory but jointly administered as part of the Adamawa Province, and the Dikwa Emirate in the extreme north, which formed a Division of the Bornu Province.

In the light of those divisions, the British Cameroons did not form a single administrative sub-unit of Nigeria. Except for the ultimate responsibility of the Governor of Nigeria, who was also Governor and Commander-in-Chief of the Southern Cameroons, there was no single administrator who had responsibility for the entire Territory. The Southern Cameroons was administered by a Commissioner of the Cameroons [an office created in April 1949] who was responsible not to the Governor in Lagos but to the Lieutenant-Governor of Eastern Nigeria. As for the Northern Cameroons, there was no separate administration until 1960 when a temporary administration was improvised under Sir Percy Wyn-Harris, with the support of officers seconded from the Nigerian service. Administrative responsibility for the British Cameroons as a whole was thus divided between the Lieutenant-Governors of Northern and Eastern Nigeria, and the parts of the Cameroons administered by them formed only a tiny portion of their overall areas of jurisdiction and

39   Victor E. Mukete, *My Odyssey, The Story of Cameroon Reunification*, (Yaounde: Eagle Publishing, 2013), p. 439.

consequently took only a fraction of their attention.

Fiscally, no separate budget was prepared, and no separate accounts were kept for the British Cameroons. Government revenues from the Territory were included without distinction in the budget of Nigeria as a whole, and expenditures were allocated to it not on the basis of its particular needs but on the basis of the overall needs of the Nigerian Regions to which it was integrated.[40] So thorough was the integration that the UN Committee on Administrative Unions reported that the Nigeria-Cameroons union had the character of a political union.[41]

The texts guiding the administration of the British Cameroons evolved with time, even though the administration itself remained essentially the same. The Order-in-Council of 1923 was amended by the Cameroons under British Mandate Order of 1932 and revoked by the Nigeria [Protectorate and Cameroons] Order-in-Council No. 1352 of August 21, 1946, which in turn was amended by the Nigeria [Protectorate and Cameroons] Order-in-Council of 1949, to provide for the administration of the Territory in accordance with the Trusteeship Agreement.

The British Cameroons quickly settled into the general pattern of Nigerian administration. Political and administrative changes in the Protectorate were immediately extended to the Territory. The Macpherson Constitution of 1952, which introduced ministerial government and confirmed the development of semi-autonomous regions in Nigeria, also provided for the representation of the British Cameroons in the executive and legislative organs of the Protectorate. In the Council of Ministers, the four Ministers from the Eastern Region had to include one representing a Division of the Southern Cameroons. The Executive Council of the Eastern Region also had to include at least one member representing the Southern Cameroons. But executive representation of the Northern Cameroons was not specifically prescribed.

In the legislature, of the eighty elected seats in the Eastern House, the Southern Cameroons was allotted thirteen; and of the ninety elected seats in the Northern House, the Provinces of the Northern Region containing the Northern Cameroons were allotted a total of twenty-one. But it was

40   GAOR, 4th Session, Supplement No. 4, Annex, p. 190.
41   T/L. 96 Chapter IV. 8 para. 8.

not specified how many of the twenty-one had effectively to come from the Northern Cameroons.

The comprehensive administrative union between Nigeria and the British Cameroons compromised the UN's role of maintaining the separate identity of the Trust Territory, supervising its development and realizing the basic objectives of the International Trusteeship System. With its partition and subsequent sub-divisions, the political identity of the British Cameroons became a mere illusion, which the UN sought to preserve as part of its supervisory functions, sending five Visiting Missions to the Territory in 1949, 1952, 1955, 1958, and 1961.

The administrative union also kindled in the British Cameroons the type of political awakening that was simmering across Nigeria. Political movements were launched in the Territory, which soon began to question the operation of the administrative union and, with time, its very essence. The future of the union was at the center of the plebiscites and the political history of the British Cameroons was, by and large, the story of the reaction to the administrative union with Nigeria.

The Rise of Nationalism

Political awakening in the British Cameroons began in the 1940s. It grew out of the regular meetings of a small group of students and workers in Lagos. Its first crystallization was the Cameroons Youth League [CYL],[42] founded in Lagos in March 1940 by Dr. E.M.L. Endeley and P. M. Kale, with the aim of representing the Southern Cameroons educationally, economically, politically, and socially.[43] Endeley proudly described it as the "genesis of Cameroons politics."[44]

The League was soon overshadowed by the National Council of Nigeria and the Cameroons [NCNC], the first veritable political party in Nigeria, formed by Hebert Macaulay and Nnamdi Azikiwe in August 1944. Initially, the elite of the Southern Cameroons identified with the NCNC, whose goals to extend democratic principles to all the peoples of Nigeria and the Cameroons, and to impart political education and

42   P. M. Kale, *Political Evolution in the Cameroons,* (Buea: Government Printer, 1967), p. 50.
43   Ibid.
44   NCNC Constitution, Lagos. September 1944, p. 1.

secure political freedom,[45] appealed to them. Some actively participated in the creation of the new party: P. M. Kale was one of the authors of its constitution and was a member of the NCNC delegation that visited London to seek repeal of the unpopular Richards Constitution.

But the intrigues of the NCNC leadership gradually created a feeling of anxiety among the Cameroonians, who felt threatened by the numerical strength and political guile of the Nigerians. They began to fall back on themselves, invoking the international status of their Territory to differentiate themselves from Nigeria. That language of differentiation would characterize the next wave of the British Cameroons political movements.

Prominent among them was the Cameroons National Federation [CNF], formed by Endeley in 1949 to fill the vacuum created by the disappearance of the CYL. The objectives of the Party indicated the new direction of Southern Cameroons nationalism. The CNF aimed at asserting the identity of the Southern Cameroons, bringing about its unification with the Northern Cameroons, and fighting for the ultimate reunification of the British and French Cameroons.[46]

The formation of the CNF marked the beginning of the politics of identity in the Southern Cameroons, which would gradually transform into a consistent opposition to Nigeria or, to be more exact, Eastern Nigeria into which the Southern Cameroons was integrated and from which the NCNC drew most of its leadership. Nigeria became the main target of the Southern Cameroons nationalist invective, in a way that the Administering Authority would never be. The illusion of the Territory's international status made the Administering Authority, as the guarantor of that status, seem rather welcome.

The real opponent was Nigeria, who effectively administered the Territory, raising concern that she might be diverting some of the benefits of trusteeship to herself. That feeling was justified by the fact that it was impossible to assess revenue from the Territory and expenditure to it. The feeling was exacerbated by the overwhelming presence of Nigerians, particularly Igbos, in almost all walks of life in the Territory. The

45   See Ndifontah mo Nyamndi, Cameroon-Nigeria Relations 1958-1978, Unpublished master's Thesis, (Yaounde: IRIC, 1979), p. 28.
46   Edwin Ardener, op. cit. p. 345. See also *West Africa* (Nos. 2147, 2148), 1958.

oppressive presence of the Igbo, whose arrogance was thought to typify the rest of Nigeria, made the people of the Southern Cameroons feel somewhat nostalgic about life in the German Kamerun where they had not experienced such domination by any ethnic group. That feeling was the genesis of a phenomenon that Edwin Ardener has called the "Kamerun Idea",[47] a desire to reconstitute the defunct German Kamerun by uniting the British and French Cameroons. It was a strange recollection, in view of the brutality of the German period and its regime of forced labor , which had been fiercely resisted in many areas. The "Kamerun Idea" was emerging as a political idea rather than a historical concept. Southern Cameroons politicians needed sentimental grounds to sustain their desire for a unit of their own.

The "Kamerun Idea" was reinforced by the fact that in forty years of trust administration, the British did next to nothing in the Southern Cameroons. Claiming that the trusteeship was only temporary, they made very little investment in the Territory. All their administrative and residential buildings were inherited from the German era: the British Commissioner for the Cameroons lodged in the residence of the former German Governor; British trading companies occupied old German structures; and they did not improve or extend the road infrastructure or any other form of development. And so the well-kept souvenirs of the German period which the British themselves found fit to use, increased the appeal of the "Kamerun Idea" to many in the Southern Cameroons.

The degree of commitment to that idea led to the first split within the CNF. In 1951, N. N. Mbile, the General-Secretary of the Party, accused Endeley of wavering in his support for unification, and broke from the CNF and joined forces with J. K. Dibonge of the French Cameroons Welfare Union to form the Kamerun United National Congress [KUNC].[48] The aim of the new party was to press for an early unification of the British and French Cameroons, leading to the emergence of "one cohesive Kamerun nation."[49]

An early electoral showdown between both parties was delayed by

47   Ibid.
48   P. M. Kale, op. cit., p. 56.
49   Ibid.

an internal leadership crisis that rocked the NCNC and engrossed the attention of the Eastern Region in 1953. Having failed to win the government of the Western Region during the elections of that year, Nnamdi Azikiwe, the leader of the Igbo-dominated NCNC, decided to return to his homeland in the Eastern Region and take over the government there. His maneuverings were resisted by those in office, inevitably leading to a crisis. As the crisis deepened, the 13 Southern Cameroons Members of the Eastern House of Assembly decided to remain neutral. But that neutrality was not appreciated by the protagonists. The Territory's only Minister in the Government of the Eastern Region, S. T. Muna, was forced to resign and the Premier rejected all calls to reinstate him.

The NCNC crisis marked a turning point in the history of the nationalist movement in the Southern Cameroons. The refusal to reinstate its lone Minister demonstrated the insensitivity of the Eastern Region towards the Territory and proved that the NCNC leadership could not be relied upon to defend the interests of the Southern Cameroons.

The reaction of the Territory's politicians was spontaneous: meeting in Mamfe in May 1953, they decided to sink their differences in the face of the more serious threat from Eastern Nigeria. They merged their two parties into the Kamerun National Congress [KNC], led first by Dibonge and from 1957 by Endeley, which they ordained to fight for a separate region for the Southern Cameroons, for the unification of the British and French Cameroons, and for the ultimate self-government or independence of a united Kamerun. The NCNC crisis moved nationalism in the Southern Cameroons to a new pitch of gravity and emphasis: it passed from the politics of differentiation to the politics of separation.

From 1953 onwards, separation from Eastern Nigeria became the trend in Southern Cameroons politics. Every party in the Territory made it a central objective, with the exception of Kale's Kamerun People's Party [KPP], formed in June 1953 with the ostentatious aim of "making parliamentary democracy a reality in the Southern Cameroons."[50] But Kale soon changed his mind and started campaigning for an autonomous region for the Southern Cameroons. However, while the idea of separation from Eastern Nigeria was accepted by all, it was not clear to many

50   Ibid. p. 58.

how far the separation should go. That uncertainty would be the central issue in the future of the Southern Cameroons.

Endeley and the KNC won an early victory for separation when, in January 1954, the Lyttleton Constitution, which replaced the Macpherson Constitution, erected the Southern Cameroons into a quasi-federal Territory, with its own Legislature and Executive Council. Endeley became Leader of Government Business. But it was a modest victory, which fell short of nationalist expectations for a full region equal to the other regions of Nigeria. It was not without detractors: the Balondo People's Convention dissociated itself from the clamor for a separate Region, arguing that the Balondo people had close affinity with the Efiks, Ibiobios and Igbos of Nigeria and therefore wished to continue to enjoy their social and cultural relations with them.[51] And it accentuated the underlying debate about the extent of the separation itself. Endeley was of the opinion that the separation should be limited to the Eastern Region, and that the best bet for the Southern Cameroons was to develop into a full region of Nigeria. But some members of his party disagreed, arguing that, as a whole, Nigeria could not be better than its eastern part. Led by John Ngu Foncha, the dissenters left the KNC in March 1955 and formed the Kamerun National Democratic Party [KNDP], with the aim of separating from Nigeria before she became independent.

The KNDP introduced a new dimension into British Cameroons politics. For the first time, a local party seriously contemplated terminating the administrative union with Nigeria. The KUNC had earlier entertained similar views, but the NCNC crisis had driven it off course and forced it to reunite with the moderate CNF. But the KNDP had no such distraction. The NCNC crisis had only strengthened the separatists, whose views the KNDP put forward convincingly enough for Foncha to oust Endeley from the premiership of the Southern Cameroons at the 1959 general elections. The KNDP victory drove Endeley to espouse the Nigeria option even more squarely than before. Once in opposition he brought his KNC into alliance with Kale's KPP, and then united both parties into the Cameroon People's National Convention [CPNC].

51   Solomon Tandeng Muna, *Journey to the Unknown*, Vol. 1 (Yaounde, S.T. Muna Foundation, 2012), p. 285.

Relations with Nigeria constituted the crux of the difference between the two movements. Foncha's strategy consisted in whipping up resentment against Nigerians, particularly Igbos, a phobia which became the bedrock of KNDP tactics. It is noteworthy that the leadership of the KNDP did not predicate the separation from Nigeria upon immediate unification with the French Cameroun. Indications are that Foncha did not conceive that unification for the medium term. He perceived the separation from Nigeria as a goal in itself, motivated "purely for the purpose of maintaining the Southern Cameroons national identity."[52]

The tactics of the KNC-KPP alliance, and later the CPNC, revolved around understating the effects of the Igbo presence in the Southern Cameroons, while highlighting the economic and financial advantages of continued association with Nigeria. CPNC leaders felt that even though highly dramatized, the Igbo presence was still a lesser evil when compared to the civil strife in the French Cameroun. As a counter to Igbophobia, Endeley raised a new scare about Cameroun as the grim alternative to separation from Nigeria.

Whatever the KNDP said about the Nigerian connection, Endeley retorted that no right-thinking person would want to live in a French Cameroun "red with the blood of thousands of innocent victims killed by terrorists and the Ahidjo regime, a land where you can be arrested without cause, beaten, searched, and imprisoned without a fair trial; where political differences are settled not by the ballot but by guns and poison."[53] The fundamental weakness of the CPNC appeal was that it contrasted a hypothetical prospect with a lived experience. By 1960, the dominant political question in the Territory was whether it should, while separating from the Eastern Region, remain a part of Nigeria, or whether it should secede from Nigeria completely.

The nationalist movement in the Southern Cameroons had a very moderate objective. While their counterparts across Africa were fighting for the total sovereignty of their respective territories, the leaders of the Southern Cameroons limited themselves to the quest for greater

52   U.N., T.C., T.1440, p. 55.
53   Strategic Committee of the CPNC, Plebiscite Message to all Voters of the Cameroons. (Lagos: Times Press, 1961), p. 7.

regional autonomy. It seems that both Foncha and Endeley did not fancy the glamour of becoming the head of a sovereign state, however small, preferring to trade that glamour for a slice of power in a bigger nation.

In the Northern Cameroons, the first ripples of nationalist activity occurred during the visit of the UN Mission in November 1949. Then, a group of Northern Cameroonians led by the Emir of Dikwa summarized their political aspirations in two demands: the separation of the Northern Cameroons from Northern Nigeria; and the unification of the Northern Cameroons with the Kanuri and Shuwa populations of the French Cameroun into a separate entity under British tutelage but outside Nigeria.[54] But the British dismissed the request, describing as mainly of historic interest any affinities between both sections of the former Empire.[55]

Following that early setback, nationalism in the Northern Cameroons changed direction. Its leaders turned their attention to the idea of uniting with the Southern Cameroons. In June of 1952, a delegation led by Mallam Abba Habib visited Buea to discuss unification with Dr. Endeley and his colleagues. Their talks culminated in a joint call "for the formation of a legislature for both the Northern Cameroons and the Southern Cameroons."[56]

But unification with the Southern Cameroons was as unwelcome in Northern Nigeria as the restoration of the Adamawa Empire. Sensing potential danger in the Endeley-Habib discussions, the Premier of Northern Nigeria hastily appointed Habib as Minister for Northern Cameroons Affairs in his Government. By the time of their next meeting in June 1953, there was little common ground between the two British Cameroons leaders.[57]

With Habib silenced, the first wave of nationalism in the Northern Cameroons entered a period of uncertainty and decline. Remnants of the movement, represented by the Emir of Dikwa and his Kamerun Socialist Convention [KSC] which sought separation from Northern Nigeria, were carefully mopped up by the British as they set about eliminating

54   TCOR., T/798, Supplement No. 2, 1950, pp. 14-19.
55   TCOR., T/517, Annex Vol. 2, 1950, pp. 385-486.
56   U.N., G.A., A/C.4.SR.1142, July 1961, p. 304.
57   Ndifontah mo Nyamndi. op. cit., p. 33.

any opinion attempting to subvert the association with Nigeria.[58]

By 1955, when another UN mission visited the Territory, the Northern Cameroons leadership reflected a completely pro-Nigeria tendency. Contradicting his previous record, the Emir of Dikwa spoke of their "avowed desire to remain within the Northern Region of Nigeria,"[59] while the Lamido of Adamawa described the Northern Cameroons as "part and parcel of the Northern Region of Nigeria with which it will live together and die together!"[60]

Still the anti-Nigeria sentiment that had been voiced in the early days simply went underground. It resurfaced in April 1959 with the formation of the Northern Kamerun Democratic Party [NKDP], whose aims included separation from Nigeria, independence for the Northern Cameroons, unification with the Southern Cameroons, and ultimate reunification with the French Cameroun.[61] The fundamental grievance of the founders of the NKDP was the feudal administration of the Territory. From the onset of the administrative union, the Northern Cameroons had been rapidly incorporated into the classic pattern of indirect rule under the powerful traditional Emirs of Northern Nigeria. Under that system, local government was neither democratic nor representative, talk less of being favorable to minority areas. In fact, representation for the Northern Cameroons was never specified by any of the Nigerian Constitutions!

The activities of the NKDP reintroduced a dichotomy of pro- and anti-Nigeria feeling similar to what had developed in the Southern Cameroons. But nationalism in the Northern Cameroons never attained the proportions of the phenomenon in the Southern Cameroons. It was always timid, often haphazard, and was never really organized into a motive force. For one thing, the geographical fragmentation of the Northern Cameroons, coupled with its administrative spread within three different Nigerian provinces constituted serious impediments to social communication and the development of a distinct political culture. Secondly, the basic pattern of politics in Northern Nigeria left little room for debate. The Region was governed by a traditional aristocracy which

58   Ibid. p. 34.
59   TCOR, T/1239, p. 12.
60   Ibid.
61   TCOR, T/1491, Nov. 25, 1959, p. 70.

coincided with the religious elite. To oppose that elite, even in a political contest, was very unpopular among the people.

Notwithstanding the differences in scale and intensity, nationalism in the Northern Cameroons, as in the Southern Cameroons, revolved around the past, present and future relationship with Nigeria. At all stages, that relationship was affected by the internal political development of Nigeria itself.

Nigerian Independence and the Fate of the British Cameroons

The 1950s witnessed great constitutional strides towards self-government in Nigeria. In January 1952, the Richards Constitution was replaced by the Macpherson Constitution, which was much more in keeping with the aspirations of Nigerians,[62] providing for a federal ministerial form of government and enlarged regional assemblies with legislative and financial powers.

But the NCNC crisis of 1953, as well as the outburst of northern hostility against the South over an Action Group motion calling for self-government in 1956, polarized Nigerian politics and convinced the Colonial Secretary, Oliver Lyttelton, that the legislative supremacy of the Central Government, which was the centralizing feature of the Macpherson Constitution, needed revision.

Lyttelton decided that the Nigerian Constitution had to be "redrawn to provide for greater regional autonomy and for the removal of powers of intervention by the center in matters that could, without detriment to other Regions, be placed entirely within regional competence."[63] He summoned a constitutional review conference of all Nigerian parties in 1954.

The Lyttleton Constitution, which emerged from the London Conference, transferred residual powers to the Regions. Areas of exclusive and concurrent legislative competence were defined, and each Region was endowed with a Premier and a Cabinet.[64] But the crucial question of self-government was again side-stepped by an ambiguous formula offering self-government to any Region that wanted it in 1956, but not to

---

62   Michael Crowder. *The Story of Nigeria,* London: Faber & Faber. 1962) p. 232
63   Quoted in Ibid., p. 234.
64   Uma O. Eleazu, *Federalism and Nation-Building,* (Devon: Arthur Stockwell Ltd., 1977) p. 48.

the whole Federation. While reorganizing and strengthening the Regions, the 1954 Constitution left the Center in some confusion, as no provision was made for the position of leader of government business.

That omission spoke to the difficulty of choosing a leader from a national scene with highly regionalized political parties -- the NCNC in the Eastern Region, the Action Group in the West, and the NPC in the North -- and none with an overall majority in Parliament.

Still, the practical needs of government called for decisive action. At a conference to review the Constitution in 1957, it was finally decided that a Federal Prime Minister should be appointed. Abubakar Tafawa Balewa, Deputy Leader of the NPC, was later installed in that position. The political evolution received a decisive boost when the Premier of the Northern Region announced that his Region would also become self-governing in 1959. From that moment, independence became the shared objective of all Nigerian political parties. It was duly achieved on October 1, 1960.

The advance of Nigeria towards independence also brought to the fore the question of the political future of the British Cameroons. For as long as Nigeria remained a dependency, Britain was content with administering the Trust Territory as an integral part of the Protectorate. But with the imminence of Nigerian independence, that situation had to be revised.

The Colonial Secretary, Lennox-Boyd, announced in 1957 that with the coming of Nigerian independence, the administrative union with the British Cameroons would have to be revisited. He saw two possible options for the Trust Territory: it could remain as part of an independent Nigeria, or it could continue under the trust administration of the United Kingdom.[65] Either way, Lennox-Boyd felt that "the people of the north and south sectors of the British Cameroons would have to say freely what their wishes were as to their future."[66]

The need to ascertain the wishes of the peoples of the British Cameroons in the plebiscites that followed arose not from their own internal progress towards self-government or independence, but because of the

---

65   Report of the UN Plebiscite Commissioner on the Plebiscite in the Northern Cameroons, U.N., T.C., T/1491. 27 November. 1959. p. 10.
66   Quoted in T/1491, p. 10.

imminent attainment of independence by Nigeria.[67]

As Nigeria approached independence, its political parties sought to consolidate themselves and acquire new gains in the crucial pre-independence elections of December 1959. Those parties, being mainly regional or even tribal parties, worked hard to consolidate their grip on their core areas, while seeking inroads in ethnic minority areas such as the British Cameroons.[68] But with the separatist KNDP in power in the Southern Cameroons, little could be gained there by way of foothold.

That left the Northern Cameroons, where the existing uncertainty was an open invitation to the political parties of Nigeria to stake their claims. They all went there in force, the NPC seeking to tighten its grip on the Territory, and the southern parties seeking to release that grip. Driven by their fear of the gigantic North, the latter began to spread the idea that the administrative union with Northern Nigeria was not only detrimental to the advancement of the Northern Cameroons, but that it was actually being forced upon the people by the NPC leadership. They reasoned that given the chance; the people of the Northern Cameroons would choose differently.

Accordingly, the political parties of southern Nigeria urged the UN to conduct a plebiscite in the Northern Cameroons to determine the future of the Territory. And so, the 1959 plebiscite was motivated not by developments within the Territory but as part of the electoral calculations of Nigerian political parties.

67   See Report on the 1958 UN Visiting Mission to Trust Territories in West Africa, para. 3, in U.N., T.C. 23rd Session, Supplement No. 2. The Report suggests that the need to ascertain the wishes of the peoples of the British Cameroons was also influenced by the progress of the French Cameroun towards independence.

68   U.N., T.C., 1/1426, Annex, 20 January 1959, pp. 8-10.

CHAPTER TWO

Organization and Conduct of the Plebiscites

International concern over the British Cameroons derived from more than the theory of trusteeship and the history of the Territory. Situated in the armpit of Africa, described by detractors as a "two-part no-man's land,"[1] the British Cameroons was the meeting point of West and Central Africa, two regions that were increasingly attracting international attention.

The location of the British Cameroons hemmed in-between two bigger neighbors that had eyes on it, intensified the international concern; while the presumed frailty of its economy made the international community more conscious of the need to assure for its people a future of some stability.

Like in many African countries, that frailty was something of a myth: it had never been conclusively established for the whole Territory; and at the best of times, economic viability is always relative. In fact, if independence were to be subject to such considerations, few African countries would be free today as the colonial powers would have found a convenient excuse to delay or deny them independence. Different studies evaluated the economic situation in the Northern Cameroons and the Southern Cameroons separately, concluding that neither was sufficiently viable; a result attributed in part to the size of the Territory. But if the British Cameroons were really that small, it was strange that the UN sanctioned its partition into two smaller parts; and no one called for its unification. Instead, the United Nations focused on the union of the fragmented Territory with one of its neighbors.

While the status of the British Cameroons as a Trust Territory lasted, international interest in its affairs was limited to the periodic reviews

---

1   *The Daily Telegraph,* London, 7 Feb. 1961.

of the report of the Administering Authority. But as independence approached, the activities of the Administering Authority came under increased scrutiny. The plebiscites which decided the fate of the Territory attracted vigorous debate at the United Nations, and their results drew varying reactions.

Prelude: The 1958 UN Visiting Mission

The idea of organizing plebiscites in the British Cameroons was first discussed at the Nigerian Constitutional Conference in London in May-June 1957. The British Colonial Secretary declared that as a result of the decisive advance of Nigeria towards independence, the trusteeship arrangement whereby the British Cameroons was administered as an integral part of Nigeria would have to be reviewed.[2] In other words, with Nigeria shedding its colonial status, the administrative union with the British Cameroons would have to be terminated. The Colonial Secretary further announced that such termination would be effected through a democratic process whereby the people of the British Cameroons would freely express their wishes regarding their future.

But the fate of the British Cameroons was not the responsibility of the United Kingdom alone. The United Nations, as the other party to the Trusteeship Agreement, had an equal role to play. So, the British government suggested that the Trusteeship Council should consider appropriate arrangements for the administration of the British Cameroons once Nigeria became independent. Such arrangements would involve either modification or termination of the Trusteeship Agreement. To that effect, the United Nations called on the United Kingdom to ascertain by appropriate means the facts of the situation and in particular the views of the inhabitants of the Trust Territory.[3] The memorandum further proposed that the 1958 UN Visiting Mission to Trust Territories in West Africa should include in its report its views on the method of consultation to be used in determining the wishes of the people of the British Cameroons regarding their future.[4] Adopted by the Trusteeship

---

2   U.N., T.C., T/1491, New York, 27 Nov. 1959, p. 10.
3   U.N., T.C., T/1393, New York, 30 June 1958.
4   Ibid.

Council, the proposal formed the basis of its Resolution 1907[XXII] of July 28, 1958, defining the terms of reference of the 1958 United Nations Visiting Mission to West Africa.

Composed of Benjamin Gerig of the USA as Chairman, Georges Salomon of Haiti, Rikhi Jaiphal of India, and Gray Thorp of New Zealand, the Mission conducted elaborate consultations in both sections of the British Cameroons to form an opinion on the wishes of the people regarding their future.

Concern for that future was voiced more strongly outside the British Cameroons than within it. Nigerian political parties flooded the Visiting Mission with memoranda, from which the idea of the plebiscite emerged as one of the most reliable ways of ascertaining the wishes of the people.

That idea was born from a conflict among Nigerian political parties over the Northern Cameroons, with the parties of southern Nigeria challenging the domination of the Northern Cameroons by the NPC. The 1958 Visiting Mission gave them an international platform from which to express their concern.

In a memorandum to the Mission, the United Middle Belt Congress/Action Group Alliance described the Northern Cameroons as "a place for adventure of the few ruling families from Yola,"[5] claiming that the people of the Northern Cameroons naturally wished "to cast away the domination of Yolaners before any decision of independence from British trusteeship."[6] The Alliance suggested that "a plebiscite should be held to allow the people to make a free choice."[7]

The idea of the plebiscite was thus aimed at terminating the close relationship between the Northern Cameroons and Northern Nigeria, and not the trusteeship itself. It was surprisingly accepted by the Government of Northern Nigeria, who saw it as a means of vindicating that relationship. The Premier of Northern Nigeria was convinced that,

> It is difficult for anyone who knows the Territory to conceive of any political future -- taking into account the factors of history,

5   U.N., T.C., T/1426, Annex IV (d), p. 8.
6   Ibid.
7   Ibid.

geography and economics -- which could bring greater benefits to its inhabitants than that they should throw their lot with an independent Nigeria and within the Northern Region.[8]

In the Southern Cameroons, opinion regarding its future was clearly divided between staying with Nigeria and separating from it. All its political parties were agreed that only the people of the Southern Cameroons, consulted by means of universal suffrage, could determine where the majority lay.[9]

Contrary to the situation in the Northern Cameroons where Nigerian political parties suggested a plebiscite on behalf of the people of the Territory, the Southern Cameroons political parties felt that a more appropriate mode of consultation should be a general election on the relationship with Nigeria, rather than a plebiscite in which "the people would have to answer with an arbitrary and irretrievable 'yes' or 'no', a question whose implications many might not fully understand, and whose consequences they would no longer be able to influence."[10]

Both the ruling KNC/KPP Alliance that supported integration into Nigeria, and the opposition KNDP which sought separation from it, agreed to regard the results of the 1959 general elections as a mandate for the victorious party to implement its electoral program.

The Visiting Mission made two critical judgments about the British Cameroons. Firstly, that the preponderant attitude in the Territory was that the moment for determining their future was at hand and could not usefully be delayed. And secondly, that

> a realistic appraisal of the present situation in the Trust Territory, as well as a realistic approach to the question of its future, require that the Territory should not be regarded as an entity but should be considered in terms of two parts and two groups of peoples, northern and southern, whose history and development have taken distinctly different courses and between whom there now

8   Ibid, Annex IV (e), p. 11.
9   T/1426, para. 183, p. 83.
10   Ibid., para. 187, pp. 85-86.

exist profound differences both in administrative systems and in political attitude and loyalties.[11]

The second finding of the Mission was manifestly ridiculous: whereas Nigeria was advancing towards independence as a single unit, the British Cameroons, which for 43 years had been administered as part of Nigeria, was suddenly thought to have developed such profound differences as to make it impossible for its future to be considered as one. The Visiting Mission recommended that the wishes of the peoples of the Northern Cameroons and the Southern Cameroons should be determined separately.[12]

For the Northern Cameroons the Mission took the view that there was "no difference of opinion on the principal question which would require or justify the holding of a formal consultation". Indeed, the Mission thought that it was "manifestly the opinion of the northern population as a whole that they should become permanently a part of the Northern Region of Nigeria." Consequently, it recommended that "if the General Assembly accepts such a union as the basis for the termination of the Trusteeship Agreement, no further consultation need be held."[13]

For the Southern Cameroons, the Mission was not so categorical, confessing that it would be difficult, without knowing the results of the January 1959 general elections, to make any precise recommendations as to the method of consulting the people, because "the majority by which a party won or the margin by which the other lost the elections would affect the course of further developments in regard to the determination of the future of the Territory."[14]

Unfortunately, neither party won a decisive majority at the elections. The KNDP captured the Government from the KNC/KPP, but only by a thin majority of two seats in a Parliament of 26 members. And reluctant to stake the future of the Southern Cameroons on such a slender majority, the UN Visiting Mission recommended that

11   Ibid., paras. 166-168, pp. 77-78.
12   Ibid. para. 170, p. 79.
13   Ibid., para. 181, pp. 82-83.
14   Ibid., paras. 193-194, p. 87.

if general agreement should develop in the newly elected House of Assembly concerning the future of the Southern Cameroons, a formal popular consultation may prove to be unnecessary, but if no such agreement emerges, it may only be through a consultation, probably a plebiscite, that it will be possible to resolve the basic issues.[15]

The report and recommendations of the 1958 Visiting Mission were debated at the resumed Thirteenth Session of the UN General Assembly in February-March 1959. The Assembly agreed with the Mission that the moment had come to determine the future of the British Cameroons, especially as it was clear by then that Nigeria would become independent on October 1, 1960.

The General Assembly also agreed that, for the purposes of the consultations, the Territory should be regarded as two separate entities. But it rejected the recommendation that there should be no plebiscite in the Northern Cameroons. It disagreed with the Mission's opinion that the people wished to remain with Northern Nigeria, arguing that the Mission had not been to all parts of the Northern Cameroons to sample views; and that the Northern Cameroons possessed no representative organs through which such views could otherwise be assessed.[16]

In concluding its debate on the Visiting Mission's report, the General Assembly recommended, in Resolution 1350[XIII], that the United Kingdom

> Take steps, in consultation with a United Nations Plebiscite Commissioner, to organize, under the supervision of the United Nations, separate plebiscites in the northern and southern parts of the Cameroons under United Kingdom administration, in order to ascertain the wishes of the inhabitants of the Territory concerning their future.

15   T/1426/Add. 1, para. 218, pp. 9-10.
16   A/C/.4/SR. 864-875, 885-886.

Dr. Djalal Abdoh of Iran was elected as the United Nations Plebiscite Commissioner for the British Cameroons.

Having settled on the idea of the plebiscites, the UN invited the people of the British Cameroons to determine their future, within the chosen framework, in a decision with limited options and limitless calculations.

The First Northern Cameroons Plebiscite, 1959

It came as a surprise that the Northern Cameroons for which the Visiting Mission prescribed no plebiscite at all should be the first to have one. In the end, it had not one but two plebiscites! While negotiations were ongoing for a plebiscite in the Southern Cameroons, the General Assembly recommended, in Resolution 1350 [XIII], that the plebiscite in the Northern Cameroons should take place around the middle of November 1959.

However, although the idea of the plebiscite was generally accepted, argument arose over the questions to be put. During consultations with the 1958 Visiting Mission, the Government of Northern Nigeria stressed the need for simple questions at the plebiscite, to avoid confusing the rural and largely illiterate electorate of the Northern Cameroons. The Premier of Northern Nigeria suggested that only one question should be put, namely: "Do you want union with the Northern Region of an independent Nigeria?" Only in the event of a negative vote could other alternatives, such as union with the Southern Cameroons or with the French Cameroun, be explored in a subsequent plebiscite.[17]

According to the Premier of Northern Nigeria, the first choice in the Northern Cameroons plebiscite should be given to Nigeria, specifically the Northern Region. The political parties of southern Nigeria were satisfied with the principle of the plebiscite and did not worry about the questions to be put.

The Premier's proposal was hotly debated at the United Nations. The African delegations, together with the Soviet Union, felt that the question as framed gave an undue advantage to Nigeria by making it possible for that option to be put a second and possibly a third time. They were of the opinion that the choice should be a straight one between immediately

17   T/1426, Annex IV (e), pp. 11-12.

uniting with Nigeria and rejecting that possibility for good. In that case, the option for uniting with the neighboring French Cameroun would have to be brought in as the other alternative.[18]

But it was argued that the conditions for union with the French Cameroun had not been sufficiently clarified for it to be put as an option at the plebiscite. And rather than postpone the consultation pending such clarification, a compromise was worked out whereby the Nigeria option would be put, but with an alternative in the form of a future decision. The proposed plebiscite would thus ask the questions:

a). Are you in favor of becoming part of Northern Nigeria when Nigeria becomes independent? Or,

b). Are you in favor of deciding the future of the Northern Cameroons at a later date?

The merit of this formula, as seen by the Indian delegate who introduced it, was that "the people of the Northern Cameroons would not be obliged to pronounce on union with the French Cameroun, the precise details of which they could not foresee."[19]

But the formula did not clarify the nature of the future consultation, neither did it say for sure what questions would be asked then; and it failed to specify that a vote for the second choice at the first plebiscite meant an outright elimination of that option in any subsequent consultation. Instead, it offered an open-ended second alternative for which every interpretation was possible.

However, the General Assembly adopted the Indian formula, and the questions comprised in it were confirmed as those to be put at the plebiscite. The people of the Northern Cameroons would be asked:

a). Do you wish the Northern Cameroons to be part of the Northern Region of Nigeria when the Federation of Nigeria becomes independent? Or,

b). Are you in favor of deciding the future of the Northern Cameroons

---

18   A/C.4/SR. 793, 20 Feb. 1959, pp. 645-646.
19   A/C.4/SR. 870, 9 March 1959, p. 703.

at a later date?[20]

But agreement on the questions did not close the argument on the plebiscite. A new controversy arose over the franchise. The 1958 Visiting Mission had endorsed a suggestion from the Premier of Northern Nigeria that in the event of a plebiscite in the Northern Cameroons, the consultation should be conducted on the basis of the electoral register then being prepared for the 1959 Nigerian general elections. The Premier argued that "preparation of a separate electoral roll purely for the plebiscite would be administratively difficult and would cause confusion in the minds of the people."[21]

The Premier's proposal had a major shortcoming — the proposed electoral register restricted the franchise to men only. And some delegations at the United Nations felt strongly against limiting the franchise in such an important consultation. They insisted on the application of universal suffrage. But there was insufficient time, between then and November when the plebiscite was scheduled, to prepare a new electoral register. So the General Assembly adopted the proposal of the Premier of Northern Nigeria, and the British Government went ahead to organize the plebiscite as provided for by Resolution 1350[XIII]. It is noteworthy that in the lead up to the exercise, the people of the Northern Cameroons had no say whatsoever. All that was heard was other people deciding for them.

The organization of the plebiscite was governed by the Nigeria [Northern Cameroons Plebiscite] Order-in-Council 1959, published in the United Kingdom as Statutory Instrument No. 1304. That Order vested responsibility for the plebiscite in the Governor-General of Nigeria, acting on behalf of the British Government. He was empowered under Article 7 of the Order to appoint a Plebiscite Administrator and constitute such other offices as he might deem necessary for the purposes of the plebiscite.

The Governor-General duly appointed Sir John Dring as Plebiscite Administrator, who brought with him the reputation of having successfully organized a similar plebiscite in the Trust Territory of Togoland under British Administration in 1956. For the Northern Cameroons plebiscite, he was placed at the head of a staff of 1,522 officers drawn

20   G.A., Res. 1350(XIII), Art. 2.
21   T/1491, p. 17.

mainly from among government and Native Authority officials of Northern Nigeria.[22] The plebiscite operation itself was supervised by a United Nations staff of 20, directed by the Plebiscite Commissioner, Dr. Djalal Abdoh.

The Northern Cameroons was divided into eight "plebiscite circles," corresponding to the electoral districts carved out for the Nigerian general elections, with a total of 131 registration areas and 334 polling stations.[23] Polling was scheduled to take place on November 7, 1959.

Following a fairly lively campaign staged by the sole local party, the Northern Kamerun Democratic Party [NKDP], and the main Nigerian political parties, approximately 80 per cent of registered voters in the Northern Cameroons actually voted in the plebiscite, which was a very high turnout, considering their low level of literacy, the poor state of transport and communications facilities, and the very limited campaign time available to the parties involved. A total of 113,859 votes were cast, of which roughly 62 per cent [70,546] voted for the second alternative.

The people of the Northern Cameroons voted by a handsome majority to postpone the decision on their future. That result was received as a victory for the local NKDP and the parties from southern Nigeria, which had all campaigned for postponement of the decision. It was a major blow for the NPC, whose claims over the Northern Cameroons had been publicly repudiated.

Table 2.1. Results of the First Northern Cameroons Plebiscite

Plebiscite Circle	First Alternative	Second Alternative
Dikwa North	7,575	7,197
Dikwa Central	8,891	11,988
Gwoza	3,356	6,773

22   Ibid.
23   Ibid, p. 5.

Cubunawa-Madagali	4,247	9,818
Adamawa North-East	6,120	13,578
Chamba	4,539	11,651
Adamawa South	4,997	9,452
Wukari East	3,063	89
TOTAL	42,788	70,546

Rejected Votes: 525
Source: U.N., T.C., T/1491, 27 November 1959, p. 32.[24]

The Plebiscite Commissioner was satisfied that the exercise had been organized "with efficiency and impartiality, in an atmosphere of freedom," and that the "exemplary" conduct of the people had been responsible for the success of the exercise. But he doubted that the result reflected its true meaning. It seemed to him that rather than vote to determine their future, the majority of the voters had used the plebiscite "to register a protest vote against the system of local administration prevailing in the Northern Cameroons."[25] Be that as it may, another consultation would have to be held.

The Southern Cameroons Plebiscite, 1961

The political parties of the Southern Cameroons were initially opposed to the idea of the plebiscite. They did not want to divert the attention of their voters from the 1959 general election. And hoping for victory in that election, each argued that its results should be taken as a decision on the future of the Territory. Unfortunately, those results produced only a slim majority for the KNDP. Reluctantly, both the KNDP and the KNC/KPP Alliance began to accept the idea of a plebiscite. They also agreed that union with Nigeria should be the main issue for decision. But they disagreed over the franchise for the election and the other

24   Ibid, p. 16.
25   Ibid., p. 34.

possible options.

Their disagreement over the other options was part of their endgame calculations. The Alliance insisted that reunification with the French Cameroun should be one of the options. Knowing that reunification was still clouded as a political objective, the Alliance saw a tactical advantage in forcing their opponents to stand on it. Not that long before, Endeley had told the UN Visiting Mission that "the partition of the German Kamerun had led to the development of sharp contrasts in the political and cultural outlook of the two sectors in consonance with the well-known divergence which characterized the cultural and political systems of Britain and France. And with the passage of time, that separation had assumed a regrettable degree of permanence."[26] Still, for electioneering purposes he now insisted that reunification with the French Cameroons be placed on the plebiscite ballot.

But the KNDP disagreed, insisting that reunification could only be effected after separation from Nigeria. That chronology of events was reflected in the first motion tabled in the House of Assembly in February 1959 by the incoming government, praying the United Kingdom:

> to implement the policy of the Government calling for the seces-
> sion of the Southern Cameroons from Nigeria before she attains
> independence in 1960, and to continue under a modified form
> of the Trusteeship Agreement for some time during which the
> possibilities of reunification with any section of the British and
> French Cameroons can be explored.[27]

The year before, the President of the Southern Cameroons Chiefs' Conference, in a Memorandum to the UN Visiting Mission, submitted that:

> At the present level of development, the people of this Territory
> honestly and relentlessly demand secession from the Federation

---

26   CF. Muna, op. cit., p. 399.
27   CF. Southern Cameroons Information Service, *Press Release No. 279*, Buea,
      13 February 1959.

of Nigeria in order to concentrate on the much harder work towards self-government and independence outside the Federation of Nigeria as a direct member of the British Commonwealth of Nations.[28]

As decision-time approached, the general feeling in the Southern Cameroons was that the choice would be restricted to the contentious issue of its relationship with Nigeria. Reunification with the French Cameroun did not seem to be an automatic option for consideration. Indeed, its inclusion in the debate was suspected and resisted by many. As John Ngu Foncha pointed out:

Neither the KNC/KPP Alliance nor the KNDP had included reunification as an alternative when interviewing the United Nations Visiting Mission in 1958. The only reason for the [KNC/KPP] adoption of that idea was that it hoped to use the terrorist murders in the Cameroons under French Administration in order to frighten the people of the Cameroons under British Administration into voting for integration with Nigeria. The majority of the people in the Southern Cameroons had demonstrated in all elections that they desired independence and separation from the Federation of Nigeria. They had never rejected the possibility of reunification: all they wanted was an opportunity to see what would happen after the attainment of independence by the adjacent Territories.[29]

At the Mamfe plebiscite conference, he was categorical: "The KNDP believes that it would be definitely wrong to include reunification as one of the alternatives at the plebiscite because it would only confuse the people."[30] And speaking in Kumba a month earlier, he had declared that

28   *Report* on the 1958 UN Visiting Mission to Trust Territories in West Africa, Annex II, p. 10.
29   GAOR 4th Committee, 14th Session, 885th meeting, 1959.
30   Speech before the Mamfe Plebiscite Conference, August 10, 1959, cf. Pius B. Soh, *Dr John Ngu Foncha* (Bamenda: Centre for Social Science Research, 1999), p. 85.

"We believe that for the time being reunification must be kept aside in order to have a place to stand before looking for reunification. Those who denounce reunification wish it to be included in the terms of the plebiscite because they see in it a chance to confuse the two issues."[31] At that point, there was something peculiar about reunification: its detractors were more vocal about it than its supporters.

Other members of the Party also weighed in. W.N.O. Efiom stated that "while his people believed in secession from the Federation of Nigeria, they did not want immediate unification."[32] I.N. Malafa contends that "Most people in the [Southern] Cameroons, either because of lack of education in the basic issues involved, or through the natural fear of sudden change, are not at present terribly enthusiastic about immediate reunification."[33] Foncha's views had been presented to the 1958 UN Visiting Mission: "The only logical issue open to our country was to allow it to secede from the Federation of Nigeria when it became independent, allowing it to continue under the British mandate until it was ready for independence. At this point it could stand alone or unite with the French Cameroons to form one nation."[34] That position was reiterated by the first National Executive Committee meeting of the KNDP following the 1959 elections. The Party decided that "After secession from Nigeria, the Southern Cameroons should stay under United Kingdom trusteeship to plan the economic development of the territory before its reunification with the French Cameroons."[35]

The KNDP thus envisaged a plebiscite with only one question: separation from Nigeria or union with it. Foncha was rather ambivalent about reunification with the French Cameroun, adopting and rejecting it by turns, depending on his audience. And not without reason: in 1959, no Southern Cameroons politician had any personal experience of the

31   J.N. Foncha, Speech at the Opening of the First Annual Conference of the National Union of Kamerun Students, Kumba, 10 July, 1959. Cf. Southern Cameroons Information Service, *Press Release No. 410*, Buea, 31 July 1959.
32   Cf. V.E. Mukete, *My Odyssey, The Story of Cameroon Reunification*, (Yaounde: Eagle Publishing, 2013), p. 322.
33   Ibid.
34   CF. Muna, op. cit., p. 400.
35   Ibid., p. 414.

German Kamerun. The German protectorate had fallen in 1916, the very year of Foncha's birth. And fearing that reunification, the ground for which had yet to be prepared, might be made a condition for separating from Nigeria, Foncha began to toy with the idea of an independent Southern Cameroons as a means of achieving that goal. It seems that that idea was not new to him. Although it did not become official party policy, Foncha threw feelers about it at various instances in the past. In 1951, he told the Victoria Divisional Council that the Southern Cameroons "should secede from Nigeria and remain an independent country."[36] At a preliminary meeting of the London Constitutional Conference of May 1957, he told delegates that the Southern Cameroons should "stand as a little independent state."[37] And during the final consultative meeting with the British Government in November 1960, Foncha continued to argue that the Southern Cameroons should be granted its independence to enable it negotiate reunification with the Cameroun Republic as equal partners. It seemed rather naïve of Foncha to expect that the British, who seemed hell-bent on the Nigeria option, would support his demand for an extended trusteeship or an independent Southern Cameroons. Endeley dismissed that possibility as "a joy ride to an unknown destination."[38] And the Colonial Secretary, Ian Mcleod, buried it by declaring that "The United Kingdom Government would never transfer sovereignty to the Southern Cameroons."[39] That stance clearly contravened the principal objective of the Trusteeship System, to prepare the people for self-government or independence. But the obsession of the British Government with the Nigeria option was such that they would do anything to keep off the table any new option that might tickle the people's imagination. They supported the KNC/KPP alliance in their push for reunification to be included as the other alternative at the plebiscite, convinced that it was not attractive enough to entice voters and hoping that its proponents would not have sufficient time to mount an effective counter-campaign. But in trying to muddy the waters for Foncha and the KNDP, Endeley and the British inadvertently made a decisive contribution to the reunification

36   Ibid., p. 353.
37   Ibid., p. 341.
38   Ibid., p. 426.
39   Ibid., p. 499.

of the Cameroons. Feeling his back against the wall, Foncha mounted a spirited campaign for reunification with the French Cameroun!

Both parties were also at variance over the franchise. The KNC/KPP felt that all foreigners resident in the Southern Cameroons should be allowed to vote in the plebiscite. But the KNDP objected because the vast majority of those foreign residents were Nigerians, who would naturally support the option involving their country.

Those differences made it difficult for the UN to recommend that the plebiscite in the Southern Cameroons should go ahead. Instead, both sides were urged to reach agreement on the alternatives to be put in the plebiscite and the voting qualifications, although the UN did set a deadline for the consultation to take place before the end of April 1960.

But neither was willing to give ground, as the issues in contention were likely to influence the outcome. Numerous discussions were held by the two leaders with the Commissioner of the Southern Cameroons; with the British Colonial Secretary, Mr. Lennox-Boyd, in May 1959; and with the Governor-General of Nigeria, Sir James Robertson, in July 1959.[40] But all those efforts yielded nothing. Not even a Conference of all Southern Cameroons parties held in Mamfe in August 1959 could reconcile the views. In the end, the leaders of the Territory agreed to seek the arbitration of the UN.

The question of the Southern Cameroons was considered anew at the fourteenth session of the General Assembly from September to November 1959. It emerged from the debate that, owing to its small size and frail economy, the Southern Cameroons could only achieve independence by association with either Nigeria or the French Cameroun. And while the Assembly was holding, African delegations brokered further negotiations between the two Southern Cameroons leaders, resulting in an agreed statement published as Document A/C. 4/414 of September 30, 1959. In that statement the two leaders proposed that there should be no plebiscite in the Southern Cameroons in 1960, that the question of the future of the Territory should be referred to the sixteenth session of the General Assembly with a view to holding the plebiscite in 1962, that the Trusteeship Agreement should be terminated not later than October

---

40   A/C.4/SR. 855, 24 Sept., 1959, p. 14.

26, 1962, and that in the meantime the administration of the Territory should be separated from that of Nigeria and the trusteeship extended.

The agreement did not address the issues that had separated the Southern Cameroons leaders. It said nothing of the questions to be put at the plebiscite or the voting qualifications. And by seeking to postpone the consultation, it conflicted with Resolution 1350[XIII], which had called for a plebiscite not later than April 1960.

The General Assembly was faced with a dilemma, whether to impose Resolution 1350 on the Southern Cameroons, or work with the agreement obtained by the African delegations. After a heated debate, the General Assembly satisfied the wishes of the Southern Cameroons leaders in half: Resolution 1352[XIV] of October 16, 1959, effectively postponed the Southern Cameroons plebiscite to 1961.

As for the alternatives to be put to the people, Endeley prevailed and reunification with the French Cameroun was placed on the ballot. But by omission or commission, the United Nations failed to meet the basic requirement of any union: it did not establish the consent of the other party involved. It did not put in place any mechanism by which the people of Nigeria or Cameroun could also be consulted to know whether they were willing to join with the Southern Cameroons. The General Assembly recommended that Southern Cameroonians be asked:

a). Do you wish to achieve independence by joining the independent Federation of Nigeria? Or,

a). Do you wish to achieve independence by joining the independent Republic of Cameroun?[41]

Each option was covered by certain guarantees: a vote for the first alternative meant that the Southern Cameroons would integrate Nigeria as "a full self-governing Region equal in all respects with the other Regions in an independent Nigeria;"[42] while a vote for the second alternative meant that the Southern Cameroons would unify with the then

41   G.A., Res. 1352(XIV), Art. 2.
42   Quoted in UN Doc. A/4727, of 11 April 1961, p. 12.

unitary Cameroun Republic "on a federal basis adaptable to conditions peculiar to all sections of the Kamerun."[43] The franchise was restricted to persons born in the Southern Cameroons or one of whose parents was born there,[44] a restriction almost impossible to implement as birth certificates were not common.

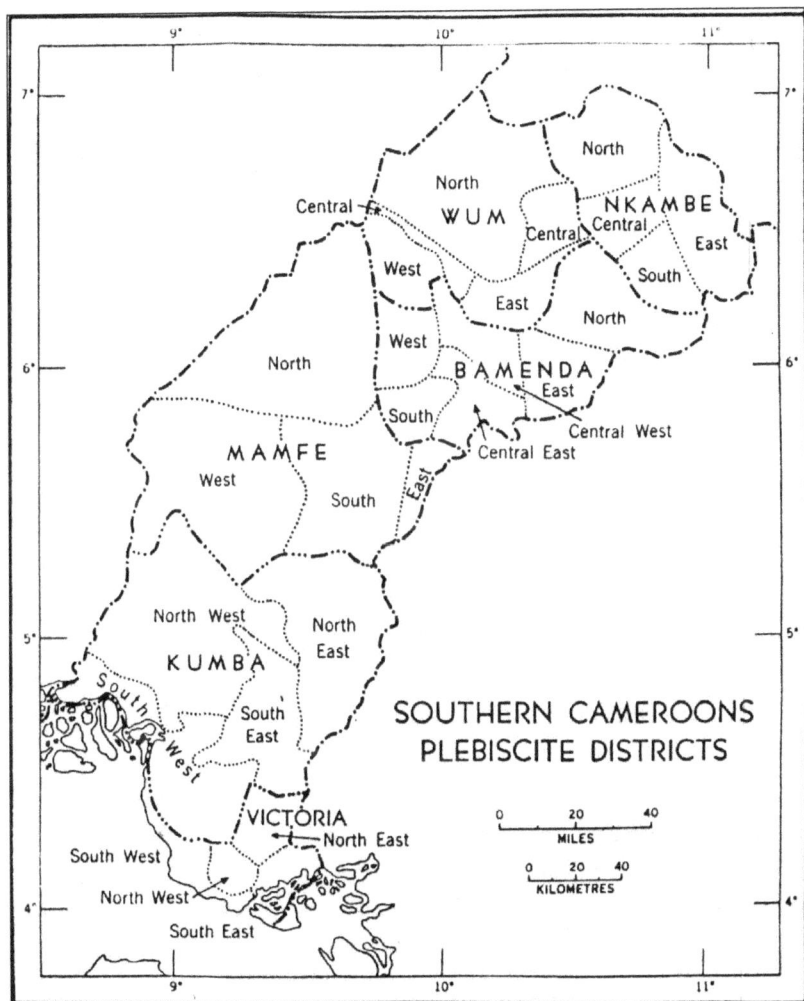

Figure 2.1. Southern Cameroons Plebiscite Districts

43   Quoted in Ibid.
44   G.A. Res. 1352 (XIV), Art. 3.

The organization of the Southern Cameroons plebiscite was governed by the Southern Cameroons Order-in-Council, 1960, published in the United Kingdom as Statutory Instrument No. 1655 of September 12, 1960. The Order vested responsibility for the conduct of the plebiscite in the Commissioner of the Southern Cameroons, who was empowered by Article 6[3] to constitute such other offices as he might consider necessary for the exercise.

He duly appointed Hubert Childs, formerly Chief Commissioner of Sierra Leone, as Plebiscite Administrator. Childs would direct an organizing staff of 4,437, of which the Deputy Administrator, five Assistant Administrators and twenty-six Supervisory Officers were expatriate officials recruited in the United Kingdom. Dr. Abdoh's UN staff of 34 supervised the plebiscite.

According to Article 3[1] of the Order-in-Council, the Southern Cameroons was divided into twenty-six plebiscite districts, corresponding to the electoral constituencies for the Southern Cameroons House of Assembly, with a register of voters for each district. And in keeping with General Assembly Resolution 1352[XIV] that the plebiscite in the Southern Cameroons be concluded not later than March 1961, the Commissioner of the Southern Cameroons decided that voting in the plebiscite would take place on February 11, 1961. In fixing that date, the wishes of the Government of the Southern Cameroons were quietly ignored. When the Deputy Plebiscite Administrator, J. Dixon, arrived Buea in August 1960 for consultations on the possible date for the plebiscite, Foncha informed him that they were leaving for London for further consultations with the British Government and that the date for the plebiscite should not be fixed before those consultations had taken place. But Dixon went ahead regardless and announced that the Southern Cameroons plebiscite shall take place on 11 February 1961.[45] It is possible that the British Government, for whom he worked, had made that decision beforehand. He could not have made it all by himself.

The plebiscite campaign was a hard-fought contest between the two main political formations of the Southern Cameroons, the KNDP and the CPNC. The latter had been formed in July 1960 by a merger of the

45   Muna, op. cit., p. 481.

KNC and the KPP, with Endeley as President. It campaigned for the union of the Southern Cameroons with Nigeria, highlighting the political upheaval in the neighboring Cameroun and the risk of the Southern Cameroons being sucked into it. For his part, Foncha campaigned for union with the Cameroun republic, using Igbophobia as his principal weapon, and accusing the hated Igbos for every ill that had afflicted the Southern Cameroons. S.T. Muna aptly summarized the KNDP argument: "Unification was an emotional and sentimental issue, brought about not by any dreams of what we were under the Germans but by how we were treated and dominated by Nigerians, especially the Igbos, in our own homeland…No one who has ever been a victim of humiliation ever forgets it."[46] In the heat of the moment, no one questioned how the fate of a people could be staked on such a leap of faith by its leaders.

The campaign was a contest of invective, characterized by scaremongering and scapegoating on either side. The protagonists sought to portray not what was good in the option they championed but what was bad in the one they opposed. Nobody talked about the advantages of what was on offer. The major difference was that while Southern Cameroonians had never experienced Ahidjo's regime, they had lived with the Igbos for forty years, enduring their domineering attitude that was resented throughout Nigeria itself. Foncha's narrative therefore had a starting advantage over Endeley's in the sense that promise was generally more attractive than performance, and he was deliberately vague about the contents of the promise.

Fon Achirimbi II of Bafut translated the perplexity of many Southern Cameroonians when he told the Mamfe Conference of 1959 that the forthcoming plebiscite offered a choice between fire and the deep sea. The options were somewhat puzzling: one from which they had been struggling to separate, and the other from which they had been separated for forty years. And while Foncha campaigned that reunification was in the natural logic of the Southern Cameroons, Endeley dismissed that logic as nothing but a figment of the imagination of the KNDP. He argued that the German Kamerun, to which reunification alluded, was barely tangible: it had been so short-lived that the Germans were still

---

46   Ibid., p. 504.

experimenting on where to establish the capital; and it was, after all, just another colonial fabrication about which an authentic African could not be unduly sentimental.[47]

The plebiscite was settled on February 11, 1961. A total of 349,652 persons registered to vote, representing roughly 90% of the potential electorate of the Southern Cameroons. Of those registered voters 94.75% actually voted, and the results showed that the people of the Southern Cameroons had voted by 70.49% [233,571 votes] to 29.51% [97,741 votes] to achieve independence by joining the Cameroun Republic.

The Plebiscite Commissioner reported that the exercise was "efficiently organized and conducted by the Administering Authority," and that "the people of the Southern Cameroons had the opportunity to express their wishes freely."[48] In evaluation, he observed that "the majority of the people may not have grasped the detailed implications of the alternatives at the plebiscite."[49]

Table 2.2. Results of the Southern Cameroons Plebiscite

	Plebiscite Districts	First Alternative (Federation of Nigeria)	Second Alternative (Republic of Cameroun)
Victoria	1. South-West	2,552	3,756
	2. South-East	1,329	4,870
	3. North-West	4,744	4,205
	4. North-East	3,291	9,251
Kumba	5. North-East	9,466	11,991
	6. North-West	14,738	555

47   A/C. 4/SR. 846, 23 Feb. 1959, p. 555.
48   A/4727, 11 April 1961, p. 52.
49   Ibid, p. 52.

	7. South-East	6,105	12,827
	8. South-West	2,424	2,227
Mamfe	9. West	2,039	8,505
	10. North	5,432	6,410
	11. South	685	8,175
	12. East	1,894	10,177
Bamenda	13. North	8,073	18,839
	14. East	1,822	18,027
	15. Central West	1,230	18,193
	16. Central East	529	17,858
	17. West	467	16,142
	18. South	220	19,426
Wum	19. North	1,485	7,322
	20. Central	3,644	3,211
	21. East	1,518	13,133
	22. West	2,137	3,440
Nkambe	23. North	5,485	1,917
	24. East	3,845	5,896
	25. Central	5,059	4,288
	26. South	7,051	2,921
	TOTALS	**97,741**	**233,571**

Source: U.N., G.A., A/4727, 11 April 1961, p. 50.

The Second Northern Cameroons Plebiscite, 1961

The results of the first Northern Cameroons plebiscite came as a shock to the United Kingdom. The British government had always maintained that the administrative union with Nigeria was the only possible way to administer the British Cameroons. But that assumption failed the very first test, as the first Northern Cameroons plebiscite revealed the depth of anti-Nigeria sentiment in the Territory.

However, although unequivocal in its rejection of integration with Nigeria, the 1959 plebiscite had been inconclusive in deciding the future of the Northern Cameroons. That plebiscite had been designed in such a way as to offer a second possibility for the Nigeria option to be put to the people. So the UN made arrangements for a further consultation in the Northern Cameroons before March 1961.[50] This time it was no longer an open-ended question but a definite choice between two clear-cut options. The General Assembly decided that the two questions to be put at the plebiscite would be:

a). Do you wish to achieve independence by joining the independent Republic of Cameroun?

b). Do you wish to achieve independence by joining the independent Federation of Nigeria?[51]

The alternatives for the second Northern Cameroons plebiscite were thus identical to those for the Southern Cameroons plebiscite, in reversed order! As in the Southern Cameroons plebiscite, either option entailed certain guarantees for the future of the people. A vote for union with Nigeria meant that the Territory "will be administered as a separate province of the Northern Region."[52] While a vote for union with the French Cameroun would offer the Northern Cameroons a choice of three possible arrangements:

a federation as envisaged for the Southern Cameroons; provincial

---

50   G.A., Res. 1473(XIV), 12 Dec. 1959, Art. 2.
51   Ibid, Art. 3.
52   Cf. A/4727, 11 April 1961, p. 18.

autonomy, with a local administration dependent of the Central Government of the Federal Republic; and administrative unification in the form of regional or provincial collectivities, under the jurisdiction of the present Constitution of the Republic of Cameroun.[53]

One of the most repeated criticisms of the first plebiscite had been its limitation of the franchise to men. Although that was said to be the general practice in Northern Nigeria at the time, the UN later felt that it had been wrong to limit the franchise in a consultation of such importance. Against opposition from various sections of the Territory,[54] the General Assembly decided that the second Northern Cameroons plebiscite should be conducted on the basis of universal adult suffrage,[55] a decision that almost doubled the electorate.

But unlike in the Southern Cameroons plebiscite where voting had been restricted to people born in the Territory or one of whose parents was born there, the second Northern Cameroons plebiscite spread the vote to anyone "ordinarily resident" in the Territory, irrespective of nationality.[56] This was to become the source of controversy following reports that Nigerians voted massively in the plebiscite.

The first Northern Cameroons plebiscite had important lessons for the second. The Plebiscite Commissioner had reported then that the majority of the voters had used the plebiscite to protest against the existing system of local government, leading the General Assembly to recommend that measures be taken "for the further decentralization of government functions and the effective democratization of the system of local government in the northern part of the Trust Territory."[57] How the UN seriously expected the administrative system operating in the Northern Cameroons for over forty years to be effectively overhauled in the two months leading up to the plebiscite is an open question. But

53   Communiqué by the Government of Cameroun, published on 31 December 1960: cf. A/4727, p. 20.
54   UN, T.C., T/SR.1086, 18 May 1960, p. 239.
55   G.A., Res. 1473(XIV), Art. 4.
56   Ibid.
57   Ibid, Art. 6.

it seems that the General Assembly wanted to satisfy its conscience that the organization of the plebiscite should not be tainted by the maligned administrative structure of the Territory.

That organization was conducted by Sir Percy Wyn-Harris, who had been appointed as the British Administrator of the Northern Cameroons when Nigeria became independent. Wyn-Harris directed a plebiscite staff of 2,142 officers and brought with him a decade of experience as Governor of The Gambia [1949-1958].

The Northern Cameroons was divided into nine plebiscite districts, corresponding roughly to the plebiscite circles established for the first plebiscite. The plebiscite districts were subdivided into 346 registration areas. Polling was scheduled to take place in two days [11 and 12 February] instead of one because the inhabitants of certain villages complained that they might be obliged to leave their villages unattended for a whole day if voting lasted for only one day, and because there were only 300 Cameroonians qualified to serve as polling agents and the Plebiscite Commissioner decided against supplementing them with Nigerian recruits, preferring to employ only Cameroonian agents for the two days.[58] As in the previous exercise, the plebiscite was supervised by Djalal Abdoh and his UN staff of 34 officials.

The campaign for the second Northern Cameroons plebiscite witnessed a major realignment of the alliance that had operated during the first exercise. This time, all political parties in southern Nigeria rallied to the support of the NPC in its campaign for the integration of the Northern Cameroons into Nigeria. Only the NKDP campaigned for joining the Cameroun Republic.

Turnout for the election was particularly high. The final register of voters included a total of 294,985 persons, roughly 50% [146,264] of whom were women. In the end, 243,865 valid votes were cast, of which 146,206 or 59.95% favored the alternative of joining the Federation of Nigeria, and 97,659 or 40.05% favored the alternative of joining the Republic of Cameroun.

58   A/C. 4/SR. 1144, 14 April 1961. p. 317.

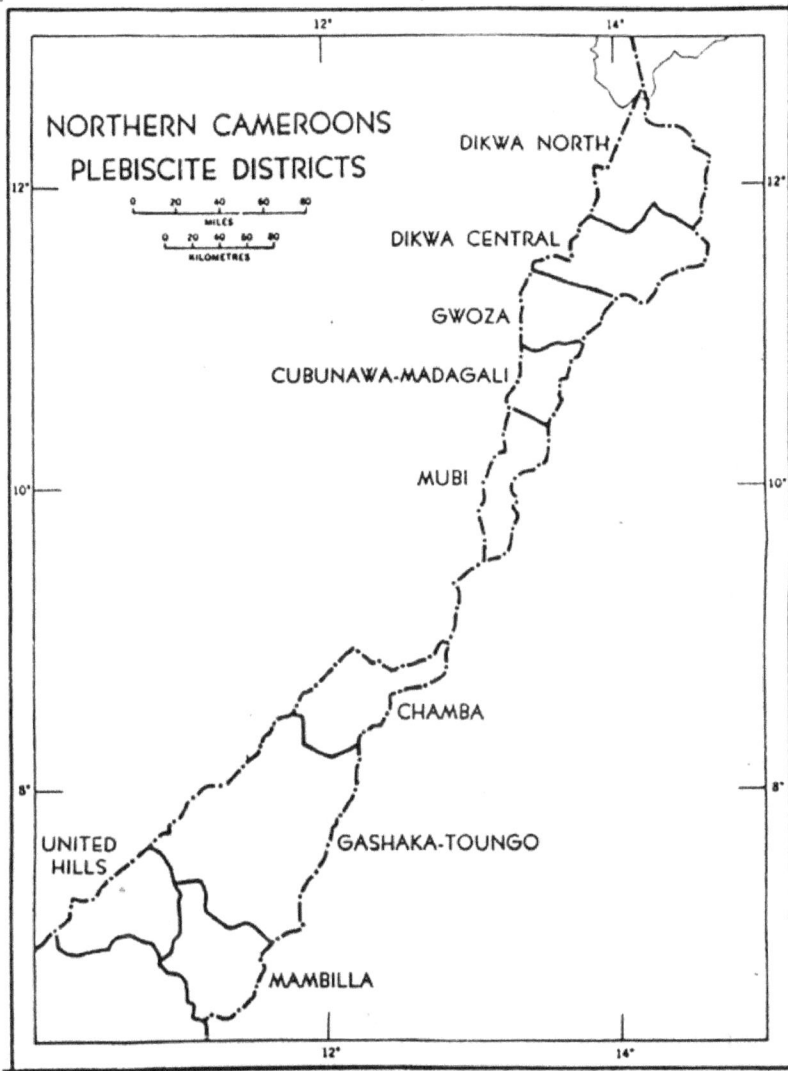

Figure 2.2. Northern Cameroons plebiscite districts

The Plebiscite Commissioner reported that the exercise was efficiently organized and conducted, and that the people of the Northern Cameroons had the opportunity to express their wishes freely and secretly.[59] In so

59   A/4727, 11 April 1961, p. 86.

doing, they chose a different future from that of the Southern Cameroons.

Table 2.3. Results of the Second Northern Cameroons Plebiscite

Plebiscite District	Republic of Cameroun	Federation of Nigeria
1. Dikwa North	10,562	22,765
2. Dikwa Central	24,203	28,697
3. Gwoza	2,554	18,115
4. Cubunawa-Madagali	16,904	13,299
5. Mubi	11,132	23,708
6. Chamba	25,177	9,704
7. Gashaka-Toungo	3,108	4.999
8. Mambilla	7,467	13,523
9. United Hills	157	7,791
TOTALS	97,659	146,206

Source: U.N., G.A., A/4727, 11 April 1961, p. 85.

The Plebiscites at the United Nations

The British Cameroons plebiscites sanctioned the termination of the trusteeship by granting independence to the people of the Territory within the framework of the choices made. The actual transfer of sovereignty took place on different dates, and between different authorities: On July 1, 1961, at Mubi, the British Administrator of the Northern Cameroons, Sir Percy Wyn-Harris, handed over the documents of the Territory to the Prime Minister of Nigeria. At a similar ceremony in Buea three months later [1 October 1961], the Acting British Commissioner of the Southern Cameroons, Malcom Milne, handed sovereignty over the Territory to

President Ahmadou Ahidjo of the Cameroun Republic. These transfers formally marked the end of the United Nations trusteeship over the British Cameroons and the independence of the Territory.

It is noteworthy that the people of the British Cameroons had very little say in the critical decisions leading to the determination of their future. The selection of the plebiscite as the means of decision was made by the UN, even though the leaders of the Southern Cameroons were agreed that the best mode of decision would be the forthcoming general election. The options of the plebiscite were chosen by the UN, even though at no point in their history had the people of the British Cameroons been openly inclined towards either option. And the timing of the plebiscites was determined by the UN, even when the leaders of the Southern Cameroons would rather not have the consultation then.

The last phase of the UN's responsibilities over the British Cameroons was the debate on the results of the plebiscites. The result of the Southern Cameroons plebiscite was virtually uncontested, except by two petitioners [N.N. Mbile and Chief Sakwe Bokwe] who requested that the tribes that had voted for integration with Nigeria be excised from the Southern Cameroons and attached to Nigeria.[60] Proponents of reunification dismissed that request as "contemptibly ludicrous."[61] It did not prosper. In contrast, the results of the second Northern Cameroons plebiscite met with a storm of protest from some Member States, who challenged the Plebiscite Commissioner's view that the people had had the opportunity to express themselves freely, arguing that the administration of the Northern Cameroons had not been separated from that of Northern Nigeria as required by Resolution 1473[XIV], and consequently, the plebiscite could not have been free or fair. Led by Cameroun and supported by France, those States called on the General Assembly to nullify the results of the plebiscite and hold fresh consultations. Their remonstration came to a head during discussions at the fifteenth session of the General Assembly to ratify the results of the plebiscites.

During that debate, French-speaking African delegations introduced a draft Resolution [L.684/Rev. 2] calling on the General Assembly to

60   V.E. Mukete, op. cit., p. 397.
61   Ibid.

send a six-member commission to the Northern Cameroons to ascertain whether the safeguards of Resolution 1473[XIV] had been implemented and make necessary recommendations "to enable the General Assembly to take appropriate measures in regard to the future of the Territory."[62]

But the majority of Members declined to censure. By 41 votes to 28, with 18 abstentions, the Assembly gave priority consideration to a rival draft Resolution [L.685] endorsing the results of the plebiscites and calling for the decisions made by the people of the British Cameroons to be immediately implemented.[63]

In the heated exchanges between both camps, the Cameroun Republic and its allies tried in vain to block draft Resolution L.685, walking out of the debate when its passage became imminent. The protest against the second Northern Cameroons plebiscite led to a situation whereby the Cameroun Republic was opposed to the Resolution granting inde-pendence to the British Cameroons, part of which had voted to join it! Draft Resolution L.685 was adopted by 57 votes to 2, with 9 abstentions, as Resolution 1608[XV] of April 21, 1961. In essence, it considered that

> The people of the two parts of the Trust Territory, having freely and secretly expressed their wishes with regard to their respec-tive futures in accordance with General Assembly Resolutions 1352 [XIV] and 1473[XIV], the decisions made by them through democratic processes under the supervision of the United Nations should be immediately implemented.

It decided that:

> The plebiscites having been held separately with differing results, the Trusteeship Agreement of 13 December 1946 concerning the Cameroons under United Kingdom administration shall be terminated, in accordance with Article 76B of the Charter of the United Nations and in agreement with the Administering Authority, in the following manner:

62   A/C. 4/L.684/Rev. 2. 15 April 1961.
63   A/C. 4/685, 18 April 1961.

(a) With respect to the Northern Cameroons, on 1st June 1961, upon its joining the Federation of Nigeria as a separate province of the Northern Region of Nigeria:

(b) With respect to the Southern Cameroons, on 1st October 1961, upon its joining the Republic of Cameroun.[64]

Commenting on the decision, the French delegate lamented "the desire of the majority to brutally and systematically impose the law of numbers on the minority."[65]

Resolution 1608(XV) had some clearly ambiguous provisions: it sanctioned the mazy termination of a single Trusteeship Agreement, following internal divisions unknown to the Agreement itself; it permitted the piecemeal liquidation of the United Nations trust over the British Cameroons, strangely allowing the same Instrument to be terminated twice. That Agreement was appropriately known as the "Trusteeship Agreement for the Territory of the Cameroons under British Administration," implying one Territory, with one administration and one Agreement. There was no separate Agreement for the Northern Cameroons and none for the Southern Cameroons. So, on June 1st, 1961, when the Trusteeship Agreement was "first" terminated upon the Northern Cameroons joining Nigeria, the trust over the British Cameroons legally ceased to exist. Being no longer in force, the Agreement could not be conjured for termination a second time on 1st October 1961 when the Southern Cameroons joined the Cameroun Republic. Between those two dates, the Southern Cameroons floated in a legal vacuum. The Trusteeship Agreement under which the United Kingdom administered it had been terminated. The administrative union with Nigeria had ended. The Southern Cameroons was on its own, without being formally independent.

---

64 UN, G.A. Res. 1608 (XIV), of 21 April 1961, Art.3, 4.
65 *Le Monde*, Paris, 22 April 1961.

CHAPTER THREE

International Involvement

The debates on the fate of the British Cameroons vividly animated the halls of the UN from 1959 to 1961. In the months preceding the plebiscites, one London newspaper commented that "though the problems of the British Cameroons seem infinitely smaller than those of the Congo, international tempers have been raised to great heights."[1]

And with good reason: the issue of the British Cameroons posed theoretical questions about trusteeship, decolonization and sovereignty, as well as practical problems of statehood, territory, wealth and population, all questions about which governments generally had very strong feelings.

The Positions of the Interested Parties

Although all Member States of the UN were directly concerned with the fate of the British Cameroons as a UN Trust Territory, some had reason to be more concerned than others, especially those States that were likely to gain or lose jurisdiction in the Territory through the plebiscites. That was true of the United Kingdom as the Administering Authority, and of Nigeria as the administrative partner. It was also true of the French Cameroun by reason of historical affiliation and geographical contiguity, and of France which, until 1960, represented Cameroun in the international community.

The policy of Great Britain towards terminating trusteeship was somewhat ambiguous. She had resisted French attempts to simply annex the former German colonies, yet she seemed reluctant to free them altogether. As one writer pointed out, "not only was the Empire a source of Britain's military and economic power and of national pride, but it also provided many individual Britons with a good income, with outlets for

1   *The Guardian*, London, 11 Nov. 1960.

their energy and opportunities for their careers."[2] In the British Cameroons, Premier Foncha accused them of "doing everything to stifle the people's march to independence."[3]

There developed among the British a strong emotional attachment to the colonial Empire, which led them to regard decolonization with suspicion and, sometimes, with systematic opposition. Many in Britain felt "a sense of personal loss, almost an amputation" whenever a part of that empire was granted independence.[4]

Britain's resistance to decolonization was influenced by the way in which the notion broke upon the world after the Second World War and the manner in which the UN pressed it forward. In his study of British foreign policy, Joseph Frankel observes that "the climate of multilateral diplomacy and the histrionics of the UN General Assembly did not correspond with Britain's notions of classical diplomacy."[5] Despite being one of the founders of the world Organization, Britain quickly became suspicious of the ever-increasing decolonizing ambitions of the General Assembly.

A veteran British colonial administrator and one-time Permanent Representative to the Trusteeship Council, Sir Alan Burns, dismissed both the Trusteeship Council and the Fourth Committee of the General Assembly as being "less concerned with the welfare of the indigenous inhabitants of the colonies than with the spread of propaganda."[6] That feeling was echoed by the Secretary of State for the Colonies, Lennox-Boyd, who wrote that:

> The proceedings of the Fourth Committee were often characterized by irresponsible and sometimes offensive speeches from certain delegations; there was little disposition to contribute constructively and objectively to the discussion of the affairs of the colonial and trust territories. Instead, the Committee

---

2   *The Times*, London, 22 April.
3   1960 Joseph Frankel, *British Foreign Policy* 1945-1973, (London: OUP, 1975) pp. 221-222.
4   John Strachey, *The End of Empire*, 1959, p. 204; Quoted in Joseph Frankel, op.cit, p. 225.
5   Ibid., p. 251.
6   Sir Alan Burns, *In Defence of Colonies*, (London: Allen and Unwin, 1975), p. 115.

zealously pursued its attempts to extend the role of the United Nations in these matters, to the detriment of the Administering Members.[7]

Britain's skepticism derived in part from the concern, in Churchill's lofty imagery, that the "fumbling fingers" of humanity might thrust independence upon peoples unprepared for the responsibility. And from the sheer unwillingness to admit that Pax Britannica had lost its shine, by yielding to pressure from outside. That resistance also veiled an underlying fear of the catalytic effect that decolonization could have in areas that Britain was not ready to leave or with which she wished to maintain a special relationship after independence.

The policy of the United Kingdom towards terminating the trusteeship over the British Cameroons was influenced by two considerations. On the one hand, the nature of the termination was guided by Britain's experience with a similar exercise in the British Togoland five years earlier, where the plebiscite had been utilized to obtain union with the Gold Coast. It was no coincidence that the questions put at the Togoland plebiscite of May 9, 1956 -- to choose between immediate integration with an independent Gold Coast and decision at a later date -- were identical to those put at the first Northern Cameroons plebiscite.

On the other hand, the practical side of terminating the trusteeship over the British Cameroons was linked to the decolonization of Nigeria. The administrative union between both Territories had been so complete that by the time Britain became firmly committed to granting independence to Nigeria, she was also committed to terminating the trusteeship over the British Cameroons.

But the UK did not always clarify her views on the future of the British Cameroons. In fact, when the Soviet Delegate to the Trusteeship Council first raised the prospect of independence for the British Cameroons, his British counterpart hushed the idea as a premature speculation about the future of the Territory.[8] Despite the noncommittal official positions,

7   Report on the Colonial Territories, 1953-54 (Cmd. 9169), para. 851: 1954-55 (Cmd. 9489), para. 840. Quoted in Alan Burns, Ibid., pp. 108-109.
8   U.N., T.C., T/SR.856, 10 Feb. 1961.

however, *The Times* of London reported that there was developing in the UK a tacit assumption that the British Cameroons would remain with Nigeria.[9]

Perhaps that assumption had always existed, going by the view that Britain had acquired the British Cameroons in order to fill in the missing links on the eastern border of Nigeria. Such an exercise was not expected to be temporary.

The closest that one came to a public statement of the British government's position on the future of the British Cameroons was at the Nigeria Constitutional Conference in London in mid-1957. The Colonial Secretary declared that there could be "no question of obliging the Cameroons to remain part of an independent Nigeria contrary to her wishes." He made it clear that although the moment of decision was at hand, the options available were limited: the British Cameroons could continue under the trust administration of the UK, an option accompanied by the ominous warning that the Territory "would not thereby be given the golden key to the Bank of England." Or the Territory could simply remain with Nigeria. The Secretary of State was categorical that this was by far the better option: "many of the best friends of the Cameroons do not foresee a destiny more likely to promote her happiness and prosperity than in continued association with Nigeria."[10]

Sensing that many Southern Cameroonians were not impressed by the Nigeria option, the British began to flirt with the idea of separate independence for the Trust Territory. In 1959, the Acting Governor-General of Nigeria, Sir Ralph Grey, proposed to N. N. Mbile of the KNC/KPP Alliance that the Southern Cameroons should suspend its fight for independence until Nigeria and Cameroun became independent, so as to negotiate its future in full appreciation of the options.[11] And in November 1960, the British hosted an all-party conference of Southern Cameroons leaders in London with a view to requesting the UN to cancel the forthcoming plebiscite and grant independence to the Southern Cameroons

---

9 *The Times*, London, 4 August, 1961.

10 Report by the Nigeria Constitutional Conference, Cmd. 287, (London: Her Majesty's Stationery Office, July 1957), p. 30.

11 Victor Julius Ngoh, *Constitutional Developments in Southern Cameroons 1946-1961*, (Yaounde: CEPER, 1990), p. 196.

as a separate entity. But when word came from the British delegation in New York that the UN would be hostile to such change of heart, the British Colonial Secretary backed out of the conference.[12]

The United Kingdom thus had a two-pronged approach in the affair of the British Cameroons: with the advance of Nigeria towards independence, the UK was eager to terminate the trusteeship over the Territory, and in the process ensure that the British Cameroons remained with Nigeria.

Nigeria's concern with the future of the British Cameroons resulted partly from geographical contiguity, and partly from nearly half a century of administrative union. The latter had gone on for so long that many Nigerians forgot that there was any real distinction in status between both Territories, less still that the administrative union was only temporary. Some were so certain of the administrative union that they included the Trust Territory in the purview of their political party, ambitiously naming it the National Council of Nigeria and the Cameroons (NCNC). After the plebiscites, its leaders would come down to earth and promptly rename the party the National Council of Nigerian Citizens!

Nigerians, especially the Igbos, felt so much at ease in the British Cameroons that they went about their business in the Territory with conceit and even arrogance. Some were surprised that the British Cameroons should have to decide on its future at all. To them, there was no such thing as the future of the British Cameroons: there was only one future, the future of Nigeria, which included the British Cameroons!

Among those who perceived a separate future for the British Cameroons, many felt that such a future threatened the territorial integrity of Nigeria. The prospect of separating the Trust Territory was branded as outright secession by many in Nigeria. As *The Guardian* of London reported on September 11, 1959, the inconclusive first Northern Cameroons plebiscite was seen by some Nigerians as "an indefensible shrinking of the Federation of Nigeria."

In a debate on the British Cameroons in February 1959, Chief Kolawole Balogun told the House of Representatives that

---

12   Ibid., pp. 195-197.

The important thing is Nigeria, the territorial integrity of Nigeria, the land, the geography added to us by the British. The greatest honor done to us by the British is to have expanded the area which we call Nigeria today, to have brought the people together and I want to say that I will be opposed to any person who wishes to disintegrate the territory that is now known as Nigeria.[13]

Another Member reminded the House that "Abubakar Tafawa Balewa did not become the first Prime Minister of the Federation to see to the liquidation of any of its parts."[14]

The continued association of the British Cameroons with Nigeria was largely taken for granted. There was a general assumption that the British Cameroons really had nowhere else to go. The prospect of separation, however frequently floated, was seldom taken seriously.

The year 1959 changed all that. Two shock electoral defeats shattered Nigeria's complacency towards the British Cameroons. By rejecting immediate union with the Northern Region, the Northern Cameroons plebiscite shook up the patronizing oligarchy of Northern Nigeria and forced them into uncharacteristic measures of local government reform in order to win back the support of the Territory.

Secondly, the KNDP defeated the KNC/KPP Alliance in the Southern Cameroons general election of January 1959, confronting Nigeria with a government that bluntly rejected the administrative union. The prospect of separation, only distantly imagined before, suddenly became a living reality in the relationship between Nigeria and the British Cameroons.

The victory of the KNDP drew varying reactions in Nigeria. Many were surprised at the collapse of the KNC/KPP appeal and regretted that the Southern Cameroons had been allowed to go that far.

Another body of Nigerian opinion was outraged, feeling that the British Cameroons was deriving more from the administrative union than it was putting into it. Some were so frustrated that they asked for

13   House of Representatives Debates, Official Report, 1959-60, Vol. 1, 7 Feb. 1959, (Lagos: Federal Gov't Printer, 1960), p. 38.
14   Ibid., 17 Feb. 1959, p. 348.

all Nigerian money spent on the Territory to be refunded and for the Southern Cameroons to be expelled from the union.

When the election was being discussed in the House of Representatives, a group emerged, urging the House to "let them go." A spokesman for the group argued that "we cannot afford to waste our money on behalf of such ungrateful people like the people of the Southern Cameroons." Nigeria was too big a country "to be begging the people of the Southern Cameroons not to go."[15] But the majority opinion in Nigeria refused to give up, hoping that the people would recover their wits and return to Nigeria.

Suspicions that the drive for separation was being instigated from outside the Territory only hardened their resolve. As one Member revealed in Parliament, "there is a bigger brother behind the whole show; and it is that bigger brother that we are aiming at. It is not small Foncha. Foncha has no power. The real power is behind him from across the border."[16] Still, Nigerians were optimistic that Southern Cameroonians "will come to realize that we in Nigeria are better associates than any new friend that they are hoping to make."[17]

Against that background, the 1961 plebiscite became even more significant. Nigeria's reaction to the exercise was varied. There were activists, like Chief Kolawole Balogun, who felt that "nobody is going to stampede us from the Cameroons," because "in all parts of the world people hold on to what they have got," that Nigerian leaders should put their heads together and reverse the tide of separation in the Southern Cameroons, and that the plebiscites "must be fought vigorously like a man."[18]

And there were moderates who argued that, for tactical reasons, Nigeria's involvement should be kept rather low key. As one Minister pointed out, the issue of the British Cameroons plebiscites "is a very delicate one, and if we are not careful, our utterances here may defeat the very intention we have in mind. The less that is said about the future of the Cameroons, the better for the reasonable elements in the Cameroons."[19]

15   Ibid., p. 347.
16   Ibid., p. 348.
17   Ibid., p. 349.
18   Ibid., 7 Feb. 1959, pp. 37-38.
19   Ibid., 17 Feb. 1959, p. 349.

Both activists and moderates shared a common goal: that Nigeria should retain the British Cameroons. In fact, the vast majority of Nigerians were in favor of their government doing something about it. And something was done. As a gesture of goodwill towards the people of the Territory, the House of Representatives decided that

> the amount of advances made by the Federal Government to the Southern Cameroons, together with the accrued interest, should be written off, and the advance of working capital made by the Federal Government to the Southern Cameroons Government together with the interest due thereon should be converted into a grant with effect from April 1, 1959.[20]

Those advances amounted to £800,000,[21] and in passing the motion, Nigerian Parliamentarians hoped to rebut the KNDP's claim that the development of the Southern Cameroons was neglected in the administrative union and convince the world as Jaja Wachuku put it that "it was Nigeria that was keeping the Southern Cameroons, and not the British Exchequer."[22]

Despite the intense parliamentary discussion on the future of the British Cameroons, the Federal Government was strangely silent on the plebiscites. It was not until 22nd January 1961, that the Federal Prime Minister, who had not set foot in the Southern Cameroons apart from two brief visits in 1958, made a broadcast appeal on Radio Nigeria to the people of the Territory.

The message was timid and circuitous, avoiding the central issue of Nigeria's preference by outlining the pros and cons of the situation in a fit of objectivity that he hoped would impress voters. As the Prime Minister saw it, the plebiscites involved a straight choice between two clearly unequal alternatives: the people could choose "certainty and security; an honorable status as an integral part of a big country in Africa," or they could throw their lot with a country "whose government has made no

---

20   Ibid., p. 352.
21   Of this sum, 450,000 had been given as advances between 1956 and 1958, 300,000 as advance working capital, and 18,000 as interest.
22   House of Representatives Debates. op.cit, p. 52.

firm promises, a country which has been torn in recent years by civil war." Balewa concluded with the warning that:

> If you vote against Nigeria, I cannot see how you can avoid living a life of poverty and hardship, and under the constant shadow of violence which the Government cannot control. You will be putting yourselves under a country which has different laws and a completely different attitude towards life.[23]

Thus, while the Nigerian Government seemed unruffled by the matter, the country was actively concerned with the British Cameroons plebiscites. Their wishes were clear -- the Trust Territory should remain with Nigeria! But as it became evident that Endeley's campaign was not gaining much traction, the Nigerian Government froze all the funds and grants voted for capital investment in the Southern Cameroons in an attempt to force the collapse of the KNDP government. The decision backfired immediately as the KNDP brandished it as proof of how the Southern Cameroons would be treated if they remained with Nigeria. Relations with the KNDP became so sour that Foncha was not even invited to Nigeria's independence celebrations on 1st October 1960.

In contrast with the tepid approach of the Nigerian Government, the Cameroun Government made no secret of its support for reunification in the British Cameroons plebiscites; it was actively engaged in influencing opinion in the Territory to that effect. The fact that both Territories were known by the same name made that intervention look entirely legitimate.

In fact, the French Cameroun, by virtue of its relative size, came to regard itself as the rightful successor of the German Kamerun, from which the British Cameroons had been removed. As one of its representatives told the United Nations, "The Republic of Cameroun looked upon the two strips of land which comprised the British Cameroons as the western part of its national territory, which had been entrusted to the administration of the United Kingdom by an accident of history."[24] That

---

23   Alhaji Sir Abubakar Tafawa Balewa. *Nigeria Speaks.* (Lagos: Longman, 1964), pp. 88-89.
24   A/C.4/SR.1143, New York, 14 April 1961, p. 308.

claim was factually incorrect, as it gave the impression that Southern Cameroonians were settled on Cameroun land. The British Cameroons had never been part of the French Cameroun and vice versa. Both had come into existence at exactly the same time, through the Franco-British Declaration of 10 July 1919, not one from the other but both from the same German colony which constituted their common heritage. In fact, the first capital of the German Kamerun was in Buea, in the zone that later became the British Cameroons. But because French Cameroun was bigger, it tended to arrogate that heritage all to itself.

Cameroun felt that, in the 33 years of its existence, the German Kamerun had developed a distinct national personality which nearly half a century of separation could not break. It sought to restore that fatherland as far as the British Cameroons was concerned. It looked upon the division of the former German colony as a casualty of the First World War, and upon the British Cameroons plebiscites as the means of putting it right. Cameroun's interest in the British Cameroons was both historical and societal. Many proponents of reunification were Camerounians, of mainly Bamileke and Bassa origin, who had fled from terrorist activity and government harassment in their country and taken refuge in the Southern Cameroons. To them, joining their relatives in Cameroun, which was the main attraction of reunification, was a genuine desire, as was the prospect of amnesty from further persecution by Ahidjo's government.

In the months preceding the plebiscites, President Ahidjo made a campaign tour of the Southern Cameroons, significantly visiting only those towns where support for Nigeria was strongest. His speeches on that tour throw light on the policy of his Government towards the British Cameroons plebiscites. That policy centered only on reunification, which he saw as the legitimate "reunion of brothers and sisters that history had separated."[25]

The theme of brotherhood was a skillful appeal to the sentiment of the people, and the Cameroun leader received a sympathetic hearing in the Southern Cameroons, aided by the many phobias that the people

25 *Agence Camerounaise de Presse* (A.CA.P.), No. 127, Yaounde, 17-18 July 1960, p. 114.

nursed against Nigeria. He dismissed those who predicted intractable problems for reunification: "to two brothers separated by history who want to be reunited, no difficulty can be insurmountable."[26] He never mentioned Nigeria, neither did he say that the people would be better off joining his country.

President Ahidjo was very coy when it came to the material attractions of reunification: "some people still say that we are poor. Maybe we are, but there is no shame in being poor, and nothing says that those who are poor today shall forever remain poor."[27] However, he had no doubt that he would be the leader of the reunited Cameroonian family: "We have never seen a poor family head sell part of his family to a rich neighbor in order to live happily."[28]

The question of reunification was beyond issues of wealth or poverty; Ahidjo saw it as "a sacred debt, not only towards our parents and grand-parents but equally towards our children."[29] And as the event approached, he felt confident that the people of the British Cameroons "shall prove their maturity to the world by voting en masse in favor of the option which follows the logic of the history of their country."[30]

As the Administering Authority in one half of the former German Kamerun, France was naturally interested in what was happening in the other half.[31] Her concern with the British Cameroons was determined by developments in its foreign policy under Charles de Gaulle.

In the early years of the Fifth Republic, Africa was a high priority area of French foreign policy. General de Gaulle was anxious to see his country undertake the delicate transition from colonial master to "friend" of the African countries, a friendship perceived as a center-periphery relationship in which the metropolis was the nerve center of a new grouping of its former colonies.

De Gaulle's initial idea of decolonization was the creation of a

---

26   Ibid., No. 131, 22 July 1960, p. 115.
27   Ibid.
28   Ibid.
29   Ibid., No. 127, 17-18 July 1960, p. 115.
30   *Le Monde,* Paris, 20 July 1960.
31   The UN regarded her as a state "directly concerned" with the British Cameroons trusteeship.

Commonwealth-style organization in which the former colonies would be granted French "assistance" in exchange for their support of France's world strategy.[32] The French Community which crystallized that idea was based partly on the need for Franco-African solidarity, following de Gaulle's conception that "development can only be achieved within a larger whole;"[33] but mainly to safeguard France's privileged links with its former colonies.

Unfortunately, the take-off of the Community was retarded by a protracted theoretical argument on its form. The debate revolved around two contending theories of Franco-African relations. One was propounded by Leopold Sedar Senghor of Senegal, conceiving the Community as a unitary organization at the African level and confederal at the Franco-African level, an approach that would arrest the balkanization of francophone Africa while increasing its independence vis-à-vis France. The other, proposed by Houphouet-Boigny of the Ivory Coast, saw the Community as territorial at the African level and federal at the Franco-African level, a strategy designed to maintain the independence of the African colonies from one another, while increasing their collective dependence on France. In the background was a subtle rivalry for leadership between the two men.

Preoccupied with the Algerian crisis, de Gaulle hesitated between both options, finally adopting a hybrid solution that entailed independence for the African colonies while maintaining privileged relations with them. But in the absence of a cohesive mechanism, the African colonies scrambled for independence, and to the dismay of the West, some soon exercised their newfound freedom by engaging with the Eastern bloc![34]

Counting his losses, a dejected de Gaulle exhorted his countrymen to «laisser nos anciens sujets disposer de leur destin. »[35] And that, «il faut

---

32   Charles de Gaulle. Press Conference of 10 Nov. 1959, CF. D. G. Lavroff, ed. *La Politique Africaine du General de Gaulle* (Paris: A. Pedone, 1980,), p. 151

33   Quoted in Lavroff, Ibid, p. 152.

34   Ibid, pp. 150-152. For a fuller discussion on the Franco-African Community, see Nicolas Martin, "De Gaulle, le Systeme Federal et la Decolonisation," in Ibid., pp. 318-328.

35   Quoted in Ibid. p. 157.

porter ailleurs l'ambition nationale.»[36] He began to concentrate on his new pet project of constructing "the union of Europe."[37]

Not that France abandoned its former African colonies. Between July 1960 and June 1962, all francophone African Heads of State were received at the Elysée Palace, where de Gaulle had some 200 meetings with them.[38] France also began to diversify its African policy and expand its sphere of influence, beginning with the former Belgian colonies, especially the troubled Congo. In 1963, de Gaulle dispatched his veteran representative at the Trusteeship Council, Kosciusko-Morizet, to take over the French embassy in Leopoldville, insisting on *"la grande importance que j'attache à votre mission au Congo."*[39]

It is revealing of French ambitions in the Congo that, less than fifteen years later, when the Shaba crisis plunged it into renewed chaos, France, and not Belgium, would be the dominant foreign presence. It is noteworthy that the man in charge of that important mission of building up French influence in the Congo had previously been entrusted with the defense of France's position during the UN debates on the British Cameroons.

De Gaulle also had his eyes on African members of the British Commonwealth, a policy that came into full perspective with his open support for Biafra during the Nigerian civil war.

Long before that, however, the British Cameroons had given him an opportunity to execute his policy towards Anglophone Africa. The case of the British Cameroons was peculiar in that it offered the prospect of direct territorial gain in the event of reunification with Cameroun, which was firmly within the French sphere of influence. Kosciusko-Morizet, narrates how on the eve of his departure for the crucial UN debates on the British Cameroons he went to see de Gaulle. During their conversation, he complained that France might be defeated in those debates by the large number of Anglophone States, a situation that was not helped by the inclination of the French Foreign Ministry to adopt a conciliatory line on the matter in order to please the British. So important was the

36   Quoted in Ibid. p. 158.
37   Quoted in Ibid. p. 160.
38   Charles de Gaulle. *Memoires d'Espoir* (Paris: Plon, 1970), p. 67.
39   Letter from de Gaulle to Kosciusko-Morizet, quoted in Lavroff, op. cit., p. 281.

issue that *"pour la première fois,"* as far as Morizet could recall, General de Gaulle took notes! He subsequently issued strict instructions to the Foreign Ministry and to former French colonies in Africa for complete francophone solidarity in the affair of the British Cameroons,[40] which was emerging as a new theatre of rivalry between Britain and France.

As the question developed, France anticipated a division at the United Nations along linguistic lines, and braced herself for the fight that would ensue. And in the conduct of foreign policy, the need arose that the question be controlled directly from the Elysée Palace rather than left to the conventional style of the Foreign Ministry at the Quai d'Orsay.

It has been suggested that France's opposition to Nigeria over the British Cameroons was in reaction to Nigeria's expulsion of French diplomats from Lagos in January 1961 in protest against the third French atomic explosion in the Sahara in December 1960.[41]

At the outset of the UN debate, the French delegate warned that the question of the British Cameroons was not the exclusive preserve of any one country or group of countries: "A question affecting the independence of an entire people was of concern to all delegations, on a footing of complete equality."[42] The French voice was thought to carry even more weight than others. Kosciusko-Morizet insisted that "due regard should be shown for the position of the Government of Cameroun,"[43] and that "since Cameroun was neither represented on the Trusteeship Council nor yet a Member of the United Nations, France, in a spirit of friendship, wished to present that Government's point of view, together with its own."[44] France had been so mandated by the Cameroun Government itself, as Premier Ahidjo revealed in 1958: *«Ce problème de réunification, je l'ai posé à nouveau aux responsables français lors de ma mission à Paris.»*[45]

That duality made it difficult to distinguish the positions of the two

---

40   Lavroff, Ibid., pp. 268-270.
41   John Major, The Emergence of African Rivalries", in D. C. Watt, *Survey of International Affairs 1961*, (London: OUP. 1965), p. 411.
42   GAOR, A/C. 4/SR.898, 7 Oct. 1959, p. 73.
43   Ibid.
44   T/SR.1086, 18 May 1960, p. 242.
45   *Agence France Presse*, No. 77, Paris, 1 April 1958. The statement translates as follows: *"This matter of reunification, I submitted it anew to French officials during my recent mission to Paris."*

countries, although it might be presumed that both were concordant, both probably decided in Paris, as Ahidjo had intimated. During the proceedings, Kosciusko-Morizet blew both hot and cold. In his preliminary statement, he declared that "France had no direct or indirect interest in the matter, its policy was based on right and justice."[46]

But France's preference was soon apparent. Although the ultimate decision on the future of the British Cameroons rested with the people themselves, Morizet felt that "The choice was necessitated by the division forty years earlier of what had once been a single unit, and it would be a choice based on both sentiment and reason."[47] It was strange for Morizet to proclaim the oneness of a German colony that France had been the first to dismember. Talk less of the sentimental value of a German project that, like other European projects in Africa, had been fiercely resisted in many areas and often only brutally imposed on the people. And he saw the reunification of both sectors of the former German protectorate as being so important that its failure would lead to the emergence of irredentist claims on both sides, and to "bitterness and tensions which could only be damaging to their stability, their prosperity and their harmony."[48]

The French approach towards the German Kamerun was very ambivalent: she openly supported the unification of the French and British Cameroons, while remaining completely silent about those areas of the same German protectorate that had been incorporated into French Equatorial Africa before the partition!

The positions of the States most directly concerned with the British Cameroons were thus diametrically opposed. That opposition was reinforced by background support from their friends and allies, further heightening the drama of the Trust Territory.

The future of the British Cameroons did not raise any obvious problems of international security to invite attention or possible intervention by the big powers. The Territory was neither large nor wealthy, not particularly strategic, and it was clear that its future could not threaten the global balance of power. In fact, apart from fleeting secret support to

46   A/C.4SR.1150, 19 April 1961, p. 357.
47   T/SR.1090. 23 May 1960. p. 266.
48   Ibid, p. 267.

proscribed political parties such as the socialist *Union des Populations du Cameroun* [UPC] of the French Cameroun, the eastern bloc had no foothold in the region. Yet both sides keenly watched the question of the British Cameroons, because the birth of every new nation raised hopes of gaining new ideological converts to one bloc or the other.

Soviet sympathy for decolonization was part of their global strategy in the struggle with the West. They considered that "colonies are the Achilles' heel of capitalism and that any attack on colonialism must weaken the western powers."[49] Accordingly, Soviet delegates in most international forums readily engaged in what Alan Burns has described as "long propaganda speeches, denouncing with monotonous regularity the wickedness of all colonial powers,"[50] in an attempt to stir up nationalist outrage in the colonies and cause international embarrassment to the colonial powers.

Although it might not lead to direct Soviet gain, each colony that gained independence was in principle one country less within the western fold, where rival communist influence could be introduced. Accordingly, the Soviet Union showed a strong desire to speed up the breakdown of Western colonial empires.

The Soviet Union viewed the question of the British Cameroons as basically a colonial question resulting "from agreements and partitions which had been arbitrarily imposed by the colonial powers upon the peoples of Africa."[51] Oberemko, the Soviet delegate, was particularly critical of the administrative union of the Territory with Nigeria, arguing that "such unions were not administrative but political unions which were inconsistent with the true objectives of the Trusteeship System."[52] Regarding the future of the British Cameroons, the Soviet Union did not only call for independence, but reiterated "the need to unify all parts of the Cameroons in one independent Cameroonian State."[53]

Unlike the Soviet Union, which was openly militant against colonialism, the US often found itself in an awkward position as far as

---

49 Sir Alan Burns. op. cit., p. 110.
50 Ibid.
51 A/C.4/SR.899. 8 Oct. 1959, p. 78.
52 Ibid, p. 79.
53 Ibid.

decolonization was concerned. Having emerged from thirteen British colonies to become the champion of freedom and democracy, it traditionally sympathized with people still fighting for their independence. Yet the vast majority of colonies belonged to America's allies. It was difficult to sacrifice them on the altar of decolonization, at a time when the mounting communist menace demanded that they close ranks. As one American Assistant Secretary of State confessed in 1953,

> Let us be frank in recognizing our stake in the strength and stability of certain European nations, which exercise influence in the dependent areas. They are our allies. A sudden break in economic relations brought about by decolonization might seriously injure the European economy upon which our Atlantic defense system depends.[54]

Moreover, as the Administering Authority of a UN Trust Territory,[55] and with overseas possessions of its own, the US could rightly be assimilated to the ranks of the colonial powers, with their impulsive skepticism towards decolonization. An American author reflected that impulse, noting that:

> Some danger exists that if nationalism succeeds too soon, the new governments may be exploited by corrupt African charlatans, under-seasoned intellectuals, and illiterate politicians on the make. Beyond doubt Africa does need further tutelage. The nationalist inflammation should not blind Africans to their immense debt to colonialism as well as their formidable lack of experience.[56]

---

54   *The Times*, London. 2 Nov. 1953.
55   The US administered the Pacific Islands under UN trusteeship as a strategic area, in accordance with Article 82 of the Charter. The Islands, previously held by Japan as a League of Nations mandate, were occupied by the US during the Second World War, and converted into a trust territory following the Security Council approval of the US draft agreement on April 2. 1947.
56   John Gunther, *Inside Africa* (1955) p. 871; Quoted in Sir Alan Burns. op. cit, p. 299.

To the Americans, most colonies contained vast reserves of strategic minerals that could not be allowed to fall into the hands of their adversaries. The decolonization dilemma of the US was that she sought to check the advance of communism without appearing to be neocolonialist, and to encourage the legitimate nationalist aspirations of dependent peoples without alienating her colonialist allies.

The result was a mostly incoherent and often ambiguous policy that tried to please both sides of the colonial divide, without satisfying either. That ambiguity was evident in the US position on the future of the British Cameroons. Commenting on developments in the Southern Cameroons, an American delegate told the UN that his country "welcomed the advent of self-determination in the Territory because it represented the will of the people to manage their own affairs." But the same delegate felt that "the results of a hasty choice might well be catastrophic."[57]

On the Northern Cameroons, another US delegate observed that "the holding of the plebiscite there on the basis of universal suffrage would have great educational value for the people," but he cautioned that "the method of voting could not be imposed from outside."[58]

The two big powers naturally found themselves in some disagreement over the future of the British Cameroons. While the US showed no clear preference, the Soviet Union was manifestly in support of the unification of the two Cameroons.

By virtue of the international questions involved, the future of the British Cameroons was a matter of concern to the other Member States of the United Nations as it was to the States most directly concerned and the big powers. But while all States showed some degree of interest in the matter, some were clearly more enthusiastic than others. The new nations, by dint of their common experience of colonialism, showed great sympathy for the people of the British Cameroons.

Those new States did not constitute a monolith, however. Three subgroups were discernible among them.

Independent African countries launched a ubiquitous onslaught against colonialism, calling for the "total liberation of Africa" during all

57   A/C.4/SR.896, 6 Oct. p. 65.
58   T/SR.1090, 23 May 1960, p. 264.

their gatherings. At the Accra Conference of Independent African States in April 1958, the eight participants[59] pledged themselves "to recognize the right of African peoples to independence and self-determination and to take appropriate steps to hasten the realization of this right."[60] They regarded the existence of colonialism in any form as "a threat to the security and independence of the African States and to world peace."[61]

Not only that, they began to claim the right to speak with authority on African colonial matters. They felt that "the problems and the future of dependent Territories in Africa are not the exclusive concern of the colonial powers but the responsibility of all the Members of the United Nations and in particular of the independent African States."[62] In other words, they began to consider themselves as states directly concerned with colonialism on the continent; they were better acquainted with the aspirations of African peoples, and they had a special interest in the satisfactory resolution of African problems.[63]

The African States were particularly interested in the British Cameroons, whose future provided a test case for the on-going whispers of continental unity. They were anxious to see how the union of two countries from different colonial backgrounds would play out in the event of the unification of the two Cameroons.

The All Africa Peoples Conference held in Accra in December 1958 noted "with satisfaction" the fact that a special session of the UN General Assembly had been called to discuss "the question of unification and independence of the Cameroons."[64] And in solidarity with the aspirations of the peoples of the Cameroons, the Conference invited "all Africans to observe the date of 20 February 1959, when the General Assembly special session on the Cameroons would open, as a 'Cameroons Day.'"[65] In the early stages of the debate on the future of the British Cameroons,

59   Ethiopia, Ghana, Liberia, Libya, Morocco, The Sudan, Tunisia, and the United Arab Republic.
60   Quoted in Vincent Bakpetu Thompson, *Africa and Unity* (London: Longman. 1969), p. 345.
61   Ibid, pp. 347-348.
62   Ibid, p. 348.
63   Ibid, p. 355.
64   Ibid, p. 356.
65   Ibid.

African States were leaning towards the option for reunification with the French Cameroun.

But that position was soon found to be divisive, in view of the fact that the future of the British Cameroons lay between Nigeria and Cameroun, both members of the African group. One African delegate at the UN noted that the problem of the British Cameroons had to be solved "in a way which would not compromise the stand of the African delegations in the struggle for African independence,"[66] by openly favoring one African Territory over another.

Moreover, it was becoming increasingly clear that African States were more excited about independence than about unity. So they began to moderate their stand on the British Cameroons. They began to talk in terms of terminating the trusteeship, leaving the people to decide for themselves who they would join in the process.

The new African position, as the Ghanaian delegate explained, was "based on the principle that all peoples of Africa should accede to independence without delay or hindrance."[67] The African countries were anxious that the question of the British Cameroons should not create unnecessary divisions among them that could divert attention from the main issue of decolonization. Neither did they want to give the colonial powers any reason to doubt the maturity of Africans and delay independence in the other Territories. African delegates had to speak with one voice, and African unity still in the making was already being put to the test.

As former colonies themselves, many Asian countries showed a natural hostility towards colonialism, an attitude reinforced at the Bandung Conference of Afro-Asian States in 1955. They were anxious that a quick end be brought to foreign domination throughout the world, because the existence of colonies reminded them all too often of the state from which they had emerged and about which they wanted to forget.

Ambitious ones secretly nursed dreams of grouping former colonies into a third force, to break the conflicting East-West dichotomy of world politics. They showed great enthusiasm in the debate on the British

66   A/C.4/SR.898, 7 Oct. 1959, p. 72.
67   A/C.4/SR.1151. 19 April 1961. p. 367.

Cameroons. The Indian delegate insisted that "India had always been identified with the cause of colonial liberation,"[68] and that his country would
"at no time subscribe to any doctrine which impeded the termination of
trusteeship or any other form of foreign authority over any Territory."[69]

Not surprisingly, India's zeal for decolonization was suspected as being
motivated by considerations of self-interest. Alan Burns has suggested
that India had colonial ambitions of her own, that her anti-colonialism
was just a cover for a secret craving: "Mr. Nehru had his eyes on Africa
and wanted the whites out of it, so that he could resettle his surplus
population there."[70] The London *Times* concurred:

> Although external influences may lead to the liquidation of
> colonialism at a comparatively early date, that does not mean
> the Africans will by then be capable of standing on their feet,
> and there is therefore a natural wish for the Asian States to stake
> an early claim for what might once more become a region open
> to external enterprise.[71]

While such a wish might be imagined in the big countries of East
Africa, Asian expansionist considerations were much less likely in a
Territory so small and so far from Asia as the British Cameroons. It is
probable that Asian interest in the future of the Territory derived from
a genuine drive for decolonization. They did not show any preference
for either option. All they were concerned about was "to see that conditions in the Territory were such that a plebiscite could be held with the
maximum of impartiality."[72] They were satisfied that "yet another Trust
Territory was on the threshold of independence."[73] Whoever they chose
to join in the process was entirely up to the people.

The Latin American countries were also keenly anti-colonialist.
That position derived from their history and was confirmed at the

---

68   A/C.4/SR.903, 9 Oct. 1959, p. 103.
69   A/C.4/SR.898, 7 Oct. 1959, p. 71.
70   Sir Alan Burns. op. cit, p. 27.
71   *The Times*, London, 31 May 1955.
72   T/SR.1086, 18 May 1960, p. 241.
73   T/SR.1091, 24 May 1960, p. 272.

Inter-American Conference of Caracas in March 1954. The Conference resolved that "it is the will of the people of America that colonialism be definitely ended," and expressed "the sympathy of the American Republics with the just aspiration of the now subject peoples to attain their sovereignty."[74]

But unlike the Asian States, which challenged the primacy of African concern in the matter, the Latin American countries felt that the question of the British Cameroons was first and foremost an African question. Their interventions were limited to general calls for independence, and veiled warnings that the strength of Africa would be undermined by the birth of tiny, vulnerable States within it.[75] They followed the general trend that the British Cameroons should attain independence by uniting with either neighbor. Like the Asian States, the Latin Americans showed no preference in that choice.

The Interested Parties and the Plebiscites

The necessity of the plebiscites was one area about which there was minimum disagreement. As a vehicle of decolonization, it met with the approval of the new nations and the Soviet Union; and as a democratic process, it appealed to the liberal traditions of the West. For considerations of self-interest, it satisfied the ambitions of Cameroun and Nigeria as well.

Only the UK was skeptical, especially with regard to the Northern Cameroons.[76] The British delegate urged the UN to implement the recommendation of the 1958 Visiting Mission that there should be no plebiscite in the Northern Cameroons:

> Firstly, the Mission was composed of four objective people with considerable experience in trusteeship matters. Secondly, the propriety of incurring the expense of the plebiscite and its supervision in a Territory where opinion was strongly in favor of one particular constitutional arrangement [integration with Nigeria] was debatable.[77]

74 Quoted in Sir Alan Burns, op.cit, p. 156.
75 A/C.4/SR.892, 2 Oct. 1959, p. 46.
76 A/C.4/SR.846, 23 Oct. 1959. p. 553.
77 T/SR.939, May 1959, p. 553.

But the General Assembly rejected both the recommendation of the Visiting Mission and the plea of the UK. Instead, it adopted Resolution 1350[XIII] of March 13, 1959, recommending the organization of plebiscites in both the Southern and the Northern Cameroons in order to ascertain the wishes of the people with regard to their future.

Yet, much as there was agreement on the necessity of the plebiscites, there was disagreement whether, for that purpose, the British Cameroons should be regarded as one territory or as two separate units. The 1958 Visiting Mission had recommended the latter view, arguing that the history and development of the two parts of the Territory had taken distinctly different courses since the administrative union with Nigeria, with the result that there now existed profound differences between them.

That view was endorsed by the UK. Andrew Cohen told the Trusteeship Council that the Administrating Authority had never thought in terms of uniting the two parts of the British Cameroons, "for the simple reason that they had never been united at any stage of history and to have brought them arbitrarily together would not have been conducive to the welfare of the people or to their advancement towards independence."[78] It is not clear which history Andrew Cohen was referring to: both sections of the British Cameroons had previously been united in the German Kamerun, and the separate Protectorates of Southern Nigeria and Northern Nigeria were amalgamated in January 1914 without compromising the welfare of the people.

No wonder, the Administrative union of the British Cameroons with Nigeria, together with the resulting division of the Territory into north and south, and the prospect of holding separate consultations in both parts, were suspect to many countries. As the Soviet delegate pointed out, Britain's purpose in placing the Trust Territory under Nigeria had been "to ensure that the ethnic, social and cultural differences between the north and the south would become more marked and that the Territory could never constitute an independent entity."[79] There were many other countries which believed in the oneness of the Trust Territory and, by implication, in the necessity for a single act of consultation on its future.

78   T/SR.1088, 19 May 1960, pp. 253-254.
79   A/C.4/SR.899, 8 Oct. 1959, p. 78.

Among those was India, whose delegate argued that "The Trusteeship Agreement for the Cameroons under British Administration applied to the whole Territory; the latter could not be divided unless a new Agreement was concluded."[80]

That was also the view of the Foreign Minister of Cameroun, Charles Okala, who submitted that

> the Trusteeship Agreement was indivisible: it was a single juridical instrument applying indissolubly to the two parts of the Territory, which constituted a single whole. Any decision providing for different dates for the termination of the Agreement in different parts of the Territory would require a modification of the Agreement.[81]

But the majority of States did not attach that much importance to the division. More important to them was the termination of the trusteeship itself. Thus, while ruling that plebiscites must be held throughout the Territory, the General Assembly accepted the recommendation of the Visiting Mission to regard the British Cameroons as two separate units for that purpose.

Agreement on the plebiscite still left other practical issues to be sorted out, on which differences became more pronounced and compromise more necessary.

The first of the contentious issues concerned the questions to be put at the plebiscite. The political evolution of the British Cameroons revolved around its relationship with Nigeria. That relationship was appraised both positively and negatively. The anti-Nigeria sentiment developed into a pro-Cameroun or a pro-reunification stance, thereby linking the future of the Territory with the future of its two neighbors.

Supporters of both sides argued that owing to the weakness of its economy, the British Cameroons could best achieve independence in association with one of its neighbors.[82]

---

80 A/C.4/SR.890, 30 Oct. 1959, p. 39.
81 A/C.4/SR.1152, 19 April 1961, p. 377.
82 A/C.4/SR.865, 24 Sept. 1959, p. 17.

At the UN, many countries agreed with that view. As the Mexican delegate pointed out,

> No satisfactory definition has ever been given to the necessary prerequisites of an independent State, but it is all too evident to what perils a country is exposed when it attains indepen-dence without possessing the requirements necessary to make it viable![83]

Other countries were worried by the danger of splitting Africa into many small States, fearing that "So small a country as the British Cam-eroons, sandwiched in-between two larger ones would be a constant source of disputes."[84] Protagonists of the viability of States felt that, for an independent country to survive, it had to be viable in economic, political and security terms to avoid becoming a pawn or a beggar State, regarded as easy pickings by aggressive neighbors.

However, the European statesmen who insisted most on this principle did not apply the same to existing small States in Europe which were cre-ated or permitted to exist as neutrals or buffers. Besides, a small State need not necessarily be weak: history abounds with examples of large States in economic shambles and some small States with vibrant economies.

Some States challenged the idea of viability as a deliberate attempt to limit the framework of self-determination in the British Cameroons by eliminating the option of outright independence. The Afghan delegate was the first to speak out, arguing that:

> The idea of subjecting a people to foreign domination for mere economic reasons was manifestly unfair. Indeed, there was a basic inconsistency in the political logic of colonialism: in the past the abundance of unexploited riches in their territories had been averred to justify the enslavement of the colonial peoples, whereas today the insufficiency of their economic resources was used as an excuse to deny freedom and independence to

---

83   A/C.4/SR.892. 2 Oct. 1959, p. 46.
84   Ibid.

certain peoples.[85]

To such delegations, union with either Nigeria or Cameroun did not constitute genuine independence for the British Cameroons, but rather the transfer from one form of foreign domination to another.

The Guinean delegate presented the case for British Cameroons independence with great fervor. Strengthened by the revolutionary élan in which his country had shaken off French colonialism, he dismissed the excuses that other countries advanced to force union of some kind on the people of the British Cameroons. He argued that economic weakness was not a peculiar characteristic of the Territory, but a general feature of the colonies. It was an inevitable sequel of colonialism which could be overcome with courage and sacrifice. As for the claim of administrative inexperience leveled on the British Cameroons, Diallo Alpha told the UN that "there were in the British Cameroons responsible and competent people whose capabilities would come to light when they were called upon to assume responsibilities."[86] He did not reject the possibility of union with either Nigeria or Cameroun; he thought it was only logical that a "country under colonial rule should first of all obtain independence and then, if it wished, it could enter into alliances."[87]

But the proponents of "complete" independence for the British Cameroons failed to rally other Member States to their view. Neither did rejection of that option imply automatic approval for the option to unify with Nigeria or Cameroun. The evidence shows that the UK did not initially want any other option apart from that of joining Nigeria. In fact, during the Fourth Committee debate on the first Northern Cameroons plebiscite, the British representative warned that his delegation would "oppose any suggestion that the people of the Northern Cameroons should be offered the choice between being part of Northern Nigeria or joining the Cameroons at present under French administration."[88]

The fact that the Cameroun option was eventually excluded from that plebiscite is an indication of the success of that threat. An African

85   A/C.4/SR.696, 6 Oct. 1959, pp. 61-62.
86   A/C/. 4/SR.898, 7 Oct. 1959, p. 76.
87   Ibid.
88   A/C.4/SR.873, 10 March 1959, p. 721.

attempt to amend draft Resolution A/C.4/L.582/Rev.1, later known as Resolution 1350[XIII], and replace the ambiguous second alternative with a clear question on joining Cameroun was narrowly defeated by 36 votes to 32, with 13 abstentions.[89]

The Soviet Union voted with the African countries, while Britain and the US voted against the amendment.[90] A similar scenario might have been adopted with regard to the Southern Cameroons, had not the Northern Cameroonians unexpectedly rejected the union with Nigeria at their first plebiscite. That decision greatly weakened the position of the UK, and the option for joining Cameroun came naturally into consideration.

The timing of the plebiscites was determined mainly by the advance of Nigeria towards independence. But whereas that advance was bilaterally coordinated between Britain and Nigeria, the timetable for terminating the trusteeship over the British Cameroons was the multilateral responsibility of the UN. That responsibility was partly discharged when the General Assembly decided that the first Northern Cameroons plebiscite should take place in November 1959.

However, the ease of that decision could not be repeated in the Southern Cameroons. Instead, the UN was stonewalled when its leaders were deadlocked over the questions to be put and the qualifications for voting in the plebiscite. To break the deadlock, African delegations organized a series of secret meetings between the two leaders, which resulted in a compromise statement, published as Document A/C.4./414 of September 30, 1959, calling for a postponement of the plebiscite to 1962.

That Compromise was greeted with mixed feelings in the Fourth Committee of the General Assembly. The UK was sympathetic because "it represented an agreement between the elected representatives of the vast majority of the inhabitants of the Southern Cameroons."[91] The US welcomed it: Mr. Zablocki warned that "The result of a hurried choice imposed on the population of the Trust Territory would be catastrophic for their political future."[92] The Pakistani delegate pointed out that "The Committee should not presume to be more Cameroonian than the

89   A/C.4/L.589.
90   A/C.44.590, 12 March 1959. p. 22.
91   A/C.4/SR.890, 30 Sept. 1959, pp. 38-39.
92   A/C.4/SR.896, 6 Oct. 1959, p. 65.

Cameroonians themselves."[93] And the French delegation welcomed the postponement because it would "facilitate the attainment of an indispensable immediate objective, namely, the complete separation of the administration of the Southern Cameroons from that of Nigeria."[94]

But other States were openly hostile to the Compromise. The Soviet Union dismissed it as being "in fact a statement by the Administering Authority;"[95] Uruguay described it as representing "a retrograde step" in the political evolution of the Territory;[96] the Indonesian delegate argued that "the idea of postponement appeared to contradict the very meaning of history;"[97] while the delegate from Burma feared "the psychological and political effects it would undoubtedly have on the Territory."[98] Some delegations went even further, arguing that the postponement raised serious legal difficulties of having to continue with the trusteeship in one part of the British Cameroons while terminating it in another part. Under such circumstances, the Trusteeship Agreement would have to be revised, something for which there were no provisions in the Charter and no legal precedents.

But they failed to realize that any legal difficulties that might arise over the fate of the British Cameroons would have been created by the General Assembly itself. By endorsing the principle of separate plebiscites in Resolution 1350[XIII], the General Assembly had tacitly admitted the possibility that the trusteeship could be terminated separately. That turned out to be the case.

The crux of the argument over the Compromise was a debate over whose interest was paramount. It opposed those who subordinated the national interest to UN resolutions and sought their strict application, and those who believed that the national will was paramount and were therefore prepared to compromise on certain UN resolutions. The argument could have developed into a stalemate if both sides did not show sympathy for the painstaking efforts of the African delegations in promoting the

93   Ibid.
94   A/C.4/SR.898, 7 Oct. 1959, p. 73.
95   A/C.4/SR.891, 1 Oct. 1959, p. 41.
96   A/C.4/SR.896. 6 Oct. 1959. p. 62.
97   A/C.4/SR.894, 5 Oct. 1959, p. 56.
98   Ibid, p. 55.

Compromise.

Although the African States themselves did not necessarily agree with some of the proposals contained in the compromise statement,[99] the simple fact that it had been reached under their aegis was critical in rallying together the opposing opinions of the Committee. The Venezuelan delegate epitomized the resignation of the anti-postponement States when he observed that "if the majority of the African delegations were in favor of that unexpected prolongation of the trusteeship regime, the Venezuelan delegation would not oppose it."[100]

It is an indication of the involvement of the African countries that they, who had abstained in the vote on Resolution 1350[XIII], now introduced draft resolution L.591, calling for the Southern Cameroons plebiscites to be held not later than March 1961 -- midway between what the General Assembly had recommended in Resolution 1350[XIII] and what the Southern Cameroons leaders asked for in their Agreed Statement. And it is an indication of the mood of compromise on the matter that the draft resolution was co-sponsored by the United States, and that such anti-postponement States as the Soviet Union voted for it.

The draft resolution was approved by 74 votes to none, with 2 abstentions, as Resolution 1352[XIV] of October 16, 1959. With the help of the African States, the Southern Cameroons plebiscite that had seemed to hang in the balance could now be held.

The spirit of compromise was also in evidence during the discussion on the second Northern Cameroons plebiscite. Without serious argument, the General Assembly adopted Resolution 1473[XIV] of December 12, 1959, recommending that the plebiscite take place not later than March 1961, and calling for reforms to ensure the decentralization and democratization of the administrative system in the Territory, as well as the separation of that system from the administration of Northern Nigeria when Nigeria attained independence.

The African countries had abstained in the vote on Resolution 1350[XIII] for two main reasons: they disagreed with the idea that the plebiscite should be conducted on the basis of the electoral register then

99   A/C.4/SR.890, 30 Sept. 1959, p. 39.
100   A/C.4/SR.894, 5 Oct. 1959, p. 56.

being prepared for the Nigerian parliamentary elections; and with the fact that the franchise should be limited to men.

An appeal by Liberia for a separate electoral register for the Northern Cameroons plebiscite[101] was rejected on grounds that it would be too costly. So too was a further Liberian proposal that the plebiscite be conducted "on the basis of universal adult suffrage,"[102] even though it had the support of the vast majority of the African States. It was a paradox of the British Cameroons that the vanguard western democracies voted against the application of universal adult suffrage in the Northern Cameroons.

At issue was the question of whether to respect local customs and exclude women from the plebiscite or impose international standards on the people by giving the vote to women. There was also the question of the uniformity of the franchise in the two parts of the Territory, given that universal adult suffrage had been in operation in the Southern Cameroons ever since the introduction of elections there. With the rejection of both Liberian proposals, the African countries refused to sanction the Resolution. But that did not prevent it from being adopted by 57 votes to none, with 24 abstentions.

Neither did its adoption discourage the African States from continuing their campaign for the enlargement of the franchise in the Northern Cameroons. Spearheaded by Miss Angie Brooks of Liberia, that campaign paid off when the General Assembly reversed its earlier decision of Resolution 1350[XIII] and agreed in Resolution 1473[XIV] to conduct the second plebiscite on the basis of universal adult suffrage.

Given that as many as 49.9% of the eventual voters in that plebiscite were women, all of whom had not participated in the first exercise, and bearing in mind the results of that exercise, it is possible that they were responsible for the dramatic switch of fortunes in that second plebiscite. Thus, the insistence of the African States on the application of universal suffrage in the plebiscite may well have been the determining factor in the fate of the Northern Cameroons.

But by far the most controversial issue of the plebiscite was the ratification of the results. The Plebiscite Commissioner's judgment that the

101   A/C.4/L.587.
102   A/C.4/L.587/Rev.1.

consultations had been efficiently organized and conducted by the Administering Authority was immediately challenged in the General Assembly, in a debate that was predictable but whose ferocity was surprising.

The controversy was limited to the second Northern Cameroons plebiscite, the results of which represented a complete turn-around from the position expressed in 1959. Those results polarized opinion within the General Assembly, and further consideration of the question of the British Cameroons was dominated by a spirited debate between those who accepted and those who rejected them.

Spearheaded by the Cameroun Republic, rejection of the results of the second Northern Cameroons plebiscite was based on two main objections: Firstly, that Britain had failed to reform the administration of the Territory as prescribed by General Assembly Resolution 1473 [XIV]. In fact, that reform was widely regarded as "a sine qua non for the validity of the future plebiscite."[103]

It seems that the disagreement was on the degree of reform rather than on the fact of it. The UK did introduce some changes in the administration of the Northern Cameroons following the first plebiscite and appointed an Administrator more or less independent of the Government of Northern Nigeria. Northern Cameroons districts formerly administered by the Adamawa or Dikwa Native Authorities were now established as separate Native Authorities, no longer subordinated to them; and all the Native Authority Councils in the Territory were to consist of people elected by secret ballot.[104]

Britain's friends praised the innovations. The delegate from New Zealand thought they represented "a sincere effort to democratize the system of local government" in the Territory.[105] And the delegate from the US was convinced that "the Administering Authority had spared neither money nor effort" in carrying them out.[106]

But Britain's adversaries derided them. The French delegate discounted them as "only a facade on a building which remained Nigerian,"[107]

103   A/C.4/SR.1150, 19 April 1961. p. 358.
104   T/SR.1085, 19 May 1960, p. 237.
105   T/SR.1090, 23 May 1960, p. 265.
106   Ibid. p. 264.
107   A/C.4/SR.1150, 19 April 1961, p. 359.

while the Cameroun Foreign Minister dismissed the newly created representative councils as "a mere coterie of princelings devoted to the Emir of Sokoto."[108] These and other countries felt that Britain's failure to fully implement the prescribed reforms cast doubt on the validity of the second Northern Cameroons plebiscite. As Kosciusko-Morizet pointed out: "the holding of a plebiscite in a country in which very important functions were still exercised by a neighboring country could well be questioned."[109]

Opponents of the plebiscite result also claimed that the consultation had been riddled with procedural irregularities, citing four distinct classes:

i). Irregularities in the preparation of the plebiscite. These included: the registration of Nigerian nationals on the electoral rolls; the distribution of voting papers by agents of the Nigerian public services; and a psychological atmosphere unsuitable for a genuine popular vote.

ii). Irregularities during the plebiscite campaign, namely: discriminatory acts against the partisans of reunification; and the active participation of the authorities and local officials on behalf of the Nigeria option.

iii). Irregularities in the conduct of the plebiscite, such as putting Nigerians or pro-Nigerians in charge of polling booths; inadequate secrecy of the ballot; and the absence of official minutes of the proceedings.

iv). Irregularities in the counting of the votes, including the inadequate supervision of ballot boxes; and the counting of votes by tellers whose impartiality could not be guaranteed, given that they were all British citizens with an obvious interest in retaining the Northern Cameroons within Northern Nigeria.

In the light of all those irregularities, the Government of Cameroun felt that the second Northern Cameroons plebiscite had been held under conditions that "from the outset the strongest objections as to its value

108   A/C.4/SR.1141, 13 April 1961, p. 296.
109   T/SR.1090, 23 May 1960, p. 267.

were bound to be entertained."[110] Those objections were duly presented in a formal petition by the Government of Cameroun for the invalidation of the results of that particular plebiscite.[111]

The Cameroun petition received strong backing from France, whose representative argued that:

> certain irregularities, no doubt harmless in themselves, had joined to bring about an atmosphere which had helped to distort the purpose of the ballot. The plebiscite was vitiated and any court of law would pronounce the results null and void because of improper procedure. The General Assembly could only take the same view.[112]

All but a few of the French-speaking African countries followed the example of France and rallied to the support of the Cameroun Republic. The instructions of General de Gaulle for francophone solidarity on the matter had not fallen on deaf ears. Ten former French colonies in Africa[113] introduced a draft Resolution [A/C.4/L.684 of 15 April 1961], asking the General Assembly to temporarily suspend consideration of the question and send a commission of six to find out whether all the prescribed safeguards had been effectively applied. They called on the Administering Authority to organize legislative elections in the Territory with a view to establishing a democratic government prior to terminating the trusteeship no later than December 1961.

But many States disagreed. Some rejected the existence of irregularities altogether. Andrew Cohen told the Committee that the UK "understood the disappointment of the Republic of Cameroun but could not accept the specious arguments which they adduced to support their

---

110   Ministry of Foreign Affairs, Yaounde, *The Position of the Republic of Cameroun following the Plebiscite of 11 and 12 February 1961 in the Northern Cameroons.* (Mimeograph).

111   Ibid, p. 6.

112   UN, G.A., A/4699, 27 Feb. 1961.

113   A/C.4/SR.1150, 19 April 1961, p. 358.

views."[114] The Nigerian delegate dismissed those objecting as "politicians of doubtful integrity."[115] Other States admitted the existence of irregularities but were not convinced that the administrative arrangements had substantially affected the results. The Tunisian delegate concluded that those irregularities "even when taken together, did not constitute sufficient reason for casting doubt on the results."[116] While the delegate from Mali argued that "the political, administrative and economic structures imposed by the colonial system had always made it possible, in colonial countries, for maneuvers and measures of intimidation to be brought into play during elections."[117]

And still other States felt that the unnecessary scrutiny of the plebiscite results would undermine the integrity of the United Nations. The Brazilian delegate pointed out that the setting up of a new fact-finding commission would "cast doubt on the value of the work so excellently performed by the Plebiscite Commissioner, question the validity of the established methods used by the United Nations and jeopardize its efforts in emancipating the remaining dependent peoples."[118]

A rival draft Resolution [A/C.4/L.685 of 18 April, 1961] was introduced, calling for the immediate implementation of the results of the second Northern Cameroons plebiscite.

The introduction of both draft resolutions set the stage for a resumed battle in the General Assembly. There were indications that some delegations were tired of the question, and impatient with any attempts to prolong it. For once, both superpowers did not participate in the debate on the two resolutions. Instead, they voted for the immediate termination of the trusteeship.

But the African States maintained a lively interest in the question. For many of them, it provided the first real opportunity to exercise their newly acquired international status. Unfortunately, that debate also exhibited the first symptoms of division within the continent, as a split appeared

---

114   Central African Republic, Congo (Brazzaville), Dahomey, Gabon, Madagascar, Niger, Senegal and Upper Volta.
115   A/C.4/SR.1148, 18 April 1961, p. 346.
116   Ibid. p. 347.
117   A/C.4/SR.1151, 19 April 1961, p. 369.
118   A/C.4/SR.1152, 19 April 1961 p. 373.

within the African group. Not unexpectedly, that split occurred along language lines, just as Kosciusko-Morizet had anticipated in 1959, with the majority of the French-speaking States backing Cameroun and France, and all the English-speaking countries supporting Nigeria and Britain.

A mini-split further occurred within the francophone group, with Guinea and Mali abstaining in all the votes on the British Cameroons. In rejecting the francophone solidarity, the Guinean delegate declared that it was "vitally important not to undermine with unjustified criticism the authority of the commissions, the visiting commissions, the commissions of inquiry and the plebiscite commissions which were sent by the UN to the Territories."[119] For his part, the Malian delegate was

> very surprised that the representative of France was concerned about conditions of impartiality and democracy in which the plebiscite had been held: since when was the French Government taking up the cause of justice in elections? It was not possible to allow the representative of a colonialist country to pose as the defender of an oppressed people by attacking another Administering Authority.[120]

The test of strength between both draft resolutions came on a proposal by the delegate of Afghanistan that a vote be taken to determine which of the drafts should receive priority consideration.[121] The result of that vote was a major disappointment for the States that sought cancellation of the plebiscite, as the General Assembly opted by 41 votes to 28, with 18 abstentions, to give precedence to draft Resolution A/C.4/L.685. From that moment, the tide turned fatally against annulment.

Its proponents resorted to systematic opposition of the victorious draft Resolution, voting against it in bloc at all stages in the hope of mustering enough muscle to defeat it. And when it became clear that they were not going to succeed, they all stormed out of the Assembly, defiantly rejecting defeat on the floor. An embittered Kosciusko-Morizet

119   A/C.4/SR.1151. 19 April 1961. p. 364.
120   A/C.4/SR.1152, 19 April 1961, p. 373.
121   A/C.4.SR.1146, 17 April 1961, p. 332.

condemned the Fourth Committee as being "nothing more than a voting machine in which the majority trampled on the minority, showing no respect either for the rules of procedure or the rules of courtesy."[122] He predicted a grim future for the Northern Cameroons:

> We hope that today's vote will not entail dramatic consequences, though we fear that a disguised annexation is being perpetrated, under the label of the United Nations, against the will of the people. We hope that all those who, in good faith, felt it their duty to vote in favor of this Resolution will not someday have cause to regret their somewhat hasty pronouncement.[123]

The ratification of the results of the second Northern Cameroons plebiscite revealed the actual depth of feeling on the question of the British Cameroons. It showed that even though concessions had been easy to make in the past, the ground for compromise grew thinner and thinner when it came to the critical issues. It did not suffice for the trusteeship over the British Cameroons to be terminated; of greater importance to some States was the way in which it was terminated, that is: which of the two neighbors the Territory joined in the event. And here expectations ran so high that either way the fate of the British Cameroons was bound to cause disappointment and dissent.

And so, the British Cameroons, which had been conceived in the secrecy of bilateral agreement between Britain and France, finally won independence in the full glare of the United Nations, in the heat and controversy of international debate, with Britain and France in opposite camps.

122　A/C.4/SR.1152, 19 April 1961, p. 380.
123　Ibid.

CHAPTER FOUR

Bone of Contention

As a result of its delicate balance between Nigeria and Cameroun, the future of the British Cameroons was a deep well of misunderstanding, a potential heightened by the unpredictable nature of the plebiscite mechanism.

Nigeria's anger towards Britain following the surprise defeat in the first Northern Cameroons plebiscite vividly illustrates the point, even if the results were also a shock to Britain. Andrew Cohen reacted rather philosophically, noting that "one of the beauties of the flower of democracy was that it did not always bloom as expected."[1]

But other voices in Britain were bewildered. *The Economist* described the results as "wildly unrealistic, however democratic," and blamed the United Nations for allowing "an inexperienced and misguided Northern Cameroons to vote to be torn bodily from the country of which they are an integral part."[2] Andrew Cohen pleaded that the results were "not to be regarded as a vote against Nigeria."[3]

Still, Nigerians felt betrayed by the United Kingdom. Several Ministers privately accused Britain of manipulating the plebiscite in order to obtain a result to their advantage.[4] The Premier of Northern Nigeria denounced British officials for organizing "great underground campaigns" in favor of postponement, adding that:

> Now that Britain has succeeded in breaking the ties between the Northern Cameroons and Nigeria, the British Chancellor of the Exchequer would go ahead with his suspected plans of

---

1   T/SR.1042. 2 December 1959. p. 2.
2   *The Economist,* London. 14 Nov 1959.
3   A/C.4/SR.438, 7 December 1959, p. 6.
4   *The Guardian,* London, 20 May 1960.

building the trust territory into an earthly paradise for whites as well as a strategic base for Britain.[5]

The Premier consoled himself that "Northern Cameroonians will soon realize their mistake and change their decision when the opportunity is offered."[6]

That strong reaction from the most influential leader of Nigeria was an *avant goût* of the depth of feeling to be expected from the parties interested in the British Cameroons. And while some of the reactions were measured, some bordered on open hostility.

Subtle Frictions

The stake of most countries in the British Cameroons was limited to the exercise of their rights as Member States of the United Nations. But the interest of some States exceeded the mere exercise of a right.

Throughout the evolution of the question, there were quiet rivalries among States whose designs for power, wealth or ideological expansion were likely to be affected by the fate of the Territory. These subtle rivalries were most noticeable between Ghana and Nigeria, and between France and Britain.

From the late 1950s, relations between Ghana and Nigeria were discordant, due in large measure to their struggle for leadership in Black Africa. Ghana's claim to that role derived from its being the first country in Black Africa to attain independence. Kwame Nkrumah saw the new Ghana as the "center to which all the peoples of Africa may come,"[7] telling his countrymen that: "history has assigned to us a great responsibility, and we must not fail all the millions of this continent who look to us as a symbol of their hopes for Africa."[8]

But at independence, Nigeria challenged Ghana's claim to African

---

5   Ibid. 11 Nov 1959.
6   *The Times, 11* Nov 1959.
7   Kwame Nkrumah, *Hands off Africa*, Accra, 1960, p.14. Quoted in Olajide Aluko. Ibid.
8   Ghanaian National Assembly Debates, Vol.12, Accra, 12 Dec. 1959, col.390. Quoted in Olajide Aluko, *Ghana and Nigeria 1957-1970* (London: Rex Collins, 1973), p. 73.

leadership, staking its own based on its sheer size and great wealth. Jaja Wachuku made the point when he observed that "Nigeria is the largest single unit in Africa and so must lead Africa. We are not going to abdicate the leadership position in which God Almighty has placed us."[9]

The relationship of both countries with other African countries, especially those still struggling for independence, was largely viewed in the context of that rivalry for leadership. So was their relationship with the British Cameroons. Ghana looked at the administrative union between the Territory and Nigeria with apprehension and was worried at the prospect of Nigeria incorporating the Trust Territory for good. As Scott Thompson has observed, "Nkrumah did not want Nigeria to get too big."[10] He was having enough problems with it already.

Ghana's approach to the question of the British Cameroons was initially determined by the desire to prevent the Territory from joining Nigeria. Nkrumah was delighted with the rise of nationalism in the Territory, especially with Dr. Endeley and his fight for the separation of the Southern Cameroons from Eastern Nigeria. As a token of his appreciation, the Ghanaian leader invited the Southern Cameroons leader to the All-African Peoples Conference in Accra in December 1958.

But when it became clear that Endeley wanted the separate Southern Cameroons to remain within Nigeria, Nkrumah quietly shifted his support to Foncha and the KNDP, who were willing to fight for all-out separation. Things went so sour between them that Endeley accused Nkrumah of "unwarranted intrusion in the domestic affairs of the Territory."[11]

Nkrumah and Foncha were very strange bedfellows: the former was a flamboyant activist, the latter a diminutive and soft-spoken conservative; their relationship indicates to what lengths the Ghanaian could go in his rivalry with Nigeria. Nkrumah secretly funded the KNDP's campaign in

9   House of Representatives Debates. Lagos, 16 Jan. 1960, col. 154-155. Quoted in Olajide Aluko, Ibid., p. 75.
10   W. Scott Thompson. *Ghana's Foreign Policy* (Princeton: Princeton University Press, 1969), p. 79.
11   *The Guardian,* London. 8 June 1960.

1959,[12] enabling Foncha to barnstorm the Territory with relative ease. After the election, Foncha was barely a day old as Premier when Nkrumah arrived in Buea for an elaborate working visit.

And given that the KNDP victory in 1959 was a turning point in the history of the Southern Cameroons, Kwame Nkrumah may have contributed to it more decisively than was realized at the time. During the campaign and after the election, Ghanaian diplomats significantly began to refer to Foncha as "our man,"[13] as opposed to Endeley who was perceived as "Nigeria's man."

Later that year, when the first Northern Cameroons plebiscite dealt a huge blow to the administrative union with Nigeria, Nkrumah's Government could hardly conceal its delight. Its delegate told the United Nations that:

> while the plebiscite had offered the people an opportunity to register their protest against the existing local administration, it had also offered them an opportunity to vote in the direction of their own sovereignty. There was no doubt that they had voted against the integration with Northern Nigeria.[14]

Nkrumah's reaction to the question of the British Cameroons, especially the Southern Cameroons, was also connected to his relations with the UPC in the French Cameroun. The Ghanaian Government was known to finance the proscribed radical party in the French territory.[15] Scott Thompson contends that Nkrumah's support for the KNDP developed into a strategy to gain a foothold next-door "to keep Ahidjo in line," when it became clear that the UPC was losing ground in Cameroun.[16]

But when the Ghanaian President realized that relations between Ahidjo and Foncha were tending to be harmonious instead, he began to

---

12   W. Scott Thompson, op. cit., pp. 66-67. There is a disagreement as to the actual amount that Nkrumah gave the KNDP. Some say £25.000. But they are all agreed that Nkrumah secretly funded the KNDP.

13   Ibid., p. 79.

14   A/C.4/SR.995, 9 Dec. 1959. p. 680.

15   Scott Thompson, op. cit., p. 76.

16   Ibid., p. 79.

reconsider his support for the KNDP. He even attempted to subvert the Southern Cameroons Government: Premier Foncha revealed in mid-1961 that arms had been discovered being smuggled into the Territory from Ghana and Guinea, for the purpose of causing disorder.[17]

In the end, Ghana viewed the 1961 plebiscite with something short of enthusiasm. Nkrumah would have been delighted that Nigeria had been deprived of the Southern Cameroons. But his satisfaction was tempered by the unhappy realization that far from joining forces with the UPC against Ahidjo, the KNDP was actually working with him.

While the British Cameroons plebiscites brought partial defeat for Nigeria, it did not bring corresponding victory for Ghana. Nkrumah ended up without the foothold that he sought on the eastern border of Nigeria. And Ghana so lost interest in the matter that during the crucial vote to decide whether to endorse or annul the result of the second Northern Cameroons plebiscite, she abstained!

Nkrumah's interest in the British Cameroons plebiscites was determined mainly by what influence he stood to gain in the region. That search for influence had a direct bearing on the subtle rivalry between Ghana and Nigeria.

Anglo-French rivalry in the British Cameroons seemed destined to occur at some point in the Territory's history. Initially, France had only reluctantly ceded to the United Kingdom the two slices of the defunct German Kamerun that constituted the British Cameroons. Had the British insisted on a larger or an equal share in the partition, friction might have developed from the beginning.

As it were, the prospect of Anglo-French discord over the British Cameroons receded as the Territory settled into the administrative union with Nigeria. But the rise of the movement for reunification brought that prospect to light, because reunification was perceived as a rejection of the administrative union with British Nigeria in favor of a new union with French Cameroun.

Although in the minds of its champions, reunification meant a sentimental return to the pre-war boundaries of the divided Kamerun, it was easily construed to mean the addition of a British territory to a French

17   *Daily Express*, London, 31 July 1961.

territory. Such misinterpretation was easy to make because the vote for reunification was a unilateral decision by the British Cameroons, leaving the French Cameroun as a mere recipient and not an active participant in the process of union.

Moreover, the fact that the two options of the plebiscites involved a choice between an anglophone and a francophone country further crystallized the misinterpretation. Some in the British Cameroons actually thought that the choice was between Britain and France, as the Premier of the Southern Cameroons revealed:

> The Opposition had distorted the meaning of the question put in the plebiscite in the Southern Cameroons in order to make the people believe that it would not be a matter of choosing between independence in union with Nigeria and independence in union with the Cameroun Republic, but of choosing between France and the United Kingdom.[18]

In the Northern Cameroons, Abba Habib reported that:

> During the 1961 plebiscite campaign, Nigerians distributed many posters intended to mislead the people by creating confusion in their minds about France and the Republic of Cameroun and urging them not to vote for France [for reunification] which had exploded an atomic bomb [in the Sahara].[19]

To many, therefore, there was a tacit Anglo-French rivalry over the British Cameroons. That reality was confirmed when the split within the African group over the Territory occurred mainly along language lines, with anglophone countries pitted against francophone countries.

The reactions of Britain and France on the question of the British Cameroons were determined partly by their agreements and disagreements, and partly by the peculiar situation in the Territory. At first sight, Britain and France seemed more inclined to cooperate over the British

18   A/C.4/SR.1150, 19 April 1961, p. 355.
19   A/C.4/SR.1142, 11 April 1961, p. 305.

Cameroons than to clash. They had concerted to set up both the mandate and the trusteeship over the Cameroons. As colonial powers, they shared the same reticence towards decolonization. And they were both concerned by the transformations within the United Nations where the most vocal campaigns for decolonization were taking place. By the late 1950s, these transformations had substantially altered the direction of the United Nations. As Robert Wood has observed:

> Whereas earlier it had been largely an instrument of western policy in its Cold War conflict with the Soviet Bloc, the modified power balances in the international system and the changes in the size and composition of United Nations membership had shifted the focus of the organization to colonial issues.[20]

Both France and Britain reacted sharply to that shift of focus. In increasingly strong terms they reiterated the conception of the United Nations as "an inter-state association bound by treaty and limited in its competence by the sovereign powers of Member States."[21] The colonial powers supported one another in their efforts to resist the decolonizing zeal of the United Nations. During the Algerian crisis, Britain defended France's claim that the question should not be discussed at the UN, because Algeria was an overseas province of France.[22] Similarly, during the Rhodesian crisis, France defended Britain's view that the UN had no competence in the matter since the Territory was already self-governing.[23]

Such mutual support explains why French diplomats were inclined to accommodate rather than oppose the United Kingdom over the British Cameroons. One London newspaper fantasized on prospects of joint Franco-British programs in African countries, wondering whether the prospective reunification of the two Cameroons might "give rise to much-needed Anglo-French cooperation on economic assistance to former

20   Robert S. Wood, *France in the World Community*, (Leiden: A. W. Sijthoff, 1973), p. 85.
21   Ibid., p. 68.
22   Mohamed Alwan, op. cit., pp. 77-78.
23   James Barros. (ed.). op. cit., pp. 155-158.

colonies in Africa."[24]

But de Gaulle had different ideas, rooted in his personal experience of history. The General never forgave Britain and the United States for sidelining him when shaping the post-war order. Although France had been raised to the status of a great power, de Gaulle was unhappy to have been left out of such an important exercise. The situation was worsened by personal differences with the British Prime Minister. Paul Addison suggests that Churchill wanted to repudiate de Gaulle as leader of the French, only persuaded against it by his Foreign Office Ministers.[25]

In the years following the War, French expectations were dampened when Anglo-French relations were seen to play second fiddle to Anglo-American relations,[26] much to the frustration of the French leader, who became more and more Anglophobic, constantly finding fault with the increasing American hegemony.[27] The rivalry with the United Kingdom reached an emphatic climax in de Gaulle's two vetoes of Britain's application to join the EEC.

It had been visible during the debate on the British Cameroons, when de Gaulle prevailed on his Foreign Ministry to adopt a tough line against the British. The freedom of action of French representatives was enhanced by the nature of the British Cameroons as a Trust Territory, which meant that France, like any other Member of the UN, had a legitimate interest in it. Kosciusko-Morizet insisted that "so long as the trusteeship had not been terminated, the Territory was still in the charge of the UN."[28] The rivalry was heightened by the fact that the fate of the British Cameroons lay between an anglophone and a francophone country. It was difficult to expect France not to take sides in such a situation, especially as the British Cameroons constituted the international frontier between British Nigeria and French Equatorial Africa, of which Cameroun was a part, and the plebiscites offered the opportunity for either power to push that frontier forward.

24   *The Guardian,* London, 11 Nov 1960.
25   Paul Addison, "Winston Churchill," in John Mackintosh, (ed.) *British Prime Ministers,* Vol.2 (London: Weidenfeld & Nicolson, 1978), p. 25.
26   Joseph Frankel, op. cit., p. 95.
27   Robert S. Wood. op. cit., p. 68.
28   A/C.4/SR.1150, 19 April 1961, p. 359.

Following de Gaulle's orders, French representatives effectively organized the opposition to Britain during the UN debates on the British Cameroons plebiscites. Significantly, French opposition did not dwell on the Southern Cameroons where the Cameroun option had been successful; it concentrated on the Northern Cameroons where that option had been defeated.

The protest discredited the administrative union with Nigeria, challenging the impartiality of the United Kingdom in organizing the plebiscites. The French delegate dismissed the administrative reforms in the Northern Cameroons as having been aimed instead at deepening "the administrative dependence of the Northern Cameroons on the central authorities of the Northern Region of Nigeria;"[29] he accused the Administering Authority of gerrymandering the plebiscite districts;[30] and deplored the rigidity and arbitrary conduct of the authorities in the Territory during the plebiscite exercise.[31]

Together with Cameroun, France spearheaded the move to annul the results of the second Northern Cameroons plebiscite. Kosciusko-Morizet argued that since the results were in doubt, the inevitable conclusion was for the plebiscite to be held again, insisting that it was better to repair a mistake in time than sanction an injustice and create an irredentist state of mind.[32] He urged the United Nations not to abandon the people of the Northern Cameroons "in such dubious circumstances."[33] And later, when Cameroun took the matter to the International Court of Justice, France gave Cameroun ample material and technical support in the nine-man Camerounian team at the Hague, there were five French legal experts![34]

All along, the United Kingdom cautiously avoided direct confrontation with France over the British Cameroons. When Kosciusko-Morizet spoke in strong terms about Britain in the Fourth Committee, Andrew Cohen was "keenly surprised at the conclusion which the representative of

---

29   A/C.4/SR.1150, 19 April 1960, p. 358.
30   A/C.4/SR.1146, 17 April 1961, p. 330.
31   A/C.4/SR.1150, 19 April 1961, p. 358.
32   Ibid., p. 359.
33   Ibid.
34   International Court of Justice: Pleadings, Oral Arguments, Documents: *Case Concerning the Northern Cameroons*, (The Hague: 1963), p. 476.

France had thought fit to draw,"[35] but refused to be drawn into the dispute.

Open Disputes

If some of the disagreement over the British Cameroons could be dip-lomatically disguised, others stubbornly refused to go away. The question of the British Cameroons was such that whatever the outcome, serious and open dispute was inevitable, between the countries that reaped direct gain or suffered perceived loss in the matter. Those open disputes were limited to the second Northern Cameroons plebiscite, with Cameroun serving as the focal point of a mainly two-pronged quarrel.

The trust administration of the British Cameroons, especially its administrative union with Nigeria, had always been questioned by Camer-oun. Britain was suspected by the political elite of that country of nursing secret intentions to hand over the Northern Cameroons to Nigeria. The result of the second Northern Cameroons plebiscite confirmed that sus-picion and created a dispute between both countries.

That result was denounced by Cameroun. Its Foreign Minister described it as having been "obtained by means of colonialist maneu-vers, in violation of General Assembly Resolution 1473[X1V]."[36] Another member of the Cameroun delegation to the United Nations warned that

> The Cameroun people asked for justice. If, however, the United
> Nations should fail to support their conclusions, it would be
> guilty of a denial of justice and the entire Camerounian people
> might well demonstrate their indignation by actions which their
> leaders would prefer to avoid.[37]

President Ahidjo ruefully regarded the result of the plebiscite in ques-tion as an "amputation" of his country, obtained by "sordid maneuvers, ranging from public intimidation and persecution, through obstructions of all kinds, to gross falsifications." He scathingly denounced Resolu-tion 1608[XV] for consecrating "such glaring inequity."[38] The flip side of

35   A/C.4/SR.1150, 19 April 1961, p. 359.
36   A/C.4/SR.1142, 13 April 1961, p. 292.
37   A/C.4/SR.1143. 14 April 1961, p. 310.
38   *Agence Camerounaise de Presse*, No. 122, Yaounde. 1 June 1961.

Cameroun's denunciation of the Resolution was that it gave the impression of also rejecting the independence of the Southern Cameroons which had voted to join it. In effect, Resolution 1608[XV] sanctioned the independence of the Southern Cameroons, which Ahidjo later went to Buea to accept; and it sanctioned the independence of the Northern Cameroons, which he vehemently rejected.

The Cameroun Government duly launched a large-scale international campaign to court world sympathy against what it felt was an erroneous decision by the General Assembly. A special "White Paper" was prepared in English, French and Spanish, setting out Cameroun's objections to the way in which the second Northern Cameroons plebiscite had been organized and conducted, and two official delegations toured African and Latin American States to lobby Government officials. The scale of the campaign had never before been achieved by any West African country.[39] Its scope was not limited to friendly or neutral States: the delegations also visited Ghana, Guinea and the United Arab Republic, all countries that were not on the best of terms with Cameroun, owing to their support for the UPC.

But it was clear that Resolution 1608[XV] which terminated the trusteeship over the British Cameroons effectively ended the political debate on the future of the Territory. More or less gracefully, Cameroun turned its attention to the legal sphere, seeking moral redress for perceived material loss. The battleground shifted from the animated halls of the United Nations to the solemn chamber of the International Court of Justice [ICJ]. In a memorandum of May 2, 1961, the Cameroun Government invited her British counterpart to join her in referring the matter to the Court. But the British Government declined, declaring that "Her Majesty's Government have carried out faithfully the wishes of the United Nations in [the Northern Cameroons]. To refer the matter to the Court would call in question the decision of the General Assembly as set out in its Resolution 1608[XV] and introduce an element of uncertainty in a matter already decided by the Assembly."[40] Consequently, they did not think that they could accept Cameroun's invitation.

---

39   *Observer Foreign News Service,* London, 21 April 1961.
40   British Embassy in Paris, Note Verbale No.1513/168/61.

But the invitation itself had been a mere formality, and its rejection did not deter Cameroun from pursuing its legal action. On May 30, 1961, through its Ambassador in France, Cameroun filed an Application to the Registrar of the ICJ, praying the Court "to adjudge and declare that the United Kingdom has, in the application of the Trusteeship Agreement of December 13, 1946, failed to respect certain obligations directly or indirectly flowing therefrom."[41]

That was the beginning of a protracted legal wrangle between Cameroun and the United Kingdom that was to drag on for over two years, at the end of which the position of both Governments remained as far apart as before.

Cameroun's position in the case concerning the Northern Cameroons was more or less a critique of the United Kingdom's administration of the Territory and of the plebiscite that had ended that administration.[42] The arguments adduced in support of that position were the same as those employed in the fight to annul the results of the plebiscite. These arguments which have been fully developed elsewhere in this work[43] shall be briefly considered here again.

1). Cameroun argued that contrary to Article 5 of the Trusteeship Agreement, the Northern Cameroons had not been administered as a separate Territory within the administrative union, but as an integral part of Northern Nigeria.

2). Article 6 of the Trusteeship Agreement called for the development of free political institutions, a progressively increasing share of the inhabitants of the Territory in the administrative service and their participation in advisory and legislative bodies and in the government of the Territory. Those objectives, in the opinion of

41   International Court of Justice, *Judgment* of 2 XII 63, (The Hague: 2 Dec. 1963). p. 18.
42   The position was elaborated in a Memorial written in Paris on 1 May 1961 and later presented to the ICJ. It was published in: ICJ. Pleadings, Oral Arguments, Documents: Case Concerning the Northern Cameroons. (The Hague: 1963), pp. 25-49. The arguments raised therein were later elucidated and substantiated in the Cameroun Government's Written Observations, Submissions and Final Submissions during the public hearings of the case in October and November 1963.
43   See Chapter Four.

Cameroun, had not been attained.

3). The Trusteeship Agreement did not authorize the United Kingdom to administer the British Cameroons as two separate parts, contrary to the rule of unity, in accordance with two administrative systems and following separate courses of political development.

4). The provisions of General Assembly Resolution 1473[XIV] calling for the administrative separation of the Northern Cameroons from Northern Nigeria were not applied.

5). The measures provided for in the same Resolution for the further decentralization of governmental functions and the effective democratization of the system of local government were not implemented.

6). The electoral lists were drawn up in a discriminatory manner by giving improper interpretation to the qualification of ordinary residence.

7). Finally, practices, acts, or omissions of the local authorities during the organization and conduct of the plebiscite altered the normal course of the consultation and involved consequences in conflict with the Trusteeship Agreement.

The crux of Cameroun's complaint was that there was a causal relationship between the violation of the Trusteeship Agreement and the irregularities in the conduct of the plebiscite on the one hand, and the result of the plebiscite on the other.

It may seem strange that the United Kingdom should come under such fierce criticism over a document that it had conceived and written single-handedly. But interest in the British Cameroons was such that interpretation of the Trusteeship Agreement was not the exclusive preserve of any one country, not even its author.

So, Cameroun, in its capacity as a State directly concerned with the British Cameroons, interpreted the administrative shortcomings and procedural irregularities in the Northern Cameroons as creating a dispute between it and the United Kingdom. The legal nature of the dispute derived from the fact that the Trusteeship Agreement was an international treaty, a breach of which was constituted by the many irregularities and omissions chronicled. According to Cameroun, the United Kingdom and none other was responsible for that breach,[44] with the United Nations exercising only a *"fonction de contrôle"*[45] over the British Cameroons.

Cameroun was also convinced about the jurisdiction of the ICJ in that dispute. Article 36 of the Court's Statute defines its competence as covering all legal disputes concerning:

a). the interpretation of a treaty, and,
b). the existence of any fact which, if established, would constitute a breach of an international obligation.

With prophetic anticipation, the Trusteeship Agreement had stated that:

> If any dispute whatever should arise between the Administering Authority and any other Member of the United Nations relating to the interpretation or application of the provisions of this Agreement, such dispute, if it cannot be settled by negotiation or other means, shall be submitted to the International Court of Justice.[46]

It was on the strength of those considerations that the Cameroun Government took the matter to the ICJ. Mindful of the fact that Resolution 1608[XV] had definitively terminated the trusteeship over the British Cameroons and that the political debate could not be reopened, the Cameroun government asked the Court "simply to state the law, and no more."[47]

But violations of international law were not overlooked merely because a General Assembly Resolution had changed the context in which those violations had been committed. Neither was Cameroun's interest in the affair strictly altruistic. As the Court observed, Cameroun:

---

44   ICJ, Case Concerning the Northern Cameroons, p. 27.
45   Ibid.
46   Trusteeship Agreement for the Territory of the Cameroons Under British Administration. Art. 19.
47   ICJ, Case Concerning the Northern Cameroons, p. 29.

contends that its interest in knowing whether the administrative union was a violation of the Trusteeship Agreement is not merely academic. It contends that there was a causal connection between the allegedly illegal administrative union and the alleged invalidity of the plebiscite.[48]

In his oral argument before the Court, Counsel for Cameroun made that point even clearer:

> The Republic of Cameroun considers that, by administering the Northern Cameroons as it did, the Administering Authority created such conditions that the trusteeship led to the attachment of the northern part of the British Cameroons to a State other than the Republic of Cameroun.[49]

That is what the Cameroun Government wanted the ICJ to determine. Its position was a legal continuation of the political battle that it had fought at the United Nations.

Britain's position was essentially a defense of the trust administration and the organization of the 1961 plebiscite.[50] In its Counter-Memorial submitted on August 14, 1962, Britain treated the complaints of Cameroun as mere allegations, even outright fabrications. Its view was based on the Plebiscite Commissioner's report that the plebiscite had been freely and fairly conducted, and the General Assembly by its Resolution 1608[XV] endorsed the results and terminated the trusteeship.

Britain reiterated the now familiar arguments concerning the impracticality of administering the British Cameroons either as a separate entity or as a single unit, insisting that both the administrative union with Nigeria and the division of the Territory into north and south were not only in the best interests of the people, but had been known to the General Assembly when the Trusteeship Agreement was approved, and "formed

---

48   ICJ. Judgment of 2 XII 63, (The Hague: 2 Dec. 1963), p. 33.
49   Ibid., p. 31.
50   That position was contained in a Counter-Memorial filed on 14 August 1962 and later supported by Written Observations, Submissions, and Final Submissions during hearings of the case.

the basis on which the Trusteeship Council and the General Assembly exercised their supervision throughout the period of the trusteeship."[51]

Britain further argued that all through the trusteeship, the administration of the British Cameroons had been under the effective control of the United Nations, either through its Visiting Missions or in debate of the annual reports of the Administering Authority. Consequently, "the complaints of the Republic of Cameroun imply that the General Assembly itself approved of and committed breaches of the Trusteeship Agreement."[52]

In fact, Britain rejected the existence of any dispute with Cameroun over the Northern Cameroons and affirmed that if at all any dispute existed, it would be between Cameroun and the United Nations:

> The dispute in this case does not appear to be between them and the Cameroun Government, but between Cameroun and the United Nations General Assembly. In administering the Cameroons, Her Majesty's Government have throughout acted under the supervision of the United Nations General Assembly and in accordance with its directives. The policies or practices with which the Cameroun Government find fault have been endorsed by the United Nations and it would not be proper for Her Majesty's Government to take upon themselves the submission to the International Court of Justice of a dispute concerning them. Moreover, Her Majesty's Government's obligations as Administering Authority are to the United Nations rather than to any particular Member.[53]

The British Government further argued that having only recently become a Member of the UN, Cameroun was not competent to institute such a case on the Northern Cameroons.

The Republic of Cameroun was never a part of the Trusteeship

---

51   ICJ. Case Concerning the Northern Cameroons, 1963, p. 69.
52   Ibid., p. 70.
53   British Embassy, Paris. *Note Verbale* No.1513/168/61.

Agreement and only enjoyed the benefits of membership of the United Nations from 20 September 1960; it is not, in the submission of the United Kingdom, entitled to rely on matters occurring during the currency of the Agreement prior to 20 September 1960 to establish a dispute before that date with the United Kingdom.[54]

Britain also felt that even if such a case were possible, the ICJ lacked the jurisdiction to hear it. The Trusteeship Agreement was a treaty, the conflicting interpretation of which would be within the jurisdiction of the Court to examine. However, as of July 1, 1961, the Agreement was no longer in force in relation to the Northern Cameroons. Article 36[1] of the Statute of the Court states that "The Jurisdiction of the Court comprises all cases which the parties refer to it and all matters specially provided for in the Charter of the United Nations or in treaties and conventions in force." Britain argued that since the Trusteeship Agreement had already been terminated, the Article giving the Court jurisdiction in case of dispute could no longer apply.

Finally, the British Government argued that by its Application of May 1, 1961, the Cameroun Republic was seeking to reverse the decision of the General Assembly contained in Resolution 1608[XV]. They did not feel that Article 19 of the Trusteeship Agreement gave the ICJ the jurisdiction to do such a thing.[55]

On the basis of all those arguments, the United Kingdom asked the International Court of Justice to reject Cameroun's claim with regard to the Northern Cameroons.[56]

Cameroun and the United Kingdom disagreed on the major issue areas of the case concerning the Northern Cameroons. While the former insisted that there was a valid case to answer, the latter held that there was no dispute at all. Cameroun argued that the United Kingdom alone was responsible for all the violations of the Trusteeship Agreement, while the United Kingdom shifted that responsibility to the United Nations

---

54   ICJ, Case Concerning the Northern Cameroons, 1963, p. 61.
55   Ibid., p. 63.
56   Ibid., p. 64.

which had approved the Agreement and supervised its implementation. Cameroun maintained that it had suffered direct prejudice as a result of those violations; while Britain rejected the idea, disputing Cameroun's right to bring a case on the matter. Finally, Cameroun held that the ICJ was competent to hear the case, while the United Kingdom felt that the dispute as conceived by Cameroun was not within the jurisdiction of the Court to adjudicate.

The role of the ICJ, which was complicated enough by the depth of the disagreement, was rendered even more difficult by the fact that one of the parties rejected both the dispute and the competence of the Court.

In its judgment, the Court made two important clarifications: firstly, that there was a dispute, and secondly, that Cameroun was perfectly entitled to bring it up. The Court declared that: "the opposing views of the Parties as to the interpretation and application of relevant Articles of the Trusteeship Agreement, reveal the existence of a dispute in the sense recognized by the jurisprudence of the Court."[57] The Court also made it clear that "The Republic of Cameroun, as a Member of the United Nations as from September 20, 1960, had a right to apply to the Court. This procedural right is by no means insubstantial."[58]

Going forward, the Court came up against two major limitations. Firstly, "The decisions of the General Assembly, as sanctioned by Resolution 1608[XV], would not be reversed by the judgment of the Court."[59] The legal effect of that Resolution was that:

> after 1 June 1961, the trust over the Northern Cameroons ceased to exist; no other Member of the United Nations could therefore claim any of the rights or privileges in the Northern Cameroons which might have been originally granted by the Trusteeship Agreement.[60]

Even the General Assembly, in the Court's view, was "no longer competent over the Northern Cameroons, pursuant to the termination of the

57   ICJ, Judgment of 2 XII 63, p. 27.
58   Ibid., p. 29.
59   Ibid., p. 33.
60   Ibid. p. 34.

trusteeship as a result of Resolution 1608[XV],"[61] because "After June 1, there was no 'Trust Territory' and no inhabitants for whose protection the trust functions could be exercised."[62] The Court was of the opinion that Article 19 of the Trusteeship Agreement, which provided for its jurisdiction in cases such as Cameroun now brought before it, was terminated along with all the other Articles of the Agreement, with the result that "after June 1, it could not be invoked as a basis for the Court's jurisdiction."[63]

The Court's opinion thus entailed a subtle legal nicety. On the one hand, it accepted the existence of a dispute based on opposing interpretations of the Trusteeship Agreement; and on the other hand, it refrained from pronouncing on the merits of the case, arguing that the said Trusteeship Agreement had already been terminated.

The second limitation from which the ICJ suffered in its consideration of the case was one imposed by its own judicial function, which requires that any legal action must have a definite purpose or object. Contrary to Cameroun's Application "simply to ask the Court to state the law, and no more,"[64] the Court felt that its judgment "must have some practical consequence in the sense that it can affect the existing legal rights or obligations of the parties involved, thus removing uncertainty from their legal relations."[65]

And even though the Court might, in appropriate circumstances, make declaratory judgments, it felt that it could not make such judgments simply for the sake of doing so. The ICJ declared that

> Whenever it adjudicates on the merits of a dispute, one or the other party, or both parties, as a factual matter, are in a position to take some retroactive or prospective action or avoidance of action which would constitute a compliance with the Court's judgment or a defiance thereof.[66]

61   Ibid., p. 35.
62   Ibid. p. 36.
63   Ibid. p. 35.
64   ICJ. Case Concerning the Northern Cameroons, 1963, p. 29.
65   ICJ, Judgment of 2 XII 63. p. 34.
66   Ibid. pp. 37-39.

As Judge Fitzmaurice separately pointed out, "Courts of law are not there to make legal pronouncements *in abstracto*. They are there to protect existing and current legal rights, to secure compliance with the existing and current legal obligations." In the light of Resolution 1608[XV], the Court found that "circumstances that have since arisen render any adjudication devoid of purpose," and, as such, "Any judgment which the Court might pronounce would be without object."[67] Accordingly, by ten votes to five, the International Court of Justice ruled that it could not adjudicate on the merits of the claim of the Republic of Cameroun.

For many countries, concern with the British Cameroons did not live beyond the termination of the trusteeship. With the adoption of Resolution 1608[XV], they easily turned their attention to other matters, quickly forgetting whatever differences they might have had over the fate of the Territory. This was partly because the British Cameroons as an entity ceased to exist after the plebiscites, and partly because, to most countries, the question of the British Cameroons had probably been only a twinkle in the sky of international relations.

To Britain and Cameroun, however, the dispute over the British Cameroons actually came to life with the plebiscites. Prior to the consultations, hopes of a desirable outcome had held off the likelihood of dispute. But after the plebiscites the dispute became inevitable. The venue shifted from the UN General Assembly to the International Court of Justice. So did the nature of the dispute, from the political to the legal.

But the actors and the prize remained the same. In this new phase of the question, Cameroun sought another international forum where the problem would be publicized, outside sympathies aroused, and where the voice of the weak could rival the voice of the strong.

The International Court of Justice satisfied those requirements. But the case concerning the Northern Cameroons ended on a legal technicality. The Court's judgment was based not on the merits of the case but on the functional limitations of the Court itself. Yet the fact that the case took place at all was a manifestation of the depth of the differences that had developed between the United Kingdom and Cameroun. It showed how the British Cameroons had changed from a "two-part no-man's land"

67   Ibid., p. 38.

into a coveted prize, worthy of an intense legal wrangle. And it showed the readiness of the new nations to challenge the old order.

But it also epitomized the keen foreign interest in the British Cameroons. In the legal dispute over the Northern Cameroons, the Territory itself was neither seen nor heard: it had not contested the results of the plebiscite; it had not been consulted on the institution of the case concerning it; and it was not represented on either side. As Counsel for the Defendant observed, "The unusual feature of this case is that it is brought in relation to an Agreement which no longer exists, about a Territory which belongs to neither Party."[68]

However, the most obvious dispute over the British Cameroons was between Nigeria and Cameroun. The impression that the Territory had been carved out of one and attached to the other was always going to be a potential source of irritation.

New complications grew out of the existence of both unions. One source estimated that by 1959, as much as one-eighth of the total population of the Southern Cameroons came from Nigeria and Cameroun![69] Such a heavy foreign presence could not be without friction between both alien communities and between their countries of origin.

One might have thought that the likelihood of such dispute would diminish with the plebiscites which ended the life of the British Cameroons by dividing it equally between them. But it seems that the plebiscites instead brought the existing tensions to a head. The claims of both were so inflated that neither was satisfied with the half-measure from the plebiscites.

With respect to the Southern Cameroons, Nigeria was embittered by the plebiscite, even though recent political trends in the Territory clearly foreshadowed the result. The plebiscite was the final act in the smoldering drama of separation that had come alive with the victory of the KNDP in 1959. In 1961, as in 1959, punitive measures were advocated against the Southern Cameroons in various circles in Nigeria. There were calls for Nigerian civil servants in the Territory to be withdrawn and for Southern Cameroons civil servants in Nigeria to be expelled; and there

---

68   ICJ, Case Concerning the Northern Cameroons, 1963, p. 399.
69   A/C.4/SR.886, 25 Sept. 1959. p. 24.

were demands for the United Kingdom to refund all Nigerian money spent on the Territory.

It is interesting to note that Nigerian anger over the Southern Cameroons plebiscite was directed not at the Government of Cameroun which stood to gain from the plebiscite, but rather at the Southern Cameroonians for failing to see the advantages of remaining with Nigeria, and to a certain extent at the United Kingdom, for not doing enough to retain the Territory. The Southern Cameroons was thus hardly a source of friction between Nigeria and Cameroun. Nigeria grieved at the loss of the Territory, without pointing accusing fingers at Cameroun.

Or so it seemed. One of the few hints of dispute came from the *West African Pilot*. The Lagos newspaper, like many other Nigerian papers at the time, regarded the question of the British Cameroons as one of prestige for Nigeria. But unlike other Nigerian papers, it refused to accept that the fate of the Southern Cameroons had been decided once and for all by the 1961 plebiscite. It called on the Nigerian Government to "do her duty to the people of Nigeria and the innocent masses of the Southern Cameroons." Nigeria wanted peace with her eastern neighbor, the paper went on, "but not at all costs."[70]

That opinion was suggestive of a dispute with Cameroun that became manifest over the Northern Cameroons, where Nigeria launched a quick counteroffensive.

Cameroun's initial strategy in the battle for the Northern Cameroons was to exclude Nigeria and concentrate on the United Kingdom as being solely responsible for the errors that had marred the plebiscite. It regarded Nigeria as an innocent party, dragged in by the United Kingdom through the administrative union. Cameroun's Foreign Minister, Charles Okala, declared that his country "had no quarrel with its Nigerian brother."[71] He accused Britain of divide-and-rule tactics, which tried to set up Cameroun against Nigeria. As far as his government was concerned, "Nigeria was not a party to the dispute and could only intervene in the debate in its capacity as a State Member of the United Nations. The only parties to the problem were the United Nations, the United Kingdom and the

70   A/C.4/SR.1141. 13 April 1961. p. 296.
71   Ibid.

Republic of Cameroun."[72]

The exclusion of Nigeria from the dispute was merely a tactic of challenging one opponent at a time. Cameroun did not really believe that Nigeria had only been a passive accomplice in the administrative union and the conduct of the plebiscites. As Okala later pointed out,

> the Native Authorities appointed in the Territory by decree of the Premier of the Northern Region, whose territorial ambitions and desire to subjugate the peoples of the Territory were well known, had played a decisive role in the organization, conduct and outcome of the plebiscite.[73]

The Cameroun Foreign Minister further described Nigeria as "an authority that for forty-five years had held the Northern Cameroons in the position of slaves."[74] Such an authority could not be regarded as an innocent party in the dispute over the Northern Cameroons.

Initially, Nigerian politicians were sympathetic towards Cameroun's frustrations. Responding to one of Okala's attacks, Jaja Wachuku, declared that: "in any game, somebody must win something, and somebody must lose something. We have lost and we have won. And the Republic of Cameroun has lost -- and has won."[75]

But they soon ran out of patience with the unrelenting criticisms of their Camerounian counterparts. And they began to challenge the exclusiveness with which Cameroun regarded the question of the British Cameroons. One of its representatives made the point that:

> It was true that the two Territories [the British Cameroons and Cameroun] had formed part of the same German colony; however, if one went somewhat further back in history, one found that a large part of the present Northern Cameroons belonged to the former Bornu and Adamawa empires, which were part of Nigeria. The most that could be said was that the Northern

72   A/C.4/SR.1142. 13 April 1961. p. 299.
73   GAOR. 15 Session, 994th Meeting, 21 April 1961.
74   Ibid.
75   A/C.4/SR.1142, 13 April 1961, p. 300.

Cameroons had had historical ties with both Nigeria and the Republic of Cameroun, but those ties did not confer any greater rights on the one than on the other.[76]

Henceforth, Nigerians reacted strongly to what they considered to be unfounded allegations of complicity made by Cameroun. When Okala criticized the administrative practices in the Northern Cameroons, and held them responsible for the result of the second plebiscite there, Wachuku accused him of trying to "draw red herrings across the trail, to befog the issue at hand with irrelevant rhetoric."[77] He urged the General Assembly not to allow "allegations of inconsequential hitches to debar it from adopting the results of the plebiscite," warning that "any delay in implementing the results of the plebiscites would be tantamount to a denial of self-determination."[78]

After the plebiscites, the border areas were fraught with danger. Skirmishes led to the destruction of property on both sides, prompting the Nigerian Prime Minister to warn that "military action will be taken against those who violate Nigeria's sovereignty along the eastern border."[79] The Premier of Northern Nigeria threatened to launch the recovery of those parts of the Cameroun Republic that were historically part of the former Fulani Empire of Sokoto.[80]

Of all the disputes over the British Cameroons, the one between Nigeria and Cameroun had the greatest potential to degenerate into open conflict. It also exposed certain secret ambitions that could change the face of the entire region. Yet both Nigeria and Cameroun recognized that their claims could not override the expressed wishes of the peoples concerned. In that sense, the plebiscites created and at the same time resolved their dispute over the British Cameroons.

76   U.N. Doc. A/C.4/492. 20 April 1961, p. 2.
77   Ibid., p. 3.
78   Ibid., p. 8.
79   *The Times*, London. 3 June 1961.
80   *West Africa*, London. 11 March 1961. p. 271.

CHAPTER FIVE

Economic Considerations

Much as the British Cameroons plebiscites were a political exercise, their underlying motivations were economic rather than political. The Territory's perceived economic weakness was the overriding consideration that led the UN to adopt a plan for it to achieve independence by joining one of its neighbors.

Most Southern Cameroons leaders themselves had no illusions about the frailty of their Territory's economy. They had been confirmed in that view by an expert investigation commissioned in 1959 to determine the fiscal viability of an independent Southern Cameroons. In his report, Sir Sydney Phillipson, who headed the enquiry, observed that revenues from an independent Southern Cameroons "might just suffice to enable it to maintain and even modestly expand its recurrent services, but that would be a precarious hand-to-mouth existence."[1] But "as a completely independent State, the Southern Cameroons, at its present stage of development, would not be viable."[2]

That report convinced Southern Cameroons leaders against "complete" independence and won them over to the brighter prospects of union with a bigger and more viable neighbor. It is now only a matter of conjecture as to how the UN might have reacted if the leaders of the British Cameroons had insisted on outright independence, irrespective of economic viability. And so, the search for a vibrant economy became the determining factor in terminating the trusteeship over the British Cameroons.

As the situation unfolded, some States were motivated by economic

---

1 Phillipson, Report, cf. Edwin Ardener, "The Nature of the Reunification of Cameroon," in Arthur Hazlewood, (ed.), *African Integration and Disintegration*, (London: OUP, 1967). p. 312.
2 Ibid.

calculations of their own; others applied economic pressure to influence the course of events; while the administrative and political changes engendered by the independence of the British Cameroons had a real impact on the flow of trade, aid, and other economic activities of the region.

The trusteeship over the British Cameroons was formally terminated in two separate ceremonies at Mubi and Buea, during which British officials handed over the instruments of State for the Northern Cameroons and the Southern Cameroons to the leaders of Nigeria and Cameroun respectively. The difference in the venue and date of those ceremonies underscores the absence of unity in the British Cameroons.

At Mubi, on July 1, 1961, Prime Minister Balewa officially received the Northern Cameroons into Nigeria at a ceremony that was routinely brief and devoid of fanfare. Thereafter, the Northern Cameroons quietly returned to the administrative arrangement that had existed during the trusteeship period, as integral parts of three separate provinces of the Northern Region, namely: Bornu, Benue, and Sardauna [formerly Adamawa], in disregard of UN Resolution 1608[XV] of April 21, 1961, which terminated the trusteeship over the British Cameroons by specifically calling for the Northern Cameroons to be constituted into a separate province of the Northern Region of Nigeria. Going forward, its story became a mere footnote in the history of Nigeria.

On the other side, differences in language and culture accumulated through nearly fifty years of separation made it impossible for Cameroun to absorb the Southern Cameroons in the same way. Among the leadership of both the Southern Cameroons and the Cameroun Republic, the hysteria of the plebiscite victory gave way to searching questions about the terms of union. Both sides were aware of embarking upon a seminal political experiment in uniting territories from two different colonial molds. It was an experiment without precedent in Africa, for which the first steps had to be cautious enough to accommodate the idiosyncrasies of either side.

At a constitutional conference in Foumban in mid-July 1961, delegates from both sides settled on a Federal republic as the framework for union, in which the then Cameroun Republic and the Southern Cameroons would become Federated States known as East Cameroon and

West Cameroon respectively.[3] John Ngu Foncha, the chief proponent of reunification, held that the federal system would "keep the two cultures [French and English] in the areas where they now operate, and blend them in the center."[4]

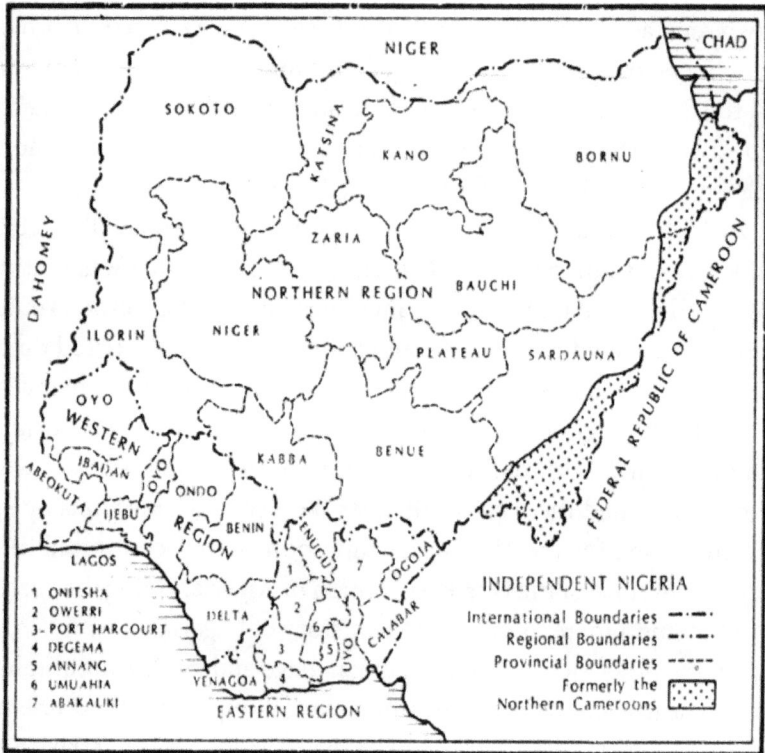

Figure 5.1. Independent Nigeria

The ceremony at Buea on October 1, 1961, symbolized the termination of the trusteeship, the independence of the Southern Cameroons and the birth of the Federal Republic of Cameroon, all at once.

In terms of land area, population, and natural resources, the British Cameroons plebiscites added more to Cameroun. At the time of union,

3   For a more detailed discussion on the working of the Federation, see the next Chapter.
4   West Cameroon, Record of the Conference on the Constitutional Future of the Southern Cameroons, held at Foumban, 17 to 21 July. 1961, cf. Willard Johnson, op. cit., p. 183.

West Cameroon accounted for about nine per cent of the land area and twenty per cent of the population of the Federal Republic of Cameroon; while the Northern Cameroons accounted for five per cent of the land area, and two per cent of the population of Nigeria. The impact of the plebiscites was bound to be greater in Cameroon than in Nigeria. And that impact was significant politically as well as economically.

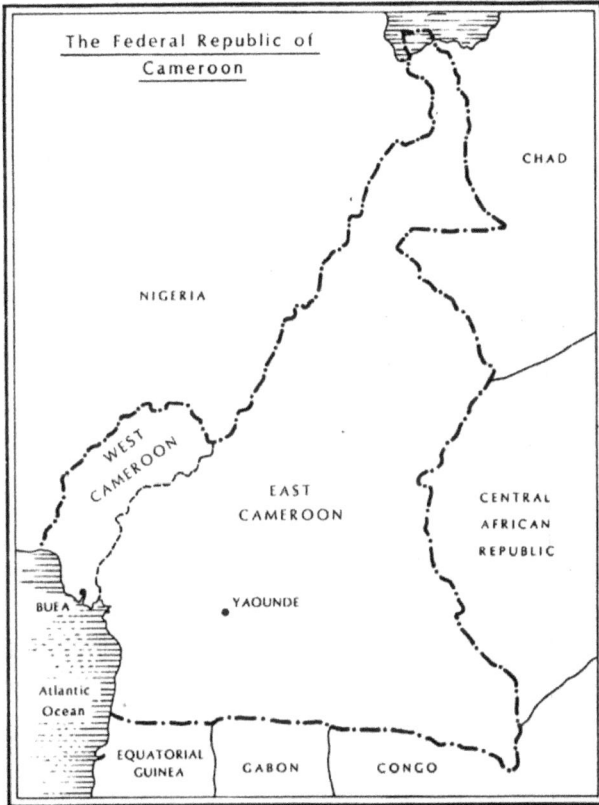

Figure 5.2. The Federal Republic of Cameroon

Trade Relations

Judging from its size, resources and infrastructure, the British Cameroons was not a large trading market. Yet by adjusting the political and administrative structure of the region, the plebiscites affected trade flows between the countries concerned.

Anglo-Cameroon Trade

Notwithstanding the agreement of the British Board of Trade in June 1962 "to do everything possible to encourage trade with the Cameroon Republic,"[5] and claims by *The Times* of London that the Federal Republic of Cameroon was "a country that Great Britain must consider as eminently worthy of friendship and assistance,"[6] Anglo-Cameroon trade relations throughout the sixties were in general decline.

There appeared to be an air of restraint about trade between Cameroon and the UK. The Commercial and Economic Cooperation Agreement signed by both governments in London in July 1963 reflected rather than dispelled that feeling. In the agreement, they acknowledged the need to develop their commercial and economic relations,[7] and undertook to encourage investments and promote import and export operations between them.[8]

But their commitment was visibly half-hearted: they mutually denied themselves the convention of "the most favored nation" treatment that was customary between former metropolis and colony, and mandatory for all members of the General Agreement on Tariffs and Trade [GATT]. France and Cameroun treated themselves thus, so did Nigeria and the UK. But Cameroon and the UK agreed instead that

> without prejudice to national legislation offering preferential treatment to certain countries, either of the Contracting Parties shall offer to the business concerns and industrial firms of the other country treatment no less favorable than that accorded to the business concerns and firms of all other foreign countries.[9]

The Agreement also provided for a Joint Commission to study

---

5   *The Daily Telegraph*, London, 28 June 1962. The agreement followed discussion in London between the British Board of Trade and the Visiting Cameroun Foreign Minister, Jean Betayene.

6   Quoted in *Le Monde, Paris*, 8 May 1963.

7   Commercial Agreement between the United Kingdom and the Federal Republic of Cameroon, London, 29 July 1963, Preamble.

8   Ibid, Article I.

9   Ibid, Article VII.

proposals for the improvement of commercial relations between them.[10] But in the characteristic malaise of their relations, the Commission was not set up until 1981!

The evolution of trade between the Southern Cameroons and the UK responded to the course of political events in the Territory. In 1958, the UK was the main trading partner of the Southern Cameroons, taking up 75% of her exports and providing 65% of her imports.[11] But as separatist tendencies intensified in the Territory, the British share of its market declined. By 1964, the UK accounted for less than 20% of the imports of the Territory. That decline was even more dramatic with regard to West Cameroon's exports to the UK, especially bananas, which was the mainstay of the Territory's economy. After Jamaica and the Windward Islands, the Southern Cameroons was the largest supplier of bananas to the UK in 1959, with 1,155,871 tons, representing 20.44% of the total UK consumption of the product.[12] By 1965, that figure had declined to a meager 8,632 tons![13] The decline was aggravated by the withdrawal of the Commonwealth preference on bananas and other West Cameroon exports to the UK.

The level of trade between the UK and the Federal Republic of Cameroon thus remained far below what was expected for a country part of which had been administered by the UK for nearly half a century. This was clearly reflected in an honest evaluation of Anglo-Cameroon trade, pronounced in 1981 by Lord Jellicoe. Speaking before the Chamber of Commerce in Douala, Lord Jellicoe, who later became the Chairman of the British Overseas Trade Board, declared that

> When, in 1961, the former British-administered Trust Territory of West Cameroon elected to merge with the independent French-speaking East Cameroon as a united Republic, it was too readily assumed by British exporters that potential business

---

10   Ibid. Article XI.
11   Wilfred A. Ndongko, *Planning for Economic Development in a Federal State: The Case of Cameroon, 1960-1971.* (Munchen: Weltforum Verlag, 1975). p. 66.
12   Board of Trade, Accounts Relating to Trade and Navigation of the United Kingdom. 1959, (London: HMSO, 1959).
13   Ibid, 1965.

in the area had come to an end. British businessmen appeared
to turn their backs on your country, merging it in their minds
with the States of former French Equatorial Africa, an area
about which to this day many British exporters know far too
little about.[14]

Cameroon-Nigeria Trade

Of all the external economic relations of Cameroon and Nigeria,
trade with each other was among the earliest. From pre-colonial times,
there was a flourishing network of local trade in the area: subsistence
food crops, salt, smoked fish, oil, spices, kola-nuts and cattle products
were exchanged at local markets in the area that now constitutes their
common border.

But at the national level, trade between the two countries remains
almost insignificant when compared with the volume of their trade
with Europe. The difference was even greater in the years following
independence.

In colonial Africa, strong economic ties were established with the
colonial powers, to the extent that the general orientation of Africa's
foreign trade was mainly the export of raw materials to Europe and the
import of manufactured goods therefrom. For Nigeria, the UK remained
the dominant trading partner, taking up nearly 50% of her foreign trade
from 1961 to 1965,[15] while for Cameroon, France was the principal trading partner, with an average 57% of her total external trade within the
same period.[16]

For both Cameroon and Nigeria, trade with the rest of Africa was
lamentably small. During the period considered above, the whole of
Africa accounted for less than 1% of Nigeria's imports and consumed only
2% of her exports. For Cameroon, Africa consumed 6% of her exports
and supplied 12% of her imports. This very low level of intra-African
trade could be attributed, among other things, to the similarity of their

---

14 Speech by Lord Jellicoe at the Douala Chamber of Commerce. 20 October 1981.
15 *Nigerian Journal of International Studies,* Lagos, Vol. 1, No. 1, July 1975, p. 92.
16 Presidency of the Republic, *Commerce Exterieur du Cameroun Oriental, 1956-
    1966,* (Yaoundé: Imprimerie Nationale, 1967), pp. 4-5.

economies as producers of raw materials, and to the appalling condition of inter-state communications networks.

Cameroon-Nigeria trade suffered particularly from this latter deficiency. Over their common frontier of more than 1,000 kilometers, there were only eleven road crossings in 1965, two river connections, and no railway links whatsoever.

And as if poor communications were not enough, the climate of mutual hostility resulting from the plebiscites made the situation worse: whereas in 1946, 2.8% of the total exports of the French Cameroons had gone to Nigeria and 1.9% of her imports had come from there, those figures declined rapidly in the years following the plebiscites to a record low of 0.15% in 1964.

Intra-Cameroon Economic Relations

The plebiscites were also of great economic significance within Cameroon. Cameroonians on both sides were conscious of the economic advantages of the union. While the Southern Cameroons needed the support of a more viable partner, Cameroun traders sought to benefit from the new market of the Southern Cameroons. Willard Johnson holds that "Bamileke traders, who dealt in all forms of small commerce, were particularly strong advocates of reunification because their major competition in the Southern Cameroons came from Nigerian traders."[17] With reunification, that competition would be contained.

The political transformations that followed the plebiscites had a profound impact on the economic structure of West Cameroon. The Territory left the sterling zone for the franc zone on April 2, 1962. The focus of its commercial activities shifted from Nigeria and Britain to East Cameroon and France. It was hoped that with entry into the franc zone, West Cameroon would become eligible for French assistance; and that in general, access to French markets already enjoyed by East Cameroon,

---

17   Willard Johnson, The Cameroon Federation: Political Integration in a Fragmentary Society, (Princeton University Press, 1970), p. 90.

would be extended to the West.[18]

Those hopes turned out to be somewhat far-fetched: as had been the case with the administrative union with Nigeria, reunification was not a magic wand for the economic woes of the Southern Cameroons. Instead, upon leaving the Commonwealth and entering the franc zone, West Cameroon was lost in the middle of nowhere: it was not able to trade with the UK as before and it was not able to penetrate French markets as expected.

The product for which West Cameroon most urgently sought new markets was bananas, which accounted for nearly 50% of the export earnings of the State, and almost all of which had previously been exported to the UK. Following its entry into the franc zone, West Cameroon was obliged to look towards France for new markets for its bananas, to replace the one it was about to lose in the UK. That search bore little fruit in the first few years, given that the French banana market was fully protected by an annually revised quota system limiting supplies exclusively to the French West Indies and African States of the French Community. Stanford Bederman explains that,

> Despite the fact that West Cameroon was a part of the Federal Republic, it did not manage to obtain a share of the country's banana quota in the French market until the end of 1966 as the producers in East Cameroon, jealous of their situation, successfully kept West Cameroon producers from infringing upon their share.[19]

West Cameroon thus left the British market without gaining access to that of France. The economic weakness that had justified the plebiscite was aggravated by the additional burden of having to look for new markets for its exports in a highly competitive world. That difficulty heralded a

18   K. Anderson, *Report on the Economic Aspects of the Reunification of the British Cameroons with the Republic of Cameroun*, (Yaoundé: 1961), mimeo. The government of the Republic of Cameroun had commissioned the investigation leading to this report.

19   Stanford H. Bederman, *The Cameroons Development Corporation: Partners in National Growth*, (London: Brown Knight and Truscott. 1968), p. 36.

decline in the export trade of West Cameroon. Edwin Ardener holds that "the West Cameroon economic situation in the 1950s was much sounder than it subsequently became": by the end of 1962, the Territory's exports had fallen by a staggering 33% from 1960 levels.[20] "The introduction of exchange control and import licensing from East Cameroon led to an increase in the tendencies of stagnation in the West Cameroon economy, and to a rapid rise in the cost of living;" by 1963, retail prices in West Cameroon had risen by 25% over the 1960 level, while private investment declined by 47%.[21]

From early indications, union did not look like the appropriate cure for the fragile economy of West Cameroon. The debate itself seemed misplaced. The issue was not how much revenue was generated from the State but how it was deployed. During the administrative union, revenues from the Southern Cameroons were included willy-nilly in the budget of Nigeria.[22] And after reunification, revenues from West Cameroon went directly into the coffers of the Federal Government, which then decided what to give the West Cameroon Government to subsidize its budget. The uncertainty of that procedure usually left the West Cameroon Government perplexed leading Prime Minister Jua to question how a State could develop itself "if it cannot know how much it has at its disposal."[23] Anyangwe contends that Ahidjo created and sustained that uncertainty on purpose: "to induce a dependency syndrome in West Cameroon and promote the view that it could not survive without East Cameroon."[24] But the discovery of oil off its coast in 1971 cut through that illusion. The existing narrative on the weakness of the West Cameroon economy, which had justified the plebiscite and later determined the distribution of power within the Federation,[25] was no longer tenable as oil from the State became the mainstay of the national economy. That narrative had initially

20   Edwin Ardener. op. cit., pp. 311-317.
21   Ibid, p. 319.
22   GAOR, 4th Session, Supplement No. 4, Annex, p. 190.
23   Carlson Anyangwe, *Imperialistic Politics in Cameroun*, (Langaa RPCIG, Cameroon, 2008), pp. 60-70.
24   Ibid.
25   That distribution was initially very lopsided: the first Federal Government of twelve ministers, included only one (S.T. Muna) from West Cameroon

been spun by the British to justify the administrative union with Nigeria, focusing on the size of the British Cameroons rather than its resources. It was later peddled by some in Cameroun to give the impression that the Southern Cameroons was coming into the union cap-in-hand. But nothing could be farther from the truth: the backbone of the economy of the German Kamerun was its coastal industrial plantations, most of which were found in the Southern Cameroons!

Initially, reunification also increased intra-Cameroon trade flows. Between 1961 and 1962, West Cameroon imports from East Cameroon jumped from 72 million to 390 million francs, while the reverse operation increased marginally, from 12 million to 14 million francs. The rise in intra-Cameroon trade was largely with regard to West Cameroon importing from East Cameroon, underscoring the fact that with reunification, East Cameroon replaced Nigeria on the West Cameroon import market.

Overall, the major economic impact of the plebiscites was the creation in the Federal Republic of Cameroon of an entirely new market, bigger, stronger, and more diversified than the economy of either Federated State. That new creation naturally resembled the bigger partner more than it did the smaller one. Through reunification, East Cameroon attracted West Cameroon into its pole of economic gravity, reshaping its practices in the process. West Cameroon emerged from that exercise much the poorer, but with hope of a brighter future.

Foreign Aid

The economic impact of the plebiscites went beyond the field of trade. Another sphere affected by the British Cameroons decisions of 1961 was that of foreign aid, especially British aid, to the region. Both French and British assistance was largely concentrated in their former colonies. In 1963, for example, over 85% of Britain's bilateral aid went to the Commonwealth and her remaining dependencies.[26] French aid was even more concentrated: no less than 94% of its bilateral aid went to the countries of the franc zone.[27]

The uncertainty over the future of the British Cameroons decisively

---

26   H. J. P. Arnold, *Aid for Development,* (London: The Bodley Head, 1966), p. 117.
27   Ibid. p. 99.

played on the grant of British aid to the Territory. As far back as 1944, the British Colonial Secretary, O.F.G. Stanley, pinpointed that uncertainty as the main obstacle to Britain's aid program in the Cameroons. Speaking before the House of Commons, Mr. Stanley attributed the slow pace of development in the British Cameroons to two related reasons:

> First of all, no private capital would go into an area whose future was uncertain. Secondly, when the Government had money to spend on capital development, on the building of roads and schools, it was not unnatural inclination to put that money into the part of the Territory [Nigeria] which they know was remaining permanently.[28]

In 1960, when a Southern Cameroons delegation visited London, the Colonial Secretary, Iain Macleod, refused to commit himself on the question of financial assistance before the plebiscites, when the uncertainty about the Territory's future would be lifted.[29] That uncertainty confronted Britain with a dilemma in formulating its aid policy towards the Territory: British aid had to be generous enough to convince the people to remain with Nigeria, but not too extravagant to constitute a significant loss in case the people decided otherwise.

While British aid to the Northern Cameroons was always contained in the aid package for Nigeria, the United Kingdom designed a separate aid program for the Southern Cameroons from 1955, following its separation from Eastern Nigeria. And for its size, the Southern Cameroons received a more-than-proportionate share of UK aid, reaching a record high of nearly £1.5 million in 1962. In fact, between 1958 and that year, as shown below, British aid to the Southern Cameroons was more important than its aid to Ghana, The Gambia, and at times Sierra Leone.

But with the plebiscites, British assistance to the Southern Cameroons dropped rapidly, by 80% between 1962 and 1963 to only £300,000, and still further to a record low of £32,000 in 1964. UK aid to the Federal Republic of Cameroon remained far below that for any of the former

---

28   Quoted in *Headlines,* No. 99, (Lagos: Daily Times Press, May 1981), p. 3.
29   *The Times,* London, 17 November 1960.

British dependencies, however small.

The impact of the plebiscites in that dramatic decline was seen in the way in which the UK withdrew from the Southern Cameroons after reunification. In Nigeria, for example, the amount of British aid in the first two years of independence stood at £32 million.[30] For Tanganyika, a former Trust Territory like the Southern Cameroons, the UK lavished some £23 million in grants and interest-free loans between 1961 and 1963.[31] To the Southern Cameroons, Britain gave a pitiful "parting gift" of £575,000 at reunification![32] Going forward, the Federal Republic of Cameroon joined the category of "foreign countries" to which the UK gave bits of assistance from time to time, as a public relations exercise. In 1963, for instance, Britain granted a total of £3.5 million in loans to Afghanistan, Algeria, Cameroon, Chile, Korea, Syria, and Vietnam. And the loans were specifically "tied to products of British industries with surplus capacity."[33]

Still, the Federal Republic of Cameroon continued to receive as much as ten times more British aid than any other country in the French Community in Black Africa, with which Community Cameroon was now associated in British minds. The plebiscites thus made it possible for East Cameroon, through its association with West Cameroon, to benefit from more British aid than was otherwise available to other former French dependencies in Africa. But the plebiscites also made it impossible for West Cameroon to receive as much aid as was normally granted to territories formerly under British control.

The greatest beneficiary of British aid to West Cameroon was the Cameroons Development Corporation [CAMDEV]. As the largest single business concern in the Territory -- employing over 20,000 people, controlling almost 20% of the cultivated land, and accounting for nearly 40% of the total export earnings of the State -- the Corporation was the perfect barometer of the economic health of the Southern Cameroons.

CAMDEV thrived on its close links with the London-based Colonial

30 H. M. Treasury. Aid to Developing Countries, 1958-1963. (London: HMSO. 1963), Cmd. 2147. September 1963, p. 24.
31 Ibid. p. 25.
32 Edwin Ardener, op. cit., p. 319.
33 Cmd. 2147. September 1963, p. 27.

Development Corporation [CDC], materialized in 1959 by the involvement of the latter as managing agents of the former and the grant of two loans worth £3,000,000, of which £1,000,000 was payable upon the signing of the Managing Agency Agreement, and the remaining £2,000,000 upon the reconstitution of CAMDEV into a joint-stock company.

Table 5.1. UK Bilateral Aid Programme with selected African Countries (in thousand pounds)

	1958	1959	1960	1961	1962	1963	1964	1965	1966	1967
GAMBIA	114	169	196	323	450	1,085	894	1,392	834	799
GHANA	574	136	114	80	130	901	2,383	575	479	494
S. LEONE	655	247	2,445	2,874	2,837	2,211	1,471	780	1,099	905
KENYA	5,284	3,313	4,099	9,617	15,235	12,117	14391	16692	10460	7,618
UGANDA	471	850	3,924	4,269	6,639	9,284	5,388	3,626	4,347	4,861
CAMEROON*	246	565	578	1,288	1,491	300	32	101	116	130
GUINEA	-	-	-	-	-	-	3	9	6	16
Ivory Coast	-	-	-	-	-	-	7	8	12	-
TOGO	-	-	-	-	-	-	6	5	7	11
SENEGAL	-	-	-	-	-	-	1	3	9	17

Source:
- 1958-1963:Figures: H. M. Treasury, Aid to Developing Countries (London: HMSO, 1963), Cmnd. 2147
- 1964-1967 Figures; Ministry of Overseas Development, British Aid Statistics, 1964-1968, (London: HMSO, 1969), pp. 24-29
* Before 1962 the figures here are for the Southern Cameroons; thereafter, they are for the Federal Republic.

But the uncertain political future of the Southern Cameroons cast an early shadow over the CDC's association with CAMDEV. That was why it insisted on CAMDEV being converted from a statutory corporation into a joint stock company, and reserved the right to cancel any further installments of the loan "if a situation had arisen which in the CDC's opinion materially alters the state of CAMDEV's affairs."[34]

34 CAMDEV, Register of Legal Documents. Vol. I, Document 9.

The results of the Southern Cameroons plebiscite confronted the CDC with a new predicament. There had been serious argument in the UK over the anachronism of the Colonial Development Corporation continuing to be involved in a territory that became independent. The controversy had first divided British opinion on the eve of the independence of the Gold Coast. Some people felt that the CDC ought to refrain from embarking on any new schemes in newly independent territories. Their main argument was that "a colony which becomes independent should take full responsibilities for that State, if it requires capital from abroad, it should be able to borrow in the ordinary way in the market."[35]

But others argued that even though such territories were no longer within the statutory ambit of the CDC, their independence meant more, not less, need for the Corporation's services. It was morally wrong, they said, "to leave a country simply to sink or swim as from the day of independence."[36]

After a long debate, the British Parliament settled for the latter view. The Overseas Resources Development Act of 1948 was amended in 1957, empowering the CDC not only to continue with projects commenced before independence, but to undertake new projects on a managing agency basis in independent Commonwealth countries. In 1963, the Colonial Development Corporation appropriately changed its name into the Commonwealth Development Corporation [CDC].

In the light of that amendment, the CDC would have been able to continue its investment in CAMDEV without controversy. But the Southern Cameroons had achieved independence by leaving the Commonwealth altogether, which was the CDC's frame of reference. A new question arose as to how to relate with countries that left the Commonwealth.

There was an obvious contradiction for the CDC to continue investing in such countries. British opinion was again divided. Officials at the Colonial Office, the Treasury and the Foreign Office felt that, notwithstanding the results of the plebiscites, the British Government should act favorably towards the Southern Cameroons in memory of Britain's

---

35   Quoted in D. J. Morgan, *The Official History of Colonial Development,* Vol. IV. (London: Macmillan. 1980), p. 122.

36   Letter from the Secretary of State for Commonwealth Relations to the Secretary of State for the Colonies, 6 December 1956, quoted in *idem.*

forty-year administration of the Territory.[37] But sections of the British Parliament, especially a group of Tory Back-benchers, argued that the CDC should not support projects in countries outside the Commonwealth, much less in those that had willingly left the Club, and that any aid to the Federal Republic of Cameroon should be channeled through the appropriate agencies.[38]

The primary attraction of the British connection was the Commonwealth preference on West Cameroon exports to the United Kingdom. By providing a protected and preferential market for West Cameroon's agricultural products, that preference was vital to the success of CAMDEV and the stability of the economy of the Territory: the price of West Cameroon products exported to the UK, especially bananas, enjoyed a 15% advantage over non-Commonwealth produce. But it was strongly targeted by a hostile lobby in the British Parliament that sought its removal. And despite vigorous representations from the Cameroon government, the lobby succeeded in ensuring that the Commonwealth preference on West Cameroon products was not extended beyond September 1963.

Although the Commonwealth preference was generally presented as an economic program, it was actually a political instrument, designed to regulate relations between the UK and the benefactor nation. It was, therefore, keenly susceptible to political change in the territories. And change of the magnitude engendered by the plebiscites was bound to impact its operation.

The history of the Southern Cameroons posed major problems for the Commonwealth preference scheme. In theory, the preference operated on the basis of membership of the Commonwealth. So, the decision of the Southern Cameroons plebiscite directly contradicted the continuation of the preference.

But in practice, there were cases of the preference being continued in countries that left the Commonwealth,[39] even though it was generally admitted that the preference could not be retained indefinitely by such countries.

37   D. J. Morgan, op. cit., p. 192.
38   Letter of 31 May 1962, from Mr. Norman A. Pannel, MP. to the Secretary of State. quoted in idem.
39   Burma, the Republic of Ireland, and South Africa.

A Norwegian expert, K. Anderson, commissioned to study the question before the plebiscites, concluded that the sudden discontinuation of the preference would have serious effects on banana exports, the incomes of producers and traders, on the Southern Cameroons government's financial position and, indeed, on the whole economy of the Territory. He recommended that an agreement be reached to phase out the preference, giving time for the Southern Cameroons to switch production from bananas to other crops.[40]

The British Government adopted Anderson's recommendations. In the UK Finance Bill of 1961, a clause was inserted specifically naming West Cameroon as a member of the preference area until September 30, 1962, a deadline later extended to September 30, 1963.[41]

The issue was debated again during the 1962/1963 session of the House of Commons. In one of the exchanges, a sympathizer of West Cameroon pleaded with the government "to do their best to ensure that the English traditions are supported" in the Territory, notwithstanding the decision of the plebiscites. He found the threatened suspension of the Commonwealth preference on the main export crop of the Territory to be a poor way of maintaining the link between the UK and West Cameroon.[42]

Another Member was against the idea that West Cameroon should be denied what had been granted to South Africa. As he queried the House: "What about South Africa? When she left the Commonwealth, what did our tired old imperialists do then? They leaned over backwards to do everything they could to give them what help they could."[43] Still another Member perceived the threatened action as a fall-out of the Franco-British rivalry over the EEC:

> I am left with the suspicion that we are deserting a people whom we have tried to help in other ways and who look to us for help in many directions, simply because we have been snubbed by the French in our efforts to get into the EEC. It seems rather hard that the people of West Cameroon, who have been linked

40   K. Anderson, Report. 1961. p. 26.
41   Edwin Ardener. op. cit., p. 316.
42   House of Commons. Debates. 22 July 1963. Col. 1210.
43   Ibid, Cols. 1206-1207.

to us in so many ways for so many years should be made the victims of a dispute between us and France and which is unrelated to their welfare.[44]

The argument against cancellation of the preference was buttressed by the new policy to continue with the CDC's investment in CAMDEV. As one Member of Parliament pointed out: "the British taxpayer is being asked to provide money to make an investment in bananas [in West Cameroon], from which the government are then to remove the preference!"[45]

Still, the case for withdrawal was compelling, based on the perception of the preference as an attribute of membership of the Commonwealth, a view forcefully summarized during the debate by one other MP: "if we attach importance to membership of the Commonwealth, then the benefits of being in must be extended with care and discrimination to any who go out."[46]

The situation was complicated by the fact that the Southern Cameroons had not only left the Commonwealth but had actually united with a country with which the UK had no special relationship. Maintaining the preference for West Cameroon products beyond a transitional period would have meant offering preferential treatment to part but not all of the Federal Republic of Cameroon, a very abnormal situation indeed.

The British Minister of Trade drew attention to the fact that even though there were several precedents for maintaining the preference in countries which had left the Commonwealth, "there was no precedent for maintaining the preference for part of an independent non-Commonwealth country."[47] The alternative would have been to grant the preference to the entire Federal Republic of Cameroon. But it was quickly pointed out that East Cameroon already enjoyed preferential treatment from France.

British opinion on the matter was further influenced by the banana-producing States of the West Indies, as the Minister of Trade informed the House of Commons:

44   Ibid. Col. 1210.
45   Ibid. Col. 1209.
46   Ibid. Col. 1211.
47   Ibid. 12 July 1962. Vol. 662. Cols. 16667-1668.

Jamaica and the Windward Islands are both concerned to
increase their export earnings and worried about the tendency, especially in the winter months, for the British market
to be over-supplied with bananas. These countries have made
it clear that they are strongly opposed to sharing their preferential advantages in our markets with West Cameroon, given
that the Territory is the only area in the world which enjoys
preference both in Britain and in the EEC.[48]

The British government finally succumbed to the pressure and withdrew the preference on September 30, 1963. In so doing, it sacrificed
the commercial health of CAMDEV on the altar of politics. The decision meant an automatic duty of £7.10s on every ton of West Cameroon
bananas entering the UK. It was not long before the impact of that decision was felt: from a profit of £36,603 in 1963, CAMDEV registered a
deficit of £85,315 in 1964, as revenue from bananas fell by a staggering
40%.[49]

Considering the result of the Southern Cameroons plebiscite, it was
to be expected that the Commonwealth preference would eventually be
withdrawn. And considering the importance of that preference, it was
not surprising that its withdrawal caused such a strain on CAMDEV and
on the economy of West Cameroon.

In purely economic terms, therefore, the greatest loser from the 1961
plebiscites was the Southern Cameroons itself, which lost its markets
in the UK, without finding alternative outlets in France. Another loser
was Nigeria, for whom the Northern Cameroons was little consolation,
having lost the more profitable markets of the Southern Cameroons.
An obvious winner was East Cameroon, which saw a net increase in its
domestic market, without losing its quota of the French market. And the
overall winner was the Federal Republic of Cameroon which could draw
from its triple colonial heritage to build a more attractive future for itself.

48   Ibid. 22 July 1963, Col. 1204.
49   D. J. Morgan, op. cit., p. 198.

CHAPTER SIX

The Plebiscites in National Politics

The impact of the plebiscites was no less important on the politics of the region and the political relations of the States concerned. Their outcome affected both Nigeria and Cameroun in different ways, internally as well as internationally. The plebiscites also adjusted their boundaries, bringing them into greater geographical proximity.[1] That neighborliness, together with the bitter-sweet memories of the plebiscites themselves, became an important element of their bilateral relations.

The Plebiscites and the Internal Politics of Nigeria

Geographical and economic indicators suggest that the plebiscites had a greater impact on Cameroun than on Nigeria. Yet the fate of the British Cameroons was more intensely debated in Nigeria than in Cameroun, because while Cameroun's claim over the British Cameroons was based on past affiliation, Nigeria's claim derived from current association, which was more difficult to give up.

Nigerian debate on the British Cameroons was more animated about the Northern Cameroons. In the Southern Cameroons, Foncha's government was focused on its desire to separate from Nigeria, entertaining little intrusion in its affairs. But with no government of its own, the Northern Cameroons remained uncertain about its future, thereby inviting speculation and manipulation from Nigeria.

Furthermore, the Northern Region, with which the Northern Cameroons was administered, was closely watched by the two southern regions, keen on maintaining the balance of power within the Federation. And to

---

1   Before the plebiscites, Nigeria and Cameroun had only 64 km of common border around the river Benue; thereafter, their new common boundary stretched all the way from Lake Chad to the Atlantic Ocean, a distance of some 1000 km.

the extent that the Northern Cameroons impacted that balance, its fate gained significance in the internal politics of Nigeria.

In spite of the rivalry between the Igbo and the Yoruba, which epitomized the wider competition between Eastern and Western Nigeria, both sides were conscious that their ultimate rival on the national scene were the Hausa-Fulani of the Northern Region. That north-south divide had been built into Nigerian politics from the inception of the Federation in 1914 by Lord Lugard's amalgamation of the Northern and Southern Protectorates of Nigeria. From that moment, a conscious, often bitter, struggle ensued between the North and the South for control of the Federation.

When political parties emerged in the country, they first attracted regional and indeed tribal followings, to the extent that ethnic rivalries were quickly transformed into political rivalries. Gradually, the political parties sought to broaden their base, focusing on any pockets of uncertainty that appeared in the peripheries of the strongholds of their rivals.

The Northern Cameroons was such a periphery of Northern Nigeria. Existing doubts about the Territory's future, coupled with the absence of a strong indigenous political structure, attracted the political parties of southern Nigeria. This Southern interest crystallized into a resolute opposition of the NPC during the first Northern Cameroons plebiscite in 1959.

The idea of the plebiscite had been born from the rivalry between the NPC and the parties of southern Nigeria. The administrative union of Northern Nigeria and the Northern Cameroons had always been criticized by those parties as having resulted in the abolition of many of the traditional institutions of the Northern Cameroons, and in its being treated more or less as a colony of Northern Nigeria.[2] It was to remedy that situation that the AG-UMBC alliance proposed to the 1958 UN Visiting Mission that a plebiscite be organized to determine the wishes of the people of the Northern Cameroons.

The magnanimity of that proposal was more apparent than real. The true aim of those parties was to test and possibly break the grip of Northern Nigeria on the Northern Cameroons. In other words, the proposed plebiscite was to be a test vote on the popularity of the administrative

2   U.N., T.C., T/1426, Annex IV, 20 Jan. 1959, pp. 8-9.

union.

Paradoxically, Northern Nigeria welcomed the plebiscite in the same spirit. The NPC was confident that any consultation would confirm the wishes of the people to remain with Northern Nigeria. In which case, the proposed plebiscite would result in a vote of confidence in the administrative union.

The rival forces espoused the opposing options of the plebiscite. The NCNC, in alliance with the NEPU, joined forces with the AG-UMBC alliance to campaign for the second alternative which entailed postponement of the decision on the Territory's future, while the NPC campaigned vigorously for the immediate integration of the Northern Cameroons into Northern Nigeria.

Curiously, the hierarchies of the southern parties did not involve themselves directly in the 1959 plebiscite campaign, preferring, as the NEPU Publicity Secretary put it, not to "dive into the internal affairs of the Northern Cameroons."[3] But their local branches were all over the field, drumming up support for postponement. In the process, they called for two basic reforms, which they calculated could be extorted through a vote for postponement, namely: reorganization of the Native Authority system, and separation of the Territory from Northern Nigeria and its constitution into an autonomous region of the Federation.

Their activities created a feeling of exasperation within the NPC, which tried at first to negotiate: in an open letter to the leaders of the other parties, the NPC leader called on them to disavow the activities of their local branches in the Northern Cameroons.[4] But Ahmadou Bello was quietly snubbed by those leaders, after which the NPC went on the offensive. Branding all the southern parties as foreign to the Northern Cameroons, it accused them of encouraging dissension in the Territory by drawing their support mainly from "a few disgruntled descendants of tyrant chiefs who were stopped from unjust and cruel treatment of the people of the Northern Cameroons."[5] The campaign turned ugly as both sides traded insults. But the voting was peaceful, and the results

3   *Nigerian Daily Times,* 29 Oct. 1959.
4   Ibid., 14 Oct. 1959.
5   T/1426, Annex IV, 20 January 1959, p. 12.

were surprising.

Considering the heavy presence of the NPC in the Northern Cameroons, the parties of southern Nigeria rejoiced when their opposition was vindicated by as much as 62 per cent of the vote against immediate integration with Northern Nigeria. A spokesman for the AG described the result of the 1959 plebiscite as "an unmistakable vote of no confidence in the NPC Government and an expression of the deep-seated resentment of the people against autocratic rule."[6]

It is difficult to assess the real concern of the parties of southern Nigeria in the plight of the people of the Northern Cameroons. True, they all advocated certain administrative reforms, which could greatly improve the lot of the people. But indications are that the reforms were of secondary concern, that their main target was the NPC, and that the plebiscite was only a platform for the wider rivalry between the political parties of Nigeria. More so because the parties of southern Nigeria based their plebiscite campaign not on the merits of postponement but on the vices of the administration, advocating only those reforms that positively set them apart from the NPC. They supported postponement only in so far as it hurt the NPC within the context of Nigerian politics. They reacted differently when the general interests of Nigeria were at stake, as was the case during the second plebiscite, even when those interests coincided with the best interests of Northern Nigeria.

The administrative union between Northern Nigeria and the Northern Cameroons was so complete that most Nigerians looked upon the latter as an integral part of the national territory. To them, the territorial integrity of Nigeria included the Northern Cameroons. And in so far as the future of the Northern Cameroons threatened that integrity, it became a question of the national interest.

The second Northern Cameroons plebiscite put that concern to the test. Nigerian politicians saw the Cameroun alternative as a threat to take away what in their view already belonged to Nigeria. They converted the plebiscite from the sole concern of the Northern Cameroons into something of a national cause, and developed a new rhetoric in the process, aimed at arousing national sentiment and rallying general support

6   *The Times,* London. 11 Nov. 1959.

for the Nigeria option. In supporting the cause, the political parties of southern Nigeria reasoned that it was better for the Northern Cameroons to be gained by the Northern Region than lost to the Federation. During the plebiscite campaign, *The Times* of London reported that "all the quarrelling parties of the Federation have for once agreed to a truce to persuade the Northern Cameroons to join Nigeria."[7]

The incorporation of the Northern Cameroons brought about a few modifications in Nigeria, but nothing on the scale prescribed by Resolution 1608 [XV]. The Northern Cameroons was not constituted into a separate province of the Northern Region. Instead, the status quo was maintained, and the Northern Cameroons continued to form parts of three different provinces of the Northern Region, namely, Borno, Sardauna [formerly Adamawa], and Benue. The Nigerian independence constitution which had anticipated the incorporation of the entire British Cameroons[8] was amended to make provision for the Northern Cameroons,[9] and membership of the Nigerian House of Representatives was enlarged from 305 to 312 to provide representation for the Northern Cameroons.[10] But by far the most important change caused by the plebiscites was the addition of the Northern Cameroons itself to Nigeria, an addition of nearly 20,000 square miles and a population of over 700,000.

In the context of Nigerian politics, the location of that addition was more important than its value. The incorporation of the Northern Cameroons into Nigeria as part of the Northern Region aggravated the regional imbalance by adding to a region that was already vastly out of proportion with the others.

However, if the South could do nothing to stop the geographical integration of the Northern Cameroons into Northern Nigeria, the political parties of southern Nigeria relentlessly contested its political absorption by the NPC. They recorded some early successes. They claimed the result of the first plebiscite as a symbolic victory over the NPC; and scored something of a *tour de force* at the general elections of December 1959: of the eight constituencies in contest in the Northern Cameroons, the

7   Ibid., 11 Jan 1961.
8   The Nigerian [Constitution] Order-in-Council, 1960. Section 16(1).
9   Nigeria Constitution, First Amendment Act, 1961.
10   Ibid.

AG captured four, the NPC three, and the NCNC-NEPU one. These two events, happening within one month of each other, suggested that the NPC was losing its grip on the Northern Cameroons, and that the AG was on the brink of a major break-through in one of the other regions.

Strengthened by those victories, the AG elbowed its way onto the UK delegation to the UN in 1960,[11] where its spokesman, Chief Ayo Rosiji, suggested that there should be three questions at the second Northern Cameroons plebiscite. Apart from the two that would pose the Nigeria and Cameroun options, there should be a third question: "Do the people of the Northern Cameroons wish to achieve independence on their own without joining either the Federation of Nigeria or the Republic of Cameroun?"[12]

The Action Group calculated that if the Northern Cameroons chose the third option, it could then rejoin Nigeria not as part of the Northern Region but as a separate unit altogether. And judging from its performance at the 1959 general elections, the AG would be the majority party in the new region, thereby controlling two of the four regions of Nigeria, especially in the Senate to which the governing party in each region sent twelve members. A separate Northern Cameroons region would thus give the AG 24 senators in the Nigerian Upper House, the same number as the NCNC and NPC combined!

However, the UN rejected Rosiji's proposals, preferring to stick to the two questions involving Nigeria and Cameroun. And in the next few months, various circumstances combined to scale down AG influence in the Territory and reinstate NPC control. First, the time lapse between the 1959 general elections and the second plebiscite enabled the NPC Government to introduce token administrative reforms which mollified the people and warmed their hearts towards Northern Nigeria. Secondly, the next plebiscite was fought as a national issue, setting aside regional or partisan rivalries. And after the plebiscite, the Northern Cameroons quietly joined the Northern Region, much to the disappointment of those who had hoped to create a separate region for its 700,000 inhabitants.

Moreover, the fact that at independence the AG found itself in the opposition did not help its chances in the north. As for the NCNC, it was

11   A. Bolaji Akinyemi. op. cit., p. 134.
12   A/C.4/SR.1081. New York, 9 Dec. 1960, p. 486.

content with playing second fiddle in the NPC-led coalition Government and would not do anything to upset its senior partner.

And so, the Northern Cameroons plebiscites, which once held vague hopes of adjusting the balance of power in favor of southern Nigeria, actually ended up reinforcing the geographical and political disproportion of Northern Nigeria *vis-a-vis* the regions of the south.

The Plebiscites and the Internal Politics of Cameroon

In contrast with the situation in Nigeria where the incorporation of the Northern Cameroons maintained the status quo, the union of the Southern Cameroons and the Cameroun Republic was breaking new ground, based on prior engagements taken by them. In its Resolution 1608 (XV), the UN General Assembly invited the Administering Authority and both sides "to initiate urgent discussions with a view to finalizing implementation" of those engagements. As S.T. Muna pointed out, "There was already a firm understanding supported by signed documents bearing the signatures of Ahidjo and Foncha which had accepted that unification would be in the form of a loose Federation."[13] However, still smarting from the results of the plebiscite, the UK took part in only one of the sessions, leaving the Southern Cameroons to find its way in the negotiations.

A peculiar feature of reunification was that throughout the plebiscite campaign, very little was said about the distribution of power within the prospective federation. The joint statement by Foncha and Ahidjo in 1960 had mapped out the broad outlines of eventual union: it would be a democratic federation, in which the Federal State would have jurisdiction over a given number of areas, while the Federated States retained control in matters of non-federal jurisdiction.[14] But while the federal prerogatives were carefully specified, those of the States were not, neither was the relationship between the State and Federal levels of government clarified. Much was left unsaid, which suited Foncha just well. He was aware that the main attraction of reunification was not its constitutional guarantees,

---

13   Muna, op. cit., p. 527.
14   Final Communique issued by A. Ahidjo and J. N. Foncha after Meeting of 10-13 October 1960. Yaoundé. mimeo.

but the sentimental attachment to the German Kamerun. He therefore tactfully based his campaign on the fact of reunification, not its form.

The vagueness of the formula concealed a sharp contrast in their view of the federation, arising from differences in their cultural background and their understanding of the reunification movement. The Southern Cameroons saw reunification as a mutual attraction from both sides, as equal partners, giving birth to an entirely new creation that was neither the Cameroun Republic nor the Southern Cameroons, but a gradual blend of both. Foncha was of the opinion that "for unification to be meaningful, it had to proceed on the basis of a federal union in which the specific character of each component of the union would be safeguarded and protected."[15] Cameroun saw it differently, as the return "home" of the part that had been taken away. And that was a fundamental difference in the story of reunification.

Owing to its small size and to the bitter memories of its union with Eastern Nigeria, the Southern Cameroons was allergic to tight unions. The entire history of the nationalist movement in the Territory was about gaining ever more autonomy. And alarmed by reports of insecurity in the Cameroun Republic, into which they feared being drawn, Southern Cameroonians were inclined to seek a rather loose form of union, from which they could extricate themselves easily. Endeley dutifully warned Foncha to guard against the Southern Cameroons being "incapacitated forever by the results of the plebiscite."[16]

Indeed, the euphoria of the plebiscite victory soon turned into a wave of introspection among the political elite of the Southern Cameroons, as disturbing signals from Yaounde cast doubt on their pre-plebiscite agreements. Direct talks between the Southern Cameroons and the French Cameroun had begun in November 1959, to explore the possibilities of union between the two territories and the form that such a union would take.

Before the plebiscite, the meetings were warm and convivial. One Southern Cameroons delegate recalls that "the Ahidjo government seemed

---

15   John Ngu Foncha, Declaration to the Constitutional Consultative Commission, Yaounde, December 1994.
16   Cf. Willard Johnson, op. cit., p. 171.

quite eager to accommodate us on the many points that we presented," to the extent that they even discussed the quota of federal ministerial portfolios to be allocated to each State.[17] The talks culminated in the signature by Ahidjo and Foncha of two important documents that established the framework of the prospective union: the Joint Communiqué of 17th October 1960 specified that unification shall be accomplished on a Federal basis; and the Communiqué on 6th December 1960 specified that the delegates chosen by both sides to work it out shall have equal status.

But after the plebiscite, Ahidjo changed his mind on all those engagements. Either he had not meant what he said during those early negotiations or he had received different advice since then. The first alarm bell was sounded by his Foreign Minister, Charles Okala, who baffled the Southern Cameroons delegation at the UN by strongly opposing the recommendation of the Fourth Committee specifying the federal form of the union and calling for the dispatch of a team of constitutional experts to assist the Southern Cameroons during the negotiations for reunification."[18] The Southern Cameroons delegation was all the more surprised because Okala had been present when Foncha and Ahidjo agreed on the federation, and could not have made such a bold switch without the approval of Ahidjo himself. It seemed that the Cameroun government wanted the federation to be a choice, not an obligation. And Okala succeeded in ensuring that Resolution 1608(XV) which terminated the trusteeship did not prescribe any mandatory constitutional framework for the Southern Cameroons as it did for the Northern Cameroons; instead it vaguely invited the parties concerned to make arrangements to implement their agreed policies on the union, even though it knew those policies, having been served all the documents signed by Ahidjo and Foncha. Also lost in the argument was the idea of sending legal experts to assist the Southern Cameroons government, with the result that some of the fine details of the post-plebiscite negotiations were not spotted by their untrained eyes.

The second alarm bell was sounded by Ahidjo himself, during the tripartite meeting that the UN had recommended. The talks were held in

17   Cf. Muna, op. cit., p. 492.
18   Ibid.

Buea in June 1961, bringing together delegates from the Southern Cameroons, the Cameroun Republic and the United Kingdom. Ahidjo began by dispelling the notion that they were negotiating as equal partners. He presented his delegation as representing an independent sovereign State with an international status and a legal personality – which the Southern Cameroons was not. And when the Southern Cameroons delegation tabled the Joint Communiqué of 17th October as the basis for discussion, Ahidjo objected. He now wanted a Federation completely different from what had been agreed before, one that was highly centralized. In Muna's recollection: "At one point he suggested to our utter amazement that the Government of the Republic would act as the Federal Government... And in complete disregard of all previous engagements, the Ahidjo government seemed to suggest that the Southern Cameroons should accept assimilation by the Republic of Cameroun."[19] Coming from such a high place, that must be the origin of the psychosis of assimilation that the English-speaking political class has been wrestling with. The Buea meeting ended without agreement, foreshadowing the difficult negotiations that lay ahead.

It was with a degree of trepidation that Southern Cameroonians approached the last phase of the reunification process, no longer certain of Ahidjo's motives and whether his word could be kept -- or trusted. To many of them, Okala's machinations at the United Nations, coupled with Ahidjo's volte-face at the tripartite conference in Buea had broken the bank of trust that had sustained their pre-plebiscite talks.

Foncha called an "All-Party" conference of the Southern Cameroons in Bamenda in June 1961, to adopt a common and safeguarded position on the federation, in preparation for the Constitutional Conference in Foumban the following month. It emerged from that conference that Southern Cameroonians desired a loose and "cooperative" federation, with a rational and balanced distribution of power between the local, State and Federal governments.[20] In his opening statement in Foumban, Foncha amplified their position: "In our desire to rebuild the Kamerun nation we must not forget the existence of the two cultures. We have

19   Ibid., p. 547.
20   Record of the Bamenda Conference, 1960.

proposed a form of Government which will keep the two cultures in the areas where they will operate and to blend them in the center. The center is therefore given very limited subjects, while the States are left largely to continue as they are now."[21]

In their view, the forthcoming federation should be a parliamentary democracy with a ceremonial president, quasi-autonomous States, and a constitution that could only be amended with the concurrence of two-thirds of each State parliament. In fact, so loose was the proposed union that, as Willard Johnson reports, the CPNC sought a provision for the "right of secession" of States to be written into the federal Constitution.[22]

There was a fundamental difference in perception of the reunification movement between the two principals: one saw it as a simultaneous coming together from both sides, while the other saw it as the geographical spread of one side over the other. The fact that the vote for reunification took place in only one side confirmed the latter view. While Foncha regarded the defunct German Kamerun as the common patrimony of both sides, Ahidjo considered his Republic as the exclusive legal continuation of the German colony, from which the British Cameroons had been removed. From that perspective, reunification was perceived in Yaoundé as the return to Cameroun of what had been lost. It was therefore only a one-way movement. In Ahidjo's view, *"le Cameroun réunifié n'apparait pas en droit international comme un nouvel Etat souverain, et juridiquement la réunification n'est analysée que comme une modification de frontière [of Cameroun!]."*[23] That misunderstanding was never cured.

Initially, Ahidjo had been rather lukewarm about reunification, not wanting to embrace an idea first enunciated by the outlawed UPC. But the popular appeal of the concept convinced him to seize its paternity from the UPC and position himself as a champion of the cause. He was encouraged by the French who saw unification not only as a process of enlarging the territory over which its influence would be paramount,

---

21   Cf. Muna, op. cit., p. 557.
22   Willard Johnson, op. cit., p. 178.
23   Speech before the National Assembly, 10 August 1961, A.CA.P., No. 182, Yaoundé, 11 August 1961. The quote translates as follows: *"the reunified Cameroon does not appear in international law as a new sovereign state, and legally reunification is analyzed only as a modification of the boundary [of Cameroun]."*

but also as a means of pacifying the moderate elements in the UPC and rallying the other political parties to his cause. He entered the negotiations with clear medium and long-term objectives. He knew that owing to existing differences between the Southern Cameroons and his Republic, reunification could only take place in the form of a federation.[24] But that arrangement was only temporary, as later events revealed,[25] and the federation would be anything but loose, as he had in mind a long list of prerogatives which, for technical reasons, could not be left to the States. That was hardly surprising: the Cameroun President had been groomed in French political thought, which viewed federalism with skepticism and disdain.

Ahidjo's thoughts on the power structure within the Federation also differed significantly from Foncha's. At issue was a contrast in the governing culture of both sides: in the Southern Cameroons, governance was based on full participation in the decision-making process through Native Authorities and elected representatives; in the Cameroun Republic, governance was based on policy directives decreed from the center. So, while Foncha sought almost autonomous States, in which local affairs would be managed locally, Ahidjo held that the powers of the States had to be controlled and directed by the Federal government.[26] Cameroun's blueprint of the power structure within the Federation was one with weak, symbolic States, and a central government so powerful as to approximate that of a unitary state.

A federal structure with such elaborate powers was incompatible with the ceremonial presidency that Foncha envisaged. With the instincts of a presidential system in which the President was all-powerful, Ahidjo conceived the Federal President as both Head of State and Head of Government, with the power to appoint State Prime Ministers, dissolve State parliaments, promulgate State laws, and repeal those that he considered to be in conflict with the Federal constitution.[27] In the parliamentary system operating in the Southern Cameroons, where government emanated from Parliament, it was unthinkable for the Prime Minister to be

24   Ibid., No. 161, Yaoundé, 18 July 1961.
25   In 1972, he abolished the Federation through a national referendum.
26   A.CA.P. No. 182, 11 August 1961.
27   Willard Johnson, op. cit., p. 186.

appointed by somebody beside Parliament!

Thus, much as the Southern Cameroons and Cameroun were in agreement over reunification in the form of a federation, they differed profoundly over the distribution of power within it. Apprehensive of tight unions, the Southern Cameroons sought a loose federation; whereas, feeling synonymous with the federal structure itself, Cameroun desired a centralized federation. It was this fundamental difference that the Foumban Conference tried to reconcile.

That Conference was not a constitutional conference per se. No new constitution was written there, and none was meant to be. Cameroun did not think that a reunified Cameroon needed a brand new constitution. As President Ahidjo later admitted, *"il revenait à la République du Cameroun d'aménager sa propre Constitution pour former un ensemble avec le territoire frère du Cameroun meridional."*[28]

In that sense, the Foumban Conference was a constitutional review conference, during which delegates from the Southern Cameroons were invited to make suggestions on the Cameroun Constitution, most of which were politely rejected. From the get-go, the Southern Cameroons delegation was hamstrung by the fact that the plebiscite leading to the union had already taken place, reducing their bargaining power and removing the pressure on the Cameroun delegation to make concessions.

Still, each side strongly defended its views, with Cameroun appearing better prepared and more focused. Its delegation of twelve was a harmonious bloc, drawn exclusively from the ranks of the UC party, with Ahidjo as its undisputed spokesman. In a winner-take-all mentality, no other party from Cameroun was represented at Foumban, not even the UPC that had initiated the idea of reunification. In contrast, the Southern Cameroons delegation of twenty-five was a heterogeneous group from all the political parties in the Territory, including some of Foncha's fiercest critics, and many who had fought against reunification and who might feel vindicated if the experiment failed. By joggling their opinions, Ahidjo easily outsmarted them, yielding little in the talks and nothing

28   *L'Unite* No. 54, Yaoundé, 28 July 1961. Translated as follows: *"it was left to the Cameroun Republic to adjust its proper Constitution so as to constitute a unit with the brotherly territory of the Southern Cameroons."*

on the key issues.

The Federation that emerged from Foumban reflected Ahidjo's vision: it was highly centralized, with a list of 30 federal prerogatives written into the Constitution;[29] the Federal Government was to be headed by an active president with very wide powers;[30] and the Federal Constitution could be revised by a simple "qualified" majority vote in the Federal Assembly.[31] The draft from Foumban was finalized during further talks in Yaounde in August 1961. Co-signed by Prime Minister Foncha and President Ahidjo, it was ratified by the Assembly of the Republic of Cameroun on 16th August 1961 and by the Southern Cameroons House of Assembly on 14th September 1961.

The great strength of the Federal Government implied the utter weakness of the Federated States. Ahidjo offered Foncha a face-saving concession in the provision of Article 38 of the Federal Constitution which granted residual but unspecified powers to the States. Henry Enonchong has dismissed that concession as a pure mirage, designed only to placate the timorous souls of the Southern Cameroons.[32]

Ahidjo also allowed the Southern Cameroons to retain its House of Chiefs,[33] but rejected the proposal for a Federal bicameral legislature on grounds that it would be too cumbersome to operate,[34] even though the Communique of 17 October 1960 foreshadowed the creation of a national Senate. Muna claims that "Ahidjo did not want any legislative instance that would require equal representation from the two States!"[35] The only substantial amendment credited to the Southern Cameroons was the mode of electing the President. The Cameroun Constitution provided for the President to be elected by the National Assembly, together with Provincial and Municipal Councils.[36] But at Foumban, the Southern Cameroons delegation proposed that in view of the extensive powers

29   *Constitution of the Federal Republic of Cameroon,* Title I, Art. 5 and 6.
30   Ibid., Title III.
31   Ibid., Title X. Art. 47.
32   H. N. A. Enonchong, *Cameroon Constitutional Law,* (Yaoundé: CEPMAE, 1967), p. 169.
33   Federal Constitution, Art. 38.
34   *L'Unite,* No. 54, Yaoundé, 28 July 1961.
35   Muna, op. cit., p. 569.
36   *Constitution of the Republic of Cameroun,* 1960, Art. 12.

of the Ahidjo version of the presidency, the President should be elected by universal adult suffrage.[37] Ahidjo quickly accepted, for reasons that we shall see later.

The anatomy of the Federal Republic reflected Cameroun's view of the federation. From the onset, the ratio between the two States determined the allocation of public office: Ahidjo assumed the presidency and made Foncha Vice-President, and the linguistic components that each represented were typecast in that order. That ratio became the deciding factor in relations between the Federated States and between them and the Federation. It also determined the relative importance of the two official languages as more people spoke one language than the other. In fact, there were areas of the administration where only one language prevailed: in the armed forces for example, French remained the sole language of command.

Yet, the act of reunification affected Cameroon politics in a way that could not have been foretold. National unity, which had eluded Cameroun during all the years of rebellion and strife, was now celebrated as a concrete national achievement. Its consolidation became the highest priority of the State. And while at home Cameroonians were learning to adapt to the new bilingual nature of their country, abroad that quality put Cameroon in a class of its own among African nations.

One of the most important consequences of the plebiscites was the creation of a sense of unity among the feuding factions in East Cameroon politics. The dominant shades of opinion in Cameroun were always in favor of reunification.[38] As early as the 1940s, the UPC regarded the unification of the British and French Cameroons as a precondition for the independence of Cameroun.[39]

Little wonder that the results of the second Northern Cameroons plebiscite caused such outrage in Cameroun. The ensuing protest eclipsed the divide in the National Assembly. It was an opposition MP, Dr. Bebey-Eyidi, who moved a motion calling on the UN to cancel the results of the

---

37   Willard Johnson, op. cit., p. 189.
38   Ibid., pp. 119-120.
39   Richard A; Joseph, *Radical Nationalism in Cameroun,* (Oxford: Clarendon Press, 1971), p. 208.

plebiscite and hold a fresh election.[40] The motion was voted unanimous-ly.[41] As Bebey-Eyidi explained, the vote *"traduisait l'unanimité nationale réalisée autour de la réunification. Ainsi, la majorité gouvernementale, l'opposition et le peuple se sont mis d'accord et ont décidé de constituer un front uni de lutte."*[42] And in the campaign to rally international support for Cameroun's case, opposition politicians worked in tandem with the Government. In the context of Cameroun politics, Jean-François Bayart claims that *"Cette collaboration porta un coup fatal à l'opposition."*[43]

And so, the British Cameroons plebiscites enabled President Ahidjo to rally his country behind him for the first time, in the fight against the Northern Cameroons plebiscite and in his conduct of reunification with the Southern Cameroons.

That newfound unity was evident during parliamentary debates on the revised Constitution. None of the opposition parties challenged it. Many voted with the Government. The UPC abstained, even though they considered the strengthened presidency as a *"porte ouverte à la dictature."*[44]

By the time the Northern Cameroons question was ended, following the Decision of the International Court of Justice in 1963, large chunks of the opposition in East Cameroon had been sucked into Ahidjo's *Union Camerounaise.* The national consensus forged to challenge the Northern Cameroons plebiscite became the catalyst for the formation of a one-party State barely five years later, leading to Ahidjo's stranglehold on power. The one-party system also put an end to the parliamentary democracy practiced in West Cameroon.

Reunification created a different type of unity among East and West Cameroonians, a type of cultural unity, built around French and English as the official languages of the Federation. Although tribal affinities persisted throughout the country, there emerged at the federal level two distinct

---

40   Jean-François Bayart, *l'Etat au Cameroun,* (Paris : Presses de la Fondation Nationale des Sciences Politiques, 1979), p. 98.

41   There were some ten political groupings represented in the Assembly in 1960.

42   Speech before the National Assembly, cf. *La Presse du Cameroun,* 13-14 mai 1961.

43   Jean-François Bayart, op. cit., p. 98. Translation: "This collaboration dealt a fatal blow to the Opposition."

44   Idem. The quote translates as: *"an open invitation to dictatorship."*

linguistic communities -- francophone and anglophone -- which had identical and therefore conflicting interests in the allocation of federal resources and the occupation of the federal space.

The epithets, anglophone and francophone, developed great significance in Cameroon, where the official languages became vectors of identification, differentiation, comparison, rivalry, solidarity, and sometimes discrimination between and among the people of the two States.

That solidarity was more evident among anglophones than among francophones, for two main reasons. Firstly, the location of the federal capital, Yaoundé, deep in the francophone sector, coupled with the continuous federalization of State powers brought increasing numbers of West Cameroonians to Yaoundé, where the strangeness of the environment and customs forced them to stick together.

Secondly, the disproportion of the population between anglophones and francophones created a feeling of insecurity among the former. That feeling was heightened by the arrogance of many in East Cameroon who, counting on their numbers, looked down on the English language and on their compatriots of that expression. Some often reduced them to an ethnic group of the Federation, counting the Bamileke, Bamoun, Bassa, Beti, Douala, Peul, and Anglophones, among the ethnic groups of the Federation! Ahidjo himself did little to endear the English-speaking population: in twenty-two years as President, he never spoke English even once! And taking their cue from him, some prominent francophone politicians suggested that the English language should be allowed to die, if not actively suppressed.[45] That tendency was actually grounded in law: Article 59 of the Federal Constitution stated that "The revised Constitution shall be published in French and in English, the French text being authentic."

The optics of the Federation presented differently on both sides. The Southern Cameroons saw it as the final station of the union, cast in stone by Article 47 of the Constitution which prohibited any amendment

---

45   Willard Johnson reports that the East Cameroon Prime Minister, Charles Assale, argued that rather than harmonize the educational systems of both States, the West Cameroon system should be reformed along the lines of the East Cameroon system to enable French to supplant English in West Cameroon. See Willard Johnson, op. cit., p. 294.

touching on the federal form of the State. But the Republic of Cameroun saw it as just a step in the journey of nation-building. Muna contends that at Foumban, the delegation of the Republic "regarded the word 'federation' merely as a cosmetic phrase that would cover up the fact that their real intention was to absorb and assimilate the Southern Cameroons into the Republic of Cameroun."[46]

Smelling the coffee, Bernard Fonlon, a leading West Cameroon thinker predicted that "With African culture moribund, with John Bullism weak and in danger of being smothered, we will all be French in two generations or three!"[47] That danger had been sensed at the Foumban Conference, as Muna recalls: "In discussing with the members of the delegation of the Republic we were made aware of the fact that they regarded the word 'federation' merely as a cosmetic phrase that would cover up the fact that their real intention was to absorb and assimilate the Southern Cameroons into the Republic of Cameroun."[48] The fear of being smothered created a feeling of anxiety and insecurity among West Cameroonians, who stuck together for survival.

East Cameroon was also united in its tacit competition with West Cameroon over the allocation of federal resources and projects. That competition led to the development of a feeling of otherness against those who spoke a different language. The banana producers of East Cameroon, irrespective of ethnic affiliation, quickly came together to protect their share of the French market from encroachment by West Cameroon producers. The linguistic dichotomy inherent in reunification created an open rivalry between both federated communities, and a sense of unity within them.

By bringing new votes, resources and contending ideas, reunification impacted the power equation in Cameroon, especially for those in office. Although, as the sole candidate, he had been elected as President of Cameroun in 1960 by 90 per cent of the votes of the Assembly,[49] and notwithstanding his attempts to form a broad-based government,

---

46   Muna, op. cit., p. 554
47   Bernard Fonlon. *"Will we Make or Mar,"* in ABBIA. No. 5, (Yaoundé: CEPMAE, March 1964).
48   Muna, op. cit., p. 554.
49   *La Presse du Cameroun,* 6 mai 1960.

President Ahidjo had not succeeded in rallying the south and pacifying the country. At the time of reunification, the presence of multiple feuding parties in the Assembly, the deployment of French troops in the country, and the recrudescence of violence in the agitated regions, indicated that his rule was far from secure.

For better or for worse, reunification would put that rule to its strongest test. By throwing its weight in one way or another, the British Cameroons could alter the balance of power in the country. Both government and opposition therefore looked to the plebiscites with eager anticipation, especially as the division of the British Cameroons into North and South fitted tantalizingly into the north-south divide in Cameroun politics. In the event, the plebiscites had both a negative and a positive impact on Ahidjo's position -- first threatening it and then consolidating it.

Victor Levine suggests that Ahidjo was more disappointed than pleased with the results of the British Cameroons plebiscites, because in his calculations the arrival of the Southern Cameroons with its mostly Christian population was not matched by the arrival of the Northern Cameroons with its predominantly Moslem population.[50] As *The Times* of London pointed out,

> He has lost the increased electoral power which he expected from the Northern Cameroons and is saddled with the Southern Cameroons which voted to join his republic but whose leaders and voters are likely to join their kith and kin in the coastal areas of the republic where the opposition forces lie.[51]

Jean-Francois Bayart holds that Ahidjo contemplated renouncing the whole idea of reunification rather than receive the Southern Cameroons alone.[52] The President's fears were compounded by the uncertainty of Foncha's loyalty. The Southern Cameroons Premier had strong ties

---

50   See Victor T. Levine. *The Cameroons from Mandate to Independence*, (Berkeley: University of California Press. 1964). p. 213: see also Jean-Francois Bayart. op. cit., p. 95.

51   *The Times*, London. 12 June 1961.

52   Jean-François Bayart. op. cit., p. 95.

with opposition leaders in Cameroun. When the UPC was proscribed in 1955, its leader, Moumie, fled to the Southern Cameroons where Foncha hosted him.[53] In 1960, Foncha offered to mediate between the Cameroun government and the UPC leadership, an offer which Ahidjo politely declined.[54] And while he failed to persuade Ahidjo to finance his reunification campaign,[55] Foncha was lavishly funded by Soppo Priso and Daniel Kemajou of the opposition.[56] V. T. Levine reports that Foncha actually contacted opposition leaders in Cameroun with a view of forming a "southern" coalition against the UUC.[57] And speculations were once rife that he intended to contest for the federal presidency in 1965. Ahidjo did not forgive him for entertaining such ambitions, and unceremoniously got rid of him in 1970.

If reunification seemed at first to threaten Ahidjo's leadership, it also offered him opportunities to consolidate his position, the most important being the Foumban Conference, which turned out to be the watershed of his entire career.

Ahidjo arrived Foumban in scheming mood. He came with a team of French lawyers, after advising Foncha that the Conference would be an all-Cameroon affair that needed no foreign presence.[58] His goal was to strengthen his position as much as possible, at the expense of Foncha's. And throughout the conference, while Foncha moralized on the virtues of renewed brotherhood, Ahidjo coldly plotted to maximize his power. His endgame was to replace the existing autonomous States with an all-powerful central government under his leadership.

The dynamics of the Conference were stacked in Ahidjo's favor. Having already voted to join the Republic without securing any clear safeguards, the Southern Cameroons delegation was forced to rely on the good faith of their opposite numbers, which turned out to be rather

---

53   Willard Johnson, op. cit. pp. 128-130. The Committee soon broke down, however, owing to differences between Moumie's militancy and Foncha's conservatism.
54   Jean-Francois Bayart, op. cit., p. 95.
55   Johnson. op. cit., p. 133.
56   Bayart, op. cit., p. 95.
57   V. T. Levine, "Calm before the storm in Cameroon," in *Africa Report*, May 1961, pp. 3-4.
58   Muna, op. cit., pp. 555-556

limited in supply as one of them recounts: "we were engaged in a most tricky encounter with 'untested brothers' who could use music and wine to lure us into complaisance..."[59]

Indeed, throughout the Conference, Ahidjo ruthlessly exploited his advantage, only yielding on matters that would serve his personal interests most. A typical example was the mode of electing the federal President. Ahidjo had been unhappy with Article 12 of the Cameroun Constitution, which provided for the President to be elected by the National Assembly and representatives of Local Councils, because those Councils were not yet operating in his native North as they were in the South. In 1960, he had used that excuse to suspend the clause in question and got himself elected by Parliament alone.

At Foumban he proposed that the Electoral College for the presidential election should be limited to the two State legislatures, calculating that the handsome UC majority in the Cameroun Assembly would be enough to secure his reelection. But when the Southern Cameroons delegation suggested that the President should instead be elected by universal suffrage, Ahidjo quickly accepted, seeing in it a further opportunity to make use of the solid northern population against the divided South.

And when the Southern Cameroons delegation contested his proposal for a four-month transitional period as being too short for viable institutions to be put in place, Ahidjo gladly increased it to six months. Article 50 of the new Constitution provided that during the transitional period, all legislative measures necessary for the establishment of constitutional institutions and the functioning of public authorities shall be taken by the President in the form of Ordinances having the force of law! That unchecked exercise of presidential power inexorably led to the totalitarian drift of Ahidjo's regime.

Assessing the events of 1961, Jean François Bayart concluded that *"En réalité, l'épisode de la réunification, qui aurait pu être fatal à M. Ahidjo, fut une étape capitale de la maximalisation de ses pouvoirs, tant au plan*

---

59   Mbile, N.N., *Cameroon Political Story: Memories of an Eyewitness* (Limbe: Presbyterian Printing Press, 1999), p. 170.

des institutions qu'à celui des forces politiques."[60]

---

60   Bayart, op. cit., p. 99. Translated as follows: "*In reality, the episode of reunification which could have been fatal to Mr. Ahidjo was a crucial step in the maximization of his powers, both institutionally and in relation to the political forces.*"

CHAPTER SEVEN

The Plebiscites and Bilateral Relations

The impact of the plebiscites was not limited to the internal structures of Nigeria and Cameroon. The plebiscites also affected their international images, as well as their relations with each other.

The Plebiscites and the Images of Nigeria and Cameroon

Notwithstanding the political capital that Nigerian parties anticipated to make from retaining the British Cameroons, the administration of the Territory was seen in some quarters as a thankless job for which Nigeria could receive nothing but criticism. And there was plenty of it. Many were suspicious of the administrative union between the two Territories. The separatists in the British Cameroons loathed it.

In fact, during the plebiscite campaign, whipping up anti-Nigeria sentiment became their most potent strategy: the hated Igbos were shown to reflect the ruthless opportunism of Nigerians, while the NPC was portrayed as the undemocratic aristocracy that had dominated the Northern Cameroons for years. Such a vision was a blemish on Nigeria's reputation abroad. It did not help its claim for African leadership; it only fostered rival claims from countries like Ghana, which had assumed much of the initiative and presented itself as the vanguard in the liberation of Africa.

Worse still, Nigeria was widely accused of complicity with the UK in corrupting the second Northern Cameroons plebiscite. During the debate on that plebiscite, Cameroun, France, and the francophone African countries had walked out of the General Assembly as much in protest against the UK as against Nigeria.

Nigeria needed to mend fences with all these States, especially with its neighbors, a task that was unduly complicated by the unseasonable declarations of some of its leaders. When the Premier of Northern Nigeria announced his intention of resurrecting the Sokoto Empire, fears were raised about Nigeria's territorial ambitions, which successive governments fought hard to allay. Tafawa Balewa felt bound to assure the UN that:

> We in Nigeria appreciate the advantages which the size of our country and its population give us, but we have absolutely no aggressive intentions. We shall never impose ourselves upon any country and shall treat every African Territory, big or small, as an equal.[1]

The damage of the plebiscites on Nigeria's international image was slight and short-lived. The plebiscite fever died down soon after the General Assembly endorsed its results. It was buried with the decision of the ICJ not to adjudicate on the case brought by Cameroun against the UK, a decision that was interpreted by the UK and Nigeria as exonerating them.

Besides, fears of Nigerian expansionism were out of proportion with reality. The conservative leadership of the ruling NPC did not portray any of the fiery continental ambitions of Kwame Nkrumah. On the contrary, Nigeria turned out to be a major check to militant Ghana, championing the status quo and advancing the cause of moderation in African politics. Balewa dismissed Nkrumah's battle cry for the immediate political unification of Africa as highly impractical and wildly unrealistic.[2]

Yet, even in moderation, Nigeria, which Professor Coleman described as the "awakened giant" of Africa,[3] quietly staked its own claim for continental leadership. Based on numbers, the claim stood on its sheer size, dense population, and immense resources. Tafawa Balewa put it with assertive humility when he reminded his countrymen that "It is towards this country that the others are looking for help and leadership."[4] And later, the 1966 Conference of Nigerian Ambassadors unequivocally declared that "Africa is Nigeria's natural sphere of influence."[5] In fact, Nigeria

1 A T. Balewa, Speech before the UN General Assembly, New York, 7 Oct 1960.
2 Ibid.
3 James S. Coleman, "Pan-Africanism or Nationalism in Africa," in American Society of African Culture, (ed.), *Pan-Africanism Reconsidered*, (Berkeley: University of California Press), p. 107.
4 A. T. Balewa, Broadcast to the Nation. 13 May 1961.
5 Quoted in Ndifontah mo Nyamndi, op. cit., p. 168.

grew so sensitive about its own size that it became a strong advocate of the sanctity of colonial boundaries in Africa. Anything that could affect that size became an important element in Nigeria's vision of itself and its role in Africa. And to the extent that the British Cameroons plebiscites increased Nigeria's size by the Northern Cameroons, they strengthened its claim to African leadership.

The impact of the plebiscites on Cameroun's international image as on its domestic politics was far-reaching. One could even say that the plebiscites created an entirely new international image for Cameroon -- from a unitary francophone republic within the French African community, to a bilingual federation that was nonaligned to both the French Community and the British Commonwealth.

The changes involved were structural as well as political. Beginning with the foreign service establishment in Yaoundé, the Foreign Minister, Charles Okala, whom Ahidjo held responsible for the failure of the Cameroun diplomatic offensive against the second Northern Cameroons plebiscite, was dismissed.[6] The post of Deputy Minister of Foreign Affairs was created, to which a West Cameroonian, Nzo Ekhah Nghaky, was appointed, his attributions being mainly to oversee relations with the UK, Nigeria, and the rest of the anglophone world about which francophone Cameroonians knew very little.[7]

With respect to foreign policy, reunification brought about a change in both ideology and rhetoric. Like all other French dependencies in Black Africa, with the exception of Guinea, Cameroun had attained independence as a member of the French African Community. But sensing the impending entanglements of that Community, some Southern Cameroonians thought that reunification might "salvage the French Cameroons from the French union."[8] At the pre-plebiscite meeting in Yaoundé in October 1960, Ahidjo and Foncha decided that the united Cameroon will not be part of the French Community or the British Commonwealth.[9]

6   Bayart, op. cit., p. 12.
7   Willard Johnson. op. cit., p. 230.
8   V.E. Mukete, Speech in the Nigerian House of Representatives, Lagos, 26 March 1957. Cf. V.E. Mukete, *op. cit.,* p. 270.
9   Final Communique issued by A. Ahidjo and J. N. Foncha after meeting of 10-13 Oct. 1960, Yaoundé, mimeo.

That posture was rather unusual. African countries naturally belonged to one post-colonial grouping or another, under the aegis of the former colonial powers.

But the sense of reunification was for Cameroon to operate a delicate balance between the two former Administering Powers. Cameroon was non-aligned, not only with respect to the two camps of the Cold War, but also in theory with respect to its two former masters.

In theory, because in practice it was impossible for the Federal Republic of Cameroon to remain exactly equidistant of France and the UK. The weight of the two Federated States played on the formulation of Cameroon's foreign policy. French influence remained dominant, mainly because francophone East Cameroon was the much bigger component, and also because the UK retained only minimal interest in the Southern Cameroons after the plebiscites.

The imbalance was heightened by the artful cunning of Ahmadou Ahidjo himself. Barely one month after that agreement with Foncha, and in total disregard thereof, the Cameroun President proceeded to sign a comprehensive pact with France.

The Franco-Cameroun Accord of November 1960 was a blanket package of ten treaties linking Cameroun to its former metropolis in the economic, military, monetary, commercial, and cultural domains. It was neither revised nor abrogated at reunification. Instead, it was tacitly extended to West Cameroon, making the Federal Republic a de facto member of the French African Community, a point underscored by Ahidjo's frequent visits to Paris and by the visit to Cameroon of every French President since de Gaulle.

At the regional level, Cameroon was an active member of the French-speaking *Organisation Commune Africaine et Malgache [OCAM]*, which it had helped found in 1960 and which grouped the former French dependencies in Black Africa. The headquarters of the Organization was in Yaoundé, until Cameroon withdrew from it in 1973, accusing OCAM of duplicating the OAU.[10]

Still, the plebiscites brought about subtle changes in Cameroon's

10   Bureau Politique National de l'UNC, *La Politique Extérieure du Cameroun.* (Yaoundé: Imprimerie Saint-Paul) p. 22.

dependence on France. In the first three decades of reunification, it symbolically stayed clear of the annual Franco-African summit conference. And although, with regard to its friends, France remained first among equals, Cameroon's vision of itself as well as its image in international relations was notably changed by reunification.

Cameroon began to see itself as having a special mission in Africa. It was a feeling based on geographical as well as cultural and historical factors. Cameroon's central location in the armpit of Africa; the diversity of its vegetation from thick tropical forest to meager desert scrub; its heterogeneous socio-cultural composition; the assortment of its historical heritage from discovery by the Portuguese,[11] through colonization by the Germans to mandate and trusteeship by the British and the French; all gave the country a unique hold on the African experience. Its reunification pointed to African unity as the synthesis of decolonization on the continent. And Cameroon began to project itself as the nucleus of African unity.

President Ahidjo's Reunification Day message highlighted that ambition:

> *Réunissant aujourd'hui les populations d'expression française et d'expression anglaise, le Cameroun sera le véritable laboratoire d'une union africaine qui doit rassembler des Etats parlant ces deux langues; il formera un pont entre ces deux Afriques.*[12]

Other sources also credited Cameroon with those unifying qualities. One London newspaper saw reunification as a political experiment

11 It is believed that the Portuguese sailor, Fernando Po, arrived at the River Wouri in Douala in 1472, and found so many shrimps in the stream that he promptly named it *"Rio dos Cameroes"* [River of Shrimps], from which the name Cameroon in all its varieties was derived.

12 Ahmadou Ahidjo, Broadcast to the Nation, in *L'Unite*, No. 64, Yaounde, 6 Oct. 1961. The statement translates thus: *"Today reuniting French-speaking and English-speaking peoples, Cameroon shall become a veritable laboratory of African unity, bringing together States speaking these two languages; it shall form a bridge between the two Africas."*

"which may point the way towards African unity on a bigger scale."[13] Another one viewed the history of the Cameroons as "a test case for all sorts of cherished African principles."[14] The Mayor of London, hoped that "the Federal Republic of Cameroon will be able to play an important part in bridging any gaps between English-speaking and French-speaking African countries by using the experience gained in handling its internal problems of unity on a wider stage."[15] Still others saw Cameroon as "an ideal staging post for British efforts to increase links with Francophone Africa."[16]

Many African countries also recognized Cameroon's unique experience in unity. In most continental organizations, Cameroon's voice was given great importance. Several set up headquarters in the country, notably, OCAM [until 1973], the Supreme Council for Sports in Africa, the *Office Africain et Malgache de la Propriéte Industrielle,* the Inter-African Phyto-Sanitary Council, and the Bank of Central African States.

At the Organization of African Unity [OAU], the lessons of reunification seemed particularly useful. In its first decade, President Ahidjo was elected to all the important dispute committees of the Organization, his peers convinced that his experience in unity at home could serve the continent as well.

The impact of Cameroon within the OAU went beyond the popularity of its President. Because of the bilingual nature of their country, Cameroonians seemed particularly suited for administrative positions in the Organization. And when the first serious challenge was posed to Diallo Telli's position as Secretary-General of the OAU in Rabat in 1972,[17] it was a little-known Cameroonian Minister of Labor, Nzo Ekhah Nghaky, who landed the coveted prize.

Ekhah Nghaky emerged victorious from a field of formidable contenders, including the Justice Minister of Upper Volta, Malick Zorome,

---

13   *Financial Times,* London, 7 May 1963.
14   *The Guardian,* London, 11 Nov. 1960.
15   Speech at the Guildhall banquet given in honor of HE the President and Madame Ahidjo, London, 7 May 1963, mimeo.
16   *West Africa,* London. 3 May 1982, p. 1181.
17   Michael Wolfers. *Politics in the Organization of African Unity,* (London: Methuen and Co. Ltd., 1976).

whose candidature had been endorsed by OCAM in Lomé in April 1972;[18] the Liberian Ambassador to the UN, Edward Peal, who counted on the support of anglophone States; Diallo Telli himself, who had lobbied to retain his post; and Ekhah Nghaky, whose greatest asset lay in the symbolism of his country of origin.

In the voting, the Cameroonian leapt into the lead from the start, soundly defeating the incumbent by thirty votes to ten.[19] In retrospect, one writer found that Ekangaki[20] had been "tailor-made" for the post of Secretary-General of the OAU[21] he was an anglophone Cameroonian, who spoke and wrote French convincingly; he had studied in Nigeria, Britain and France; and had been nominated by Nigeria!

Two years later, when Ekangaki resigned in the heat of the "Lonrho Affair,"[22] the Assembly of Heads of State was deadlocked in election between Omah Arteh of Somalia and Vernon Mwaanga of Zambia for over eleven hours.[23] Then an exhausted Somali President proposed that Cameroon, in whose name Ekangaki had been elected, be asked to name a candidate. The proposal was adopted, and Cameroon found itself with the single-handed power to appoint the Secretary-General of the OAU. It duly appointed William Eteki Mboumoua, a francophone Cameroonian who had been Minister of Education before becoming Special Adviser to President Ahidjo.

Incidentally, Eteki Mboumoua had been in the contest from the beginning, but was withdrawn after the first ballot, having received only five votes.[24] And then, with the compromise worked out by President

18   Ibid., p. 69.
19   Ibid. p. 70.
20   The new Secretary-General simplified his name from the tongue-twisting Ekhah-Nghaky to Ekangaki following his election.
21   Michael Wolters, op. cit., p. 71.
22   Ekangaki was fiercely criticized for appointing, as OAU technical consultants, the British firm Lonrho that was known to have strong business connections with the white minority regime of South Africa. Ekangaki argued that he had acted in good faith, with the knowledge of the OAU Council of Ministers. But it was obvious that he had forfeited the confidence of many States, so he opted to resign.
23   Michael Wolfers, op. cit., p. 79.
24   Ibid., p. 80.

Siad Barre, Eteki found favor in an Assembly that had overlooked him earlier in the day. That favor was based on the perception of Cameroon as a symbol of unity within the OAU.

With all the changes they brought, the British Cameroons plebiscites affected the international images of Nigeria and Cameroon in different ways. For the former, they increased the size of the country, which was its most important asset in international relations. For the latter, they introduced an element of diversity that made it unique in Africa. For both, the plebiscites left a mixed impact on their bilateral relations.

The Plebiscites and Cameroon-Nigeria Relations

Some of the most important relations that a State entertains with the outside world are those with its neighbors. A country's neighborhood has such enormous bearing on its internal security that governments no longer need reminding to attach importance to bilateral relations with their neighbors.[25] For Cameroon and Nigeria, the plebiscites, coming so soon after independence, had a strong impact on their bilateral relations, first as a source of conflict, and then as a catalyst for cooperation.

The British Cameroons plebiscites created two kinds of misunderstandings between Cameroon and Nigeria. One was the general bitterness resulting from the half-fulfilled hopes of the plebiscites. The other concerned border disputes emanating from the boundary adjustments brought about by the plebiscites.

The competing expectations of Cameroun and Nigeria over the British Cameroons were such that disagreement was inevitable between them. That disagreement first came to light during the UN debate on the plebiscites. It persisted for years afterwards.

Cameroon-Nigeria relations in the early years were ominously uneasy. Following the second Northern Cameroons plebiscites, there was such fierce indignation in Cameroun against Nigeria that President Ahidjo felt obliged to caution his countrymen *"de ne pas se livrer à des manifestations*

---

25   In colonial times, African countries were linked "vertically" with the metropolitan powers, not "horizontally" with themselves, the result being that they had relatively little knowledge about their own environments.

*de xénophobie contre les Nigerians qui résident chez nous.*²⁶ Even so, the date of June 1, 1961, when the Northern Cameroons formally joined Nigeria, was officially declared a Day of National Mourning in Cameroun.

In announcing that decision, Ahidjo told his compatriots that "Henceforth, when we shall be talking of Cameroon, we shall always bear in mind our 800,000 brothers who are beyond our frontiers [in Nigeria], and who share our hopes and joys. They shall be with us in spirit before being totally with us."²⁷ He vowed to do everything in his power to end "this cruel separation."²⁸

One way of doing so was by instituting legal proceedings to annul the results of the disputed plebiscite. And should that fail, Ahidjo counted on the irredentist fervor of the people. Drawing from the lessons of history, he declared that *"le Cameroun septentrional restera ce que l'Alsace-Lorraine a été pour la France à une époque de son histoire."*²⁹

While individual Nigerian politicians were willing to pick bones with their Cameroun counterparts, the Federal Government was intent on consolidating the gains of the plebiscites rather than disputing their losses. Balewa was anxious that instability in Cameroun should not spill over into Nigeria and called for "adequate military forces to safeguard Nigeria's long land frontier with Cameroun"³⁰.

The situation was more restive than either government admitted. The antipathy of people on both sides of the border reached alarming proportions, with several violent clashes. One source put the death toll in the first few months of 1961 at nearly 150, in a situation that was "fraught with danger."³¹ The tension persisted for years after the plebiscites. June 1 continued to be observed as a Day of National Mourning throughout Cameroon until 1966, the year that Nigeria came to the brink of disintegration.

---

26 *L'Unite*, No. 32, Yaounde. 24 Feb. 1961. Translation: *"not to indulge in manifestations of xenophobia against Nigerians residing in our country."*
27 A.CA.P., No. 122, Yaounde, 1 June 1961.
28 Idem.
29 Ibid., No. 103, Yaounde. 5 May 1961. Translation: *"the Northern Cameroons shall remain for us what Alsace-Lorraine represented for France at a certain period of its history."*
30 House of Representatives Debates, January Session, Lagos, 1960.
31 *Observer Foreign News Service*, London, 21 April 1961.

The Nigerian crisis of 1966 had one obvious effect on relations with Cameroon - the civil war so engrossed Nigeria's energies that it could no longer afford clashes with its neighbors. Instead, it needed their sympathy in the existential crisis that had engulfed it.

The outbreak of war in Nigeria was an important divide in Cameroon-Nigeria relations — from conflict to sympathy. However, if the trauma of the civil war proved to be a soothing hand on the rugged surface of Cameroon-Nigeria relations, there was one problem area that survived its passage with positions unaffected. That was the problem of boundaries between the two countries.

The task of protecting national boundaries in Africa was rendered burdensome by the casual manner in which those boundaries had been drawn. Armed with superficial and hearsay knowledge of Africa, the European diplomats who met in Berlin in 1884 to share the continent did not care about the natural features of the lands they were partitioning, less still about the people who inhabited those lands. The resulting boundaries were mostly works of fiction. One British Prime Minister captured with cynical humor, probably after a few drinks, the unfathomable absurdity of some of the boundary-making processes in colonial Africa:

> We have been engaged in drawing lines upon maps where no white man's foot ever trod; we have been giving away mountains and rivers and lakes to each other, only hindered by the small impediment that we never knew exactly where the mountains and rivers and lakes were.[32]

Or whether they existed at all! For an emerging continent, such imaginary boundaries were a recipe for disaster, to the extent that today virtually every African country has one claim or another, whether territorial or boundary, against one or all of its neighbors! The situation was rendered all the more complicated when, as happened between Nigeria and Cameroun, the boundaries had to be adjusted after independence.

The boundary changes engendered by the plebiscites were a source

---

32   Quoted in J. C. Anene, *The International Boundaries of Nigeria 1885-1960*, (London: Longman, 1970), p. 3.

of deep friction between the two countries. In essence, the changes concerned the two artificially contrived borderlines that at one stage or another had demarcated the Territories, namely, the Anglo-German colonial boundary between Nigeria and Kamerun, and the Franco-British partition line within the former German colony. Before the First World War, the former had been the international boundary between Nigeria and Kamerun. After the War, the latter became the international boundary between the two Cameroons, or rather, in view of the administrative union, between Nigeria and Cameroun.

But while the Anglo-French or Milner-Simon partition line had been carefully supervised throughout the mandate and trusteeship periods as the international frontier between the British and French spheres, the Anglo-German frontier was reduced to a regional boundary within the administrative union of the British Cameroons and Nigeria. In the Northern Cameroons, that boundary quietly disappeared as the coterminous provinces of Northern Nigeria swallowed the Territory. The Southern Cameroons later recovered its territorial integrity, although the old German boundary remained as the regional boundary with Eastern Nigeria. The plebiscites revoked and maintained both international boundaries in parts. In the north, the Milner-Simon line became the international boundary between Cameroon and Nigeria; in the south, the almost forgotten Anglo-German boundary was resurrected as their international boundary.

Those changes produced ripples of migration among some peoples of the British Cameroons who disagreed with the verdicts of the plebiscites. In the Northern Cameroons, ardent supporters of reunification moved across the border into the Southern Cameroons;[33] in the Southern Cameroons, its determined opponents moved over into Nigeria. In the south in particular, the rejuvenation of an international boundary in an area where people had been used to roaming about freely for nearly half a century destroyed many habits and sundered anew certain communities that had found their unity in the erosion of that frontier.

A community so affected was the Ekoi group which, Professor Anene reckons, was split almost in half by the new frontier, with nearly 40,000

33   *Cameroon Times*, Victoria. 1 Nov. 1962.

in the Southern Cameroons and 50,000 in Nigeria.[34] By the same token, the abolition of the southern portion of the Milner-Simon line, which now became the internal boundary between East and West Cameroon, reunited many communities that had been arbitrarily divided by the Anglo-French partition.

The resurrection of the old Anglo-German boundary did more than sunder the Ekoi community. It turned out to be one of the sticking points between Cameroon and Nigeria. For long after the plebiscites, the existence of an international frontier did not dawn on some of the border peoples. One part of Mamfe Division in West Cameroon called Akwaya had no communications links with the rest of Cameroon, save across two worn-out German footbridges over the Cross River. All their links were with Nigeria; Cameroonians there continued to live as though they were still part of Nigeria; and Nigerians there found it hard to believe that they were now in a foreign country.

The consequence was that the Cameroon armed forces found it extremely difficult to protect that portion of their international frontier without clashes with their Nigerian counterparts. The situation was not helped by the fluid nature of the boundary, leading to recurrent clashes.

In order to forestall such clashes, the Cameroon-Nigeria Joint Commission was established in 1965, to delimit their maritime and land boundaries. The Commission held its first meeting in the Nigerian border town of Ikom on 11 October 1965. But only a few months after that introductory session, Nigeria walked into the teeth of a civil war that threatened its very existence, and the work of the Commission was suspended for the five years that the war lasted.

From 1966 to 1970, border problems between the two countries were eclipsed by the Nigerian Civil War. Ironically, the end of the war renewed the problems. In June 1970, it was reported that many Nigerians had been killed by Cameroon customs officials, in a border incident that the Yaoundé Government vigorously denied.[35]

That incident resurrected the activities of the Cameroon-Nigeria Joint Commission. It met in Douala in August 1970 and again in Yaoundé in

34   J. C. Anene, op. cit., p. 88.
35   Ndifontah mo Nyamndi, op. cit., p. 175.

June 1971. But the meetings ended in deadlock owing to disagreement over the sketchy maps presented by both sides, a fact which one Nigerian newspaper attributed to the probability of profitable oil prospection around the maritime frontier.[36] But it was also a reflection of how ill-defined the boundary was in the first place.

Matters were made worse in October 1971 when Nigeria unilaterally extended its territorial waters from twelve to thirty nautical miles. That decision caused bitter resentment in Cameroon, because it threatened its flourishing fishing industry which employed nearly a thousand people and yielded nearly two million dollars annually, two-thirds of the catch being in waters that under the new Nigerian law were now prohibited.[37]

The decision led to a reinforcement of Cameroon's military presence in the border areas, increasing the risk of confrontation. In July and August 1973, there were repeated clashes in which Nigerian fishermen were reportedly driven from Cameroonian villages along Rio del Rey.[38] And for the first time, the Nigerian Government officially acknowledged the existence of a boundary dispute with Cameroon.[39]

That dispute was the central topic of discussion during President Ahidjo's visit to Nigeria in August 1974. As a reprieve, the two Presidents agreed to create a four-kilometer corridor along their common boundary, within which mineral prospection was forbidden. That decision was formalized in the Maroua Declaration issued by both Presidents during Yakubu Gowon's visit to Cameroon the following year. The Declaration was said to have "theoretically settled the constantly nagging problem of border clashes overfishing and land rights."[40]

Only theoretically, because in reality the Maroua Declaration was more of a non-solution, the buffer zone concept being completely ill-suited for the protection of an undemarcated boundary. The border clashes continued. Not long after the Maroua Declaration, one Nigerian newspaper wondered whether "these armed forays against our citizens

---

36   *Sunday Post,* Lagos. 1 May 1972.
37   Jean-François Bayart, «La Politique Extérieure du Cameroun 1960-1971,» in *Revue Française d'Etudes Politiques Africaines,* No. 75, Paris, Juin 1975, p. 60.
38   *African Contemporary Record,* 1973-1974, London.
39   *Daily Times,* Lagos, 22 March 1974.
40   Nigerian Observer, 5 June 1975.

are not actually acts of commission by the Cameroon authorities?"[41]

Such outcries notwithstanding, both governments behaved as if all was well on their common border. On a visit to Cameroon in 1977, General Olusegun Obasanjo called on both sides to avoid "purposeless emotions" in tackling their border problems, arguing that they were "unfortunately an unavoidable aspect of human existence which, in a way, serve to strengthen our faith in ourselves and in our common destiny."[42] For his part, President Ahidjo felt that border problems between Cameroon and Nigeria although inevitable, "are so quickly resolved that they become a matter for individuals rather than for the dignitaries of our two countries."[43]

Consoling as they were, those declarations only cushioned a thorny frontier problem, and postponed the pain of solving it. A shoot-out between the armed forces of both countries in the creeks of Rio del Rey in May 1981 in which seven people died, brought the two nations to the brink of war, reminding them of the explosive potential of their unsolved boundary problems.

If Cameroon-Nigeria relations were all about the boundary, they would be a constant headache to both sides. Fortunately, there were other areas of relationship in which there was less cause for conflict and increased propensity to cooperate.

Like other newly independent African countries, Cameroon and Nigeria faced similar challenges in the world and nursed similar aspirations for the future. They were both strongly anti-colonialist, and both felt insecure in a world where the weak and the poor found it difficult to survive alongside the strong and the rich. And like all other neighbors they too had their areas of disagreement and their areas of agreement. The areas of agreement grew from the similarity of their views in foreign policy and their identical domestic concerns. They shared the same interest in world peace, which Balewa described as a pre-requisite for the well-being of all mankind,[44] and Ahidjo saw as the business of all the

---

41   *The Punch,* Lagos. 24 August 1978.
42   Olusegun Obasanjo, Speech in Garoua, 8 August 1977.
43   Ahmadou Ahidjo, Speech in Garoua. 8 August 1977, mimeo.
44   A. T. Balewa, Statement to the House of Representatives, Lagos. 20 August 1960.

nations of the world.[45] They had strong faith in the United Nations, an organization that to Balewa was "the effective machinery for inducing peace,"[46] and "the only sure guarantee for preserving the sovereignty of the States that are weak,"[47] an Organization whose moderating role in international affairs Ahidjo found to be "irreplaceable!"[48] As developing countries, they both ardently wished for increasing international cooperation. And they were fundamentally non-aligned: they would not align themselves "as a matter of routine" with any of the power blocs,[49] or entertain "motivated prejudice against anyone."[50]

At the continental level, their objectives were similar. Both Cameroon and Nigeria were keenly committed to the respect of the sovereign equality of nations. That has always been a major African concern, lest their independence be undermined. They were also committed to the related principle of non-interference in the domestic affairs of other States, a policy motivated by anxiety that radical exiles operating from countries like Ghana were constantly seeking to de-stabilize their regimes and overthrow their governments. Nkrumah had incurred the wrath of both countries by offering asylum to members of the radical Dynamic Party of Nigeria,[51] and the exiled UPC of Cameroun

Commensurate with their aspirations for continental leadership, both countries were committed to the total liberation of Africa. Ahidjo felt that Cameroon's liberty was "umbilically linked to the liberty of all African peoples;"[52] while Balewa held that "On the question of colonialism and racial discrimination, we in Nigeria will never compromise."[53]

Finally, both Cameroon and Nigeria had a similar attachment to African unity. They were convinced that the ultimate strength of Africa

45   A. Ahidjo, Speech to the First National Council of the CNU. Yaoundé, 5 Nov. 1966.
46   A. T. Balewa, Speech to the UN General Assembly, New York, 7 Oct. 1960.
47   A. T. Balewa, Speech to the US Congress, Washington, 26 July 1960.
48   A. Ahidjo. Speech to the Fourth Congress of the UC, Ebolowa, 4 July 1962.
49   A. T. Balewa Statement to the House of Representatives, Lagos, 20 August 1960.
50   A. Ahidjo, Speech to the 5th Congress of the UC, Bafoussam, 30 Nov. 1965.
51   *Sunday Post,* Lagos, 18 Feb. 1962.
52   A. Ahidjo, Speech to the 4th Congress of the UC, Ebolowa, 4 July 1962.
53   A. T. Balewa, Address to the Conference of African and Malagasy Heads of State and Government, Addis Ababa, 24 May 1963.

lay in its unity. As Balewa pointed out, "Africa with its diverse and unique problems cannot afford to be divided. Nor can it afford the dissipation of energy resulting from speaking in diverse voices."[54]

But they were opposed to the summary approach to African unity propounded by Kwame Nkrumah and the militant Casablanca Group of African States. In contrast, Cameroon and Nigeria were active members of the moderate Monrovia Group, which believed in progressive African unity by concentric circles. As Ahidjo pointed out:

> Africa will move towards her unity by passing through gradual, limited regional constructions, all converging on the ultimate goal. This shall be done by the progressive alignment of geographical entities already homogenized by identical structures which renders the various parts interdependent.[55]

The similarity of views and the congruity of predispositions between Nigeria and Cameroon inclined them to cooperate rather than to clash. The case for cooperation was strengthened by the simple fact that they were neighbors.

The plebiscites increased the zone of direct geographical contact between them from sixty-four to nearly a thousand kilometers. That lengthy contiguity became a cardinal element of their bilateral relations. It was with that in mind that the Nigerian Foreign Minister, Jaja Wachuku, hoped that the British Cameroons "should be a bond to link the two Territories together."[56]

However, in the early days as Cameroon grieved over the Northern Cameroons, she was in no mood for cooperation. It took time to come to terms with the stubborn fact of bilateral cooperation with Nigeria. Cameroon approached that cooperation grudgingly at first, then somewhat gingerly, and finally with resignation. Ahidjo captured the changing moods of his country in that regard:

---

54   Cf. *West African Pilot*, Lagos, 27 Jan. 1962.
55   A. Ahidjo, Speech to the 5th Congress of the UC, Bafoussam, 30 Nov. 1965.
56   A/C.4/SR.994, New York, 21 April 1961.

Since our accession to independence, we have held out our hands, trying to forget in spite of painful and serious events, the resentment that subjective irritability would have amply justified. We turned our backs on it, feeling that all gathering must begin around oneself, based on relations of good neighborliness, friendship and fraternity.[57]

It could not have been otherwise when the two countries shared such a long frontier, with so many nationals of each country in the other. Significantly, one of their first acts of cooperation was about the movement of persons and goods across that frontier. In an Agreement signed in Yaoundé in February 1963, Cameroon and Nigeria agreed to facilitate the "legitimate movement of persons and personal effects across the boundary between them."[58] They also simplified travel requirements by abolishing the use of visas.

They further agreed to crack down on illicit cross-border traffic, of which there was a lot in the forest and creek areas, depriving both countries of substantial customs revenue. The smugglers were so wily that both governments needed concerted efforts to root them out. So they decided to establish common customs stations on the frontier in juxtaposition. As part of the joint effort, they agreed to allow their vessels to carry out anti-smuggling operations in the territorial waters of each other and to facilitate the exchange of professional information among their customs officials.[59] From concealed hostility in 1961, both countries moved into open dialogue by 1963. With time, their language mellowed. In a general Agreement on bilateral cooperation, they expressed their desire to cooperate in the economic, scientific, educational and cultural fields; and to consult each other on all matters of common interest.[60]

That Agreement reflected the new spirit of their relationship, one of

57   A. Ahidjo, Speech to the 5th Congress of the UC, Bafoussam, 30 Nov. 1965.
58   Agreement on the Control of Movement of Persons and Goods between Cameroon and Nigeria, Yaounde, 6 Feb. 1963, Art. 1.
59   Ibid., Art. IX.
60   Agreement on Bilateral Cooperation between Cameroon and Nigeria, Yaounde, 6 Feb. 1963, Art. 1.

brotherhood, understanding, and mutual respect.[61] If the British Cameroons plebiscites had been the source of temporary frictions and sporadic clashes between Cameroon and Nigeria, they condemned the two countries, in the long run, to wider and more lasting cooperation.

The greatest test of their solidarity came during the Nigerian Civil War, a test that also demonstrated the striking similarity of their domestic concerns. In an important sense, Cameroon and Nigeria had identical domestic worries, deriving from their internal composition. Apart from the general problems of development that confronted all African countries, Cameroon and Nigeria faced acute problems of internal cohesion. Both were made of hundreds of distinct ethnic groups loosely held together by States that were patiently trying to crystallize a sense of nationhood. In Nigeria, the three free-wheeling regions were perpetually at each other's throats. In Cameroon, the chemistry of reunification was such that the two linguistic components had to remain distinctly alive for the whole entity to be truly united. In both, the quest for national unity occupied a choice position among their priorities. And there was always the fear that a threat to the unity of one country might produce a knock-on effect in the other. In that case, their neighborliness was both a blessing and a risk.

The Nigerian crisis put that neighborliness to its strongest test. As the sole country in geographical contact with the seceding region, Cameroon's attitude was critical. Any sympathy for the insurrection would have compromised the Federal war effort. That temptation was great, after the loss of the Northern Cameroons. But Ahidjo surprised everyone by categorically denouncing the Biafran secession. Addressing the Press in Bamenda, he declared that "So long as I shall be at the head of Cameroon, there shall be no question of recognizing a secessionist State in Nigeria."[62] In the volatile context of the Nigerian civil war, that was a very brave position to take.

Francophone African Presidents do not normally contradict French foreign policy options. For Ahidjo to contravene the French position on the Nigerian crisis seemed like a reckless gamble. As he later admitted: *"les*

---

61   Ibid., Preamble.
62   A. Ahidjo, Press Conference, Bamenda, 8 May 1969.

Français ne m'ont jamais pardonné ma prise de position lors de la guerre civile au Nigeria, pour l'intégrité de ce pays, alors que la France prenait position en faveur du Biafra."[63]

Ahidjo's unequivocal denunciation of the Biafran secession, pronounced in the heart of West Cameroon, was meant for domestic as well as foreign consumption. It was based on the fear that secession in Nigeria might threaten the unity of Cameroon. And it was directed at the increasing number of West Cameroonians who, conscious of their status as a national minority, nervously watched developments in the minority Eastern Region of Nigeria.

Ahidjo had not forgotten the CPNC's attempts to legalize the right of secession during negotiations for reunification. And he was aware of the growing disenchantment of West Cameroonians over the insidious advance of the Federation into areas of presumed State competence. To make matters worse, the Biafran leader was reported to have sent emissaries to West Cameroon offering support for any secession there.[64] It was no coincidence, therefore, that Ahidjo travelled to West Cameroon to denounce the Biafran secession.

He did not only denounce the secession. He was actively engaged in international efforts to resolve the crisis. By virtue of Cameroon's unique proximity with the secessionist region, Ahidjo was a key member of the OAU Committee on the Nigerian crisis. And hardly had the war ended than he dispatched his Foreign Minister, Nko'o Etoungou, to assure Gowon that "Nigeria's victory is of tremendous joy to my people."[65]

Perhaps Ahidjo's greatest contribution in resolving the crisis was that he did not allow Cameroonian territory to be used in the conflict, rejecting advances from both sides to traverse his country,[66] and strengthening his border security just in case. His neutrality went to the extent that textiles

---

63   A. Ahidjo, Interview with Henri Bandolo, cf. *La Flame et la Fumee,* (Yaounde: Editions SOPECAM), 1986, p. 404. Translation: *"the French never forgave me for the stand I took during the Nigerian Civil War, for the integrity of that country while France took position in favour of Biafra."*

64   John J. Stremlau, *The International Politics of the Nigerian Civil War,* (Princeton: Princeton University Press), 1977, p. 74.

65   *Daily Times,* Lagos, 29 May 1970.

66   John Stremlau, op. cit., p. 74.

with the images of the protagonists were banned throughout Cameroon.[67]

That neutrality helped tighten the quarantine that ultimately choked the break-away region. In an appraisal of Cameroon's role in the conflict, Yakubu Gowon declared that "Nigeria might never have been what it is today if the Republic of Cameroon allowed its territory to be used as a communications link against Nigeria during the civil war."[68] And he knew better. It was to convey his country's gratitude to Cameroon for that tacit support that he came to Yaoundé in April 1971. During the visit, the Nigerian leader declared that Cameroon's attitude during the war had made her a trusted companion and a faithful friend of his country.[69] Gowon's claim was not mere hyperbole. The Nigerian civil war had lifted Cameroon-Nigeria relations from the frigid state of mutual suspicion to the warmth of mutual sympathy. At the beginning of the crisis, Cameroon was still in mourning over the Northern Cameroons; after the war, the story of the Northern Cameroons was seldom mentioned by either side.

The end of the war opened the floodgates of high-level consultations between the two countries. President Ahidjo, who had not been to Nigeria after the British Cameroons plebiscites, visited Nigeria five times in the six years following the Nigerian civil war -- in 1970, 71, 72, 74, and 75. During the first of those visits, he announced that he was "profoundly happy to be in Lagos, because I consider Nigeria as my second home."[70]

What Ahidjo meant is not entirely clear, although rumor once circulated that his father was actually of Nigerian origin! But it appears that he now felt at home in a country which, a few years before, had been the cause of national mourning in Cameroon. His recurrent visits indicate how much relations between Cameroon and Nigeria had improved. It was an irony that it needed an attempted secession in Nigeria and fear of such an attempt in Cameroon to turn on that improvement.

In regional and continental organizations, they supported each other. Their mutual support was demonstrated during the election of the Secretary-general of the OAU in June 1972. Resisting pressure from Commonwealth African countries to nominate a candidate, Nigeria

67   Ibid.
68   Nigeria: Bulletin on Foreign Affairs, Vol. 1, No. 3, Lagos, July 1972, p. 22.
69   Federal Ministry of Information, Lagos, Press Release, No. 93, 1975.
70   Cf. *Sunday Times*, Lagos, 27 Sept. 1970.

instead proposed a Cameroonian, Nzo Ekhah Nghaky, and lobbied strongly for his election.[71]

And later on, in gratitude for his nomination, Ekangaki reshuffled the OAU Secretariat and promoted the Nigerian Assistant Secretary-General, Peter Onu, to the high-profile portfolio of Political Affairs and Spokesman of the Organization. The reshuffle aroused criticism that Ekangaki had operated a "palace coup" in favor of Nigerian interests.[72] But it was only reasonable for the Secretary-General to appoint a spokesman that he could trust. Their collaboration within the OAU secretariat reflected the wider cooperation between their two countries.

The political impact of the British Cameroons plebiscites was greatest on the two countries which benefitted territorially from the exercises. That impact was felt both separately and jointly by Nigeria and Cameroon. In Nigeria, the Northern Cameroons was briefly a bone of contention between the major political parties, before quietly settling into the Northern Region, aggravating the much talked-about regional imbalance. In Cameroon, reunification introduced a new cultural dichotomy that was as important at home as it was strategic abroad. For both, the plebiscites became a significant determinant of their bilateral relations, serving as a source and a solvent of frictions between them, as an obstacle and a catalyst of mutual cooperation.

71   *West Africa*, London, 30 June 1972.
72   Michael Wolfers, op. cit., p. 76.

Conclusion

The size of the British Cameroons, which played such a key role in its history, was entirely fortuitous. Its contiguity with the British Protectorate of Nigeria led the United Kingdom to bring both Territories into administrative union. And its location, sandwiched between two big neighbors, led the United Nations to arrange a permanent union with one of them, based on the view that on its own the British Cameroons was too small to constitute an economically viable unit. The economic potential of the Territory was repeatedly assessed by eminent experts, often with contrasting results: Sydney Phillipson found that an independent Southern Cameroons would be doomed to a precarious hand-to-mouth existence;[1] but Kenneth Berill concluded that the country was fertile and full of promise;[2] and the Commissioner for the Cameroons confirmed that the Southern Cameroons was financially viable to run its own government.[3] The UN agreed with Phillipson and decided to unite the Territory with one of its neighbors, even if that meant departing from the basic objective of the Trusteeship System, to promote the progressive development of the people towards self-government or independence.

However, much as enhancing the economic prospects of the British Cameroons was an entirely noble concern of the United Nations, there was no guarantee that union with either neighbor would achieve that goal, when forty-five years of association with Nigeria had failed to do so, and when the union of the two sections of the Territory itself had never been contemplated. The irony of the British Cameroons was that the failure of one union to develop its economy became the pretext for engaging the people in a second union, on the back of an unsuccessful experiment!

Besides, strictly speaking, independence and union are antithetical

1   Phillipson, *Report*, op. cit.
2   Kenneth Berill, Report, cf. *West Africa*, No. 2277, London, 21 Jan. 1961, p. 73.
3   Muna, op. cit., p. 275.

concepts. Independence means freedom from control by others, while union leads to the surrender of part or total control over oneself to others. The phrase "independence by joining", which qualified the plebiscite options, was therefore something of an absurdity. Throughout the administrative union, the Southern Cameroons fought hard to cast off the yoke of the Eastern Region of Nigeria. So it was more than paradoxical to consider union with the same Nigeria as an option for the independence of the Southern Cameroons.

As the process unfolded, the critical decisions on the fate of the British Cameroons were not taken by the people of the Territory but by the international community, based on reasons that were not clearly compelling. Although they voted in the plebiscites, the exercise itself was imposed upon them, against the better judgment of their leaders. Furthermore, the debate on the British Cameroons took place far from its shores, between people who had never set foot in the Territory, in an Assembly where the subject itself was not directly represented.

The implementation of the results of the plebiscites raised further questions about the exact purpose of the exercise. At ceremonies at Mubi and Buea, intended to mark the independence of the British Cameroons, departing British officials handed over the Instruments of the Territory to the leaders of Nigeria and Cameroun.

Both ceremonies aroused heated controversy. Many queried why the Instruments of a Territory should be handed to non-citizens of the Territory, without conjuring the image of a trade-off of some kind, given that Balewa and Ahidjo were totally unknown in most parts of the Territory, and neither had any mandate from the people to act on their behalf. And others wondered how joining another country made the country in question "independent". If anything, the British Cameroons switched from trusteeship into union, without pausing to formally proclaim and popularly celebrate its independence. It was a form of independence by proxy, watched from the sidelines by the veritable leaders of the Territory, and it was the first time in history that a people were granted independence while the relevant instruments were taken elsewhere!

Also, at issue was whether the plebiscite, as conceived and framed, could truly reflect the wishes of the people. The UN deemed it appropriate, having successfully applied a similar format elsewhere. But the

188 THE BRITISH CAMEROONS PLEBISCITES

Plebiscite Commissioner raised doubts that the majority of the voters may not have grasped the detailed implications of the alternatives before them.[4] Which was hardly surprising. In all previous elections, the people of the British Cameroons were presented with clear-cut choices of candidates or programs. But the 1961 plebiscites were far more sophisticated. Enlightened electorates would have a hard time conceptualizing, in the same breath, the combination of independence and union with another country. For the uneducated electorate of the British Cameroons, that proposition was harder still. Independence was generally seen as the transition from an existing situation of colonial domination to a new dispensation of national sovereignty. However, the ruffling presence of Nigerians led many British Cameroonians to regard the administrative union as a form of foreign domination. And the plebiscites offered them the peculiar option of gaining their freedom by uniting with the country from which they sought that freedom!

The question of the British Cameroons caused considerable friction within the United Nations as the plebiscite options opposed two neighbors that participated in the process as both judge and interested party. Each made its own calculations, drawing support from its circle of friends. Both sought to sway the electorate, and both were accused of unduly influencing the election. In the Southern Cameroons, Endeley complained that "many people had come from the Republic of Cameroun and received voting cards;" in the Northern Cameroons, Habib grumbled that over 100,000 Nigerians, disguised as Public Works laborers, had voted in the second plebiscite.[5] Against that backdrop, the true verdict of the 1961 plebiscites may never be known.

The integration of the Northern Cameroons into Northern Nigeria was facilitated by the cultural and religious similarities of the population on both sides. But the union of the Southern Cameroons and the Cameroun Republic was impacted by the linguistic and systemic differences developed during the long period of separation. Essentially, it was a delicate graft of their two political systems, both inherited from rival colonial regimes with contrasting perceptions of governance. Both systems were

---

4   UN. Doc. A/4727, New York. 11 April 1961. p. 52.
5   A/C.4/SR.1142, New York, 13 April 1961, pp. 303-306.

soon locked in a subtle existential rivalry in which Ahidjo's endgame, as reported by Henri Bandolo, was to *"casser les Foncha, Endeley, Ngom Jua, et autres ténors politiques de la partie anglophone du pays."*[6]

Not surprisingly, many of them were relieved when the high-handed president resigned in 1982. They welcomed his successor, Paul Biya, hoping that he would address their growing concerns. Indications are that the new President was well aware of those expectations, having pledged to moralize government action. During his very first visit to the English-speaking region in February 1983, he addressed the sensitive nerves of the English-speaking community: "Your frankness," he said, "your love for the truth, and your attachment to social justice are values which should be respected and preserved."[7] The President acknowledged that those core values of truth and justice had not received much respect before.

In bringing together two Territories from different colonial backgrounds, the unification of the Cameroons was a seminal experiment in African history. Some feared that it might become a new theater in the age-old rivalry between France and Britain, leading to a precarious union that would be prone to internal conflict. But many saw it as a foretaste of the possibility of mending the brokenness of the African continent by bridging the colonial divide and restoring the original harmony of its natural diversity.

6   Henri Bandolo, *La Flame et la Fumee*, Yaounde, Editions SOPECAM, 1986, pp. 108-109. Translation: *"to bring down Foncha, Endeley, Ngom Jua and other political leaders of the English-speaking regions of the country."*
7   Paul Biya, Speech in Bamenda, 9 February 1983. CF. *The New Deal Message, Speeches and Interviews of President Paul* Biya, Vol. 1, p. 68, Editions SOPE-CAM, Yaoundé, 1983.

Select Bibliography

Ahidjo, Ahmadou, *Contribution à la Construction Nationale*. Paris: Présence Africaine, 1964.

Ardener, Edwin O., "The Kamerun Idea." *West Africa*: Nos 2147 and 2148, June 1958.

"The Nature of the Reunification of Cameroon", in A. Hazelwood (ed.), *African Integration and Disintegration*. London: OUP, 1967.

Azikiwe, Nnamdi, "Nigeria in World Politics." *Présence Africaine*, Vols 4 and 5, 1960.

Bayart, Jean-François, *L'Etat au Cameroun*. Paris : Presse de la Fondation Nationale des Sciences Politiques, 1979.

Crowder, Michael, *The Story of Nigeria*. London: Faber and Faber, 1962.

El-Ayouty, Yassin, *The United Nations and Decolonization*. The Hague: Martinus Nijhoff, 1971.

Enonchong, H.N.A., *Cameroon Constitutional Law*. Yaounde: CEPMAE, 1967.

Eyongetah and Brain *A History of the Cameroon*. London: Longman, 1974.

Ezera, Kalu, "Self-Determination in Southern Cameroons". *West African Pilot*, 27 February 1959.

Farley, Lawrence, *Plebiscites and Sovereignty*. Boulder Westview Press, 1986.

Federation of Nigeria, *House of Representatives Debates. Official Records, 1959-1961*. Lagos: Federal Government Printer.

Fonlon, Bernard, "Will We Make or Mar." Yaounde: *ABBIA*, March 1964

Gardinier, David E., *Cameroon: UN Challenge to French Policy*. London: OUP, 1963.

Gonidec P.F., "Les Institutions politiques de la République Fédérale du Cameroun". *Civilisations*: Vol. 2, No. 4, 1961, and Vol. 12 No.1, 1962.

Great Britain, Colonial Office: *Annual Report of H.M. Government to the Assembly of the United Nations on the Cameroons under United Kingdom Administration, 1946-1960*.

Hall, Duncan, *Mandates, Dependencies and Trusteeship*. London: Stevens and Sons, 1948.

International Court of Justice, *Case Concerning the Northern Cameroons*. The Hague, 1963.

Joseph, Richard A., *Radical Nationalism in Cameroon*. Oxford: Clarendon Press,

1971.

Kale, P.M., *Political Evolution in the Cameroons*. Buea: Government Printer, 1976.

Lavroff, D.G. (ed.) *La Politique Africaine du General de Gaulle*. Paris: A. Pedone, 1980.

Le Vine, Victor T., *The Cameroons from Mandate to Independence*. Bekerley: University of California Press, 1964.

"A Reluctant February Bride: The Other Cameroons." *Africa Report,* February, 1961.

Mabileau, Albert, *Décolonisation et Régimes politiques en Afrique noire*. Paris: A. Colin, 1967.

Mattern, Johannes, *The Employment of the Plebiscite in the Determination of Sovereignty*. The John Hopkins Press, 1920.

Morgan, D.J., *The Official History of Colonial Development*. London: Macmillan, 1980.

Muna, Solomon Tandeng, *Journey to the Unknown*. Yaounde: S.T. Muna Foundation, 2012.

Mveng, Engelbert, *Histoire du Cameroun*. Paris: Présence Africaine, 1963.

Ngoh, Victor Julius, *Constitutional Developments in Southern Cameroons*. Yaounde: Pioneer Publishers, 1990.

Robinson, Kenneth, *The Dilemmas of Trusteeship*. London: OUP, 1965.

Ronen, Dov., *The Quest for Self-Determination*. New Haven, Yale University Press, 1979.

Rubin, N., *Cameroon: An African Federation*. London: Pall Mall Press, 1971.

Sady, Emil J., *The United Nations and Dependent Peoples*. Washington D.C.: Brookings Institute, 1965.

Schwarzenback, Edmund, "Cameroon Experiment in Federation." *Swiss Review of World Affairs*, Zurich, May 1968.

Southern Cameroons, *Record: Conference on the Constitutional Future of the Southern Cameroons, Foumban, July 1961*. Buea: Government Printer, 1961.

United Nations, *General Assembly. Official Records, Fourth (Trusteeship) Committee*. By Session up to 1962. New York.

Trusteeship Council Official Records. By Session up to 1962.

Wildstrand, Carl (ed.) *African Boundary Problems*. Uppsala: 1969.

Wood, Robert S., *France in the World Community*. Leiden: A.W. Sijthoff, 1973.

APPENDIX I

TRUSTEESHIP AGREEMENT FOR THE TERRITORY OF THE CAMEROONS UNDER BRITISH ADMINISTRATION

Whereas the Territory known as the Cameroons under British Mandate and hereinafter referred to as the Territory has been administered in accordance with Article 22 of the Covenant of the League of Nations under a mandate conferred on His Britannic Majesty; and Whereas Article 75 of the United Nations Charter, signed at San Francisco on 26 June 1945, provides for the establishment of an International Trusteeship System for the administration and supervision of such territories as may be placed thereunder by subsequent individual agreements; and Whereas, under Article 77 of the said Charter, the International Trusteeship System may be applied to territories now held under mandate; and Whereas His Majesty has indicated the desire to place the Territory under the said International Trusteeship System; and Whereas, in accordance with Articles 75 and 77 of the said Charter, the placing of a territory under the International Trusteeship System is to be effected by means of a trusteeship agreement, Now, therefore, the General Assembly of the United Nations hereby resolves to approve the following terms of trusteeship for the Territory.

ARTICLE 1

The Territory to which this Agreement applies comprises that part of the Cameroons lying to the west of the boundary defined by the Franco-British Declaration of 10 July 1919, and more exactly defined in the Declaration made by the Governor of the Colony and Protectorate of Nigeria and the Governor of the Cameroons under French mandate which was confirmed by the exchange of Notes between His Majesty's Government in the United Kingdom and the French Government of 9 January 1931. This line may, however, be slightly modified by mutual agreement between His Majesty's Government and the Government of the French Republic where an examination of the localities shows that it is desirable in the interests of the inhabitants.

ARTICLE 2

His Majesty is hereby designated as Administering Authority for the Territory, the responsibility for the administration of which will be undertaken by His Majesty's Government' in the United Kingdom of Great Britain and Northern Ireland.

ARTICLE 3

The Administering Authority undertakes to administer the Territory in such a manner as to achieve the basic objectives of the International Trusteeship System laid down in Article 76 of the United Nations Charter. The Administering Authority further undertakes to collaborate fully with the General Assembly of the United Nations and the Trusteeship Council in the discharge of all their functions as defined in Article 87 of the United Nations Charter, and to facilitate any periodic visits to the Territory which they may deem necessary, at times to be agreed upon with the Administering Authority.

ARTICLE 4

The Administering Authority shall be responsible: (a) for the peace, order, good government and defence of the Territory and (b) for ensuring that it shall play its part in the maintenance of international peace and security.

ARTICLE 5

For the above-mentioned purposes and for all purposes of this Agreement, as may be necessary the Administering Authority:

    a). Shall have full powers of legislation, administration and jurisdiction in the Territory and shall administer it in accordance with the Authority's own laws as an integral part of its territory with such modification as may be required by local conditions and subject to the provisions of the United Nations Charter and of this Agreement;

    b). Shall be entitled to constitute the Territory into a custom, fiscal or administrative union or federation with adjacent territories under its sovereignty or control, and to establish common services between such territories and the Territory where such measures are not inconsistent with the basic objectives of the International Trusteeship System and with the terms of this Agreement;

c). And shall be entitled to establish naval, military and air bases, to erect fortifications, to station and employ its own forces in the Territory and to take all such other measures as are in its opinion necessary for the defence of the Territory and for ensuring that it plays its part in the maintenance of international peace and security. To this end the Administering Authority may make use of volunteer forces, facilities and assistance from the Territory in carrying out the obligations towards the Security Council undertaken in this regard by the Administering Authority, as well as for local defence and the maintenance of law and order within the Territory.

ARTICLE 6

The Administering Authority shall promote the development of free political institutions suited to the Territory. To this end the Administering Authority shall assure to the inhabitants of the Territory a progressively increasing share in the administrative and other services of the Territory; shall develop the participation of the inhabitants of the Territory in advisory and legislative bodies and in the government of the Territory, both central and local, as may be appropriate to the particular circumstances of the Territory and its people; and shall take all other appropriate measures with a view to the political advancement of the inhabitants of the Territory in accordance with Article 76[b] of the United Nations Charter. In considering the measures to be taken under this Article the Administering Authority shall, in the interests of the inhabitants, have special regard to the provisions of article 5[a] of this Agreement.

ARTICLE 7

The Administering Authority undertakes to apply in the Territory the provisions of any international conventions and recommendations already existing or hereafter drawn up by the United Nations or by the specialized agencies referred to in Article 57 of the Charter, which may be appropriate to the particular circumstances of the Territory, and which would conduce to the achievement of the basic objectives of the International Trusteeship System.

ARTICLE 8

In framing laws relating to the holding or transfer of land and natural resources, the Administering Authority shall take into consideration native laws and customs, and shall respect the rights and safeguard the interests, both present and future, of the native population. No native land or natural resources may be transferred except between natives, save with the previous consent of the competent public authority. No real rights over native land or natural resources in favor of non-natives may be created except with the same consent.

ARTICLE 9

Subject to the provisions of article 10 of this Agreement, the Administering Authority shall take all necessary steps to ensure equal treatment in social, economic, industrial and commercial matters for all Members of the United Nations and their nationals and to this end:

a). Shall ensure the same rights to all nationals of Members of the United Nations as to its own nationals in respect of entry into and residence in the Territory, freedom of transit and navigation, including freedom of transit and navigation by air, acquisition of property both movable and immovable, the protection of persons and property and the exercise of professions and trades;

b). Shall not discriminate on grounds of nationality against nationals of any Member of the United Nations in matters relating to the grant of concessions for the development of the natural resources of the Territory, and shall not grant concessions having the character of a general monopoly.

c). Shall ensure equal treatment in the administration of justice to the nationals of all Members of the United Nations.

The rights conferred by this article on nationals of Members of the United Nations apply equally to companies and associations controlled by such nationals and organized in accordance with the law of any Member of the United Nations.

ARTICLE 10

Measures taken to give effect to article 9 of this Agreement shall be subject always to the overriding duty of the Administering Authority in accordance with Article 76 of the United Nations Charter to promote the political, economic, social and educational advancement of the inhabitants of the Territory, to carry out the other basic objectives of the International Trusteeship System, and to maintain peace, order and good government. The Administering Authority shall in particular be free:

a). To organize essential public services and works on such terms and conditions as it thinks just;

b). To create monopolies of a purely fiscal character in order to provide the Territory with the fiscal resources which seem best suited to local requirements, or otherwise to serve the interests of the inhabitants of the Territory;

c). Where the interests of the economic advancement of the inhabitants of the Territory may require it, to establish or permit to be established, for specific purposes, other monopolies or undertakings having in them an element of monopoly, under conditions of proper public control; provided that, in the selection of agencies to carry out the purposes of this paragraph, other than agencies controlled by the Government or those in which the Government participates, the Administering Authority shall not discriminate on grounds of nationality against Members of the United Nations or their nationals.

ARTICLE 11

Nothing in this Agreement shall entitle any Member of the United Nations to claim for itself or for its nationals, companies and associations, the benefits of article 9 of this Agreement in any respect in which it does not give to the inhabitants, companies and associations of the Territory equality of treatment with the nationals, companies and associations of the State which it treats most favorably.

ARTICLE 12

The Administering Authority shall, as may be appropriate to the circumstances of the Territory, continue and extend a general system of elementary education designed to abolish illiteracy and to facilitate the vocational and cultural advancement of the population, child and adult, and shall similarly provide such facilities as may prove desirable and practicable in the interest of the inhabitants for qualified students to receive secondary and higher education, including professional training.

ARTICLE 13

The Administering Authority shall ensure, in the Territory, complete freedom of conscience and, so far as is consistent with the requirements of public order and morality, freedom of religious teaching and the free exercise of all forms of worship. Subject to the provisions of article 8 of this Agreement and the local law, missionaries who are nationals of Members of the United Nations shall be free to enter the Territory and to travel and reside therein, to acquire and possess property, to erect religious buildings and to open schools and hospitals in the Territory. The provisions of this article shall not, however, affect the right and duty of the Administering Authority to exercise such control as he may consider necessary for the maintenance of peace, order and good government and for the educational advancement of the inhabitants of the Territory, and to take all measures required for such control.

ARTICLE 14

Subject only to the requirements of public order, the Administering Authority shall guarantee to the inhabitants of the Territory freedom of speech, of the press, of assembly and of petition.

ARTICLE 15

The Administering Authority may arrange for the co-operation of the Territory in any regional advisory commission, regional technical organization, or other voluntary association of states, any specialized international bodies, public or private, or other forms of international activity not inconsistent with the United Nations Charter.

ARTICLE 16

The Administering Authority shall make to the General Assembly of the United Nations an annual report on the basis of a questionnaire drawn up by the Trusteeship Council in accordance with Article 88 of the United Nations Charter. Such reports shall include information concerning the measures taken to give effect to suggestions and recommendations of the General Assembly and the Trusteeship Council. The Administering Authority shall designate an accredited representative to be present at the sessions of the Trusteeship Council at which the reports of the Administering Authority with regard to the Territory are considered.

ARTICLE 17

Nothing in this Agreement shall affect the right of the Administering Authority to propose, at any future date, the amendment of this Agreement for the purpose of designating the whole or part of the territory as a strategic area or for any other purpose not inconsistent with the basic objectives of the International Trusteeship System.

ARTICLE 18

The terms of this Agreement shall not be altered or amended except as provided in Article 79 and Article 83 or 85, as the case may be, of the United Nations Charter.

ARTICLE 19

If any dispute whatever should arise between the Administering Authority and another Member of the United Nations relating to the interpretation or application of the provisions of this Agreement, such dispute, if it cannot be settled by negotiation or other means, shall be submitted to the International Court of Justice, provided for in Chapter XIV of the United Nations Charter.

APPENDIX II

United Nations General Assembly Resolution 1350 [XIII] of 13 March 1959: The Future of the Trust Territory of the Cameroons under United Kingdom Administration

The General Assembly

Recalling its Resolution 1282 [XIII] of 5 December 1958 requesting the Trusteeship Council to examine, as early as possible during the twenty-third session, the reports of the United Nations Visiting Mission to Trust Territories in West Africa, 1958, on the Cameroons under French Administration and the Cameroons under United Kingdom Administration, and to transmit them, with its observations and recommendations, to the General Assembly not later than 20 February 1959, to enable the Assembly, in consultation with the Administering Authorities to take the necessary measures in connection with the full attainment of the objectives of the Trusteeship System.

Having examined, in consultation with the Administering Authority, the special report of the Trusteeship Council, as well as the report of the Visiting Mission on the Cameroons under United Kingdom Administration;

Noting the statements made in the Fourth Committee by the representatives of the Administering Authority, and by the Premier of the Southern Cameroons, by the Leader of the Opposition of the Southern Cameroons House of Assembly, and by the leader of the Northern Cameroons Affairs in the Government of the Northern Region of Nigeria;

1). Recommends that the Administering Authority, in pursuance of Article 76b of the Charter of the United Nations, take steps, in consultation with a United Nations Plebiscite Commissioner, to organize, under the supervision of the United Nations, separate plebiscites in the northern and southern parts of the Cameroons under United Kingdom Administration, in order to ascertain the wishes of the inhabitants of the Territory concerning their future;

2). Recommends further that in the northern part of the Territory the plebiscite should take place about the middle of November 1959, that the people of the northern part of the Territory should be asked:

"(a) Do you wish the Northern part of Cameroon to be part of the Northern Region of Nigeria when the Federation of Nigeria becomes independent?" or

"(b) Are you in favor of deciding the future of the Northern Cameroons at a later date?"

and that the plebiscite should be conducted on the basis of the electoral register at present being compiled for the elections to the Federal House of Representatives;

3). Recommends further that the plebiscite in the southern part of the Territory should be conducted during the next dry season between the beginning of December 1959 and the end of April 1960;

4). Decides that the two alternatives to be put to the southern part of the Territory and the qualifications for voting in the plebiscite there should be considered by the General Assembly at its fourteenth session;

5). Expresses the hope that all concerned in the territory will endeavour to reach agreement before the opening of the fourteenth session of the General Assembly on the alternatives to be put in the plebiscite in the Southern Cameroons and the qualifications for voting in it;

6). Decides to appoint a United Nations Plebiscite Commissioner who shall exercise, on behalf of the General Assembly, all the necessary powers and functions of supervision, and who shall be assisted by observers and staff to be appointed by the Secretary General in consultation with him;

7). Requests the United Nations Plebiscite Commissioner to submit to the Trusteeship Council a report in two parts on the organization, conduct and results of the plebiscites, the first part of the report, which shall deal with the northern part of the Territory, to be submitted in time for transmission to the General Assembly for consideration before the end of its fourteenth session;

8). Requests the Trusteeship Council to transmit to it the reports of the United Nations Plebiscite Commissioner, together with any recommendations and observations it considers necessary.

794th plenary meeting,
13 March 1959

1). Official Records of the General Assembly, Thirteenth Session, Annexes, Agenda Item 13. Document A/4094.
2). Official Records of the Trusteeship Council, Twenty-third Session, Supplement No. 2 [T/1440].
3). See Official Records of the General Assembly, Thirteenth Session, Fourth Committee. 846th, 847th, 849th and 850th meetings.

APPENDIX III

A/C.4/414 30 September 1959
Fourteenth session of the General Assembly of the United Nations
FOURTH COMMITTEE Agenda Item 41

THE FUTURE OF THE TRUST TERRITORY OF THE CAMEROONS UNDER UNITED KINGDOM ADMINISTRATION

Agreed statement by Mr. John Foncha, Premier of the Southern Cameroons and Dr. E.M.L. Endeley, Leader of the Opposition in the Southern Cameroons House of Assembly

Coming back to the United Nations after six months, we, the elected leaders of the government and political parties of the Southern Cameroons House of Assembly, have been greatly encouraged, as we were at the resumed thirteenth session, by the friendly interest of delegations and their concern for the welfare of our people. We for our part are anxious, by reaching agreement among ourselves as to the next step to be taken, to help the work of the Fourth Committee and still more important to promote the future well-being of our people.

We have had the advantage of discussions with the representatives of African Member States in the United Nations, whose sympathy and help we greatly appreciate, and with our colleagues in the United Kingdom delegation, who share with us the task of interpreting to the United Nations the wishes and aspirations of the people of the Southern Cameroons.

We are both of us of course anxious that the Southern Cameroons should attain independence as early as circumstances permit in the form most suited to its circumstances and the wishes of the people. But, since the parties represented in the House of Assembly were not able to agree during the recent discussions in the Southern Cameroons on the arrangements for a plebiscite in 1960, we think that it will be wiser to defer consultation with the people for the time being.

Subject therefore to the agreement of the General Assembly, we are

203

agreed as follows:

1). There should be no plebiscite in the Southern Cameroons in 1960.

2). Pending settlement of its future, the Southern Cameroons should continue to be administered under the present Trusteeship Agreement, but separately from Nigeria. We understand that the United Kingdom would be prepared to continue to administer it on this basis.

3). The separation of the administration of the Southern Cameroons from that of the Federation of Nigeria should be completed not later than the date on which the Federation of Nigeria becomes independent.

4). The Administering Authority, in consultation with the Government and Legislature of the Southern Cameroons, should take steps to complete the separation of the administration of the Southern Cameroons from that of the Federation of Nigeria not later than 1 October 1960, the date on which the Federation of Nigeria becomes independent.

5). The Administering Authority, in co-operation with the Government and people of the Southern Cameroons, should work towards the achievement of the objectives of the Trusteeship System in accordance with Article 76 [b] of the Charter.

6). In the light of the above we suggest that the General Assembly should decide to consider this question not later than its sixteenth session with a view to ascertaining the wishes of the people of the Territory in 1962 as to their future.

7). We should be agreeable if the General Assembly should recommend that, in agreement with the Administering Authority, the Trusteeship Agreement should be terminated not later than 26 October 1962, in accordance with Article 76 of the United Nations Charter.

APPENDIX IV

United Nations General Assembly Resolution 1352[XIV]of 16 October 1959:

The future of the Trust Territory of Cameroons under the United Kingdom Administration: organization of the Plebiscite in the southern part of the Territory

The General Assembly,

Recalling its Resolution 1350[XIII] of 13 March 1959 concerning the future of the Trust Territory of the Cameroons under United Kingdom Administration, which expressed the hope that all concerned in the Territory would endeavor to reach agreement before the opening of the fourteenth session of the General Assembly on the alternatives to be put in the plebiscite in the Southern Cameroons and the qualifications for voting in it,

Noting the statements made by the representative of the Administering Authority, by the Premier of the Southern Cameroons and by the Leader of the Opposition in the Southern Cameroons House of Assembly to the effect that no agreement was reached before the fourteenth session of the General Assembly as to the alternatives to be put in the plebiscite and the qualifications for voting in it, and that a postponement of the plebiscite in the Southern Cameroons to a later date will help to establish more favorable conditions for ascertaining the freely expressed wishes of the population,

Noting the opinions expressed during the debate on this question at the fourteenth session of the General Assembly,

Noting the statements made by the Premier of the Southern Cameroons and by the Leader of the Opposition in the Southern Cameroons House of Assembly at the 898th meeting of the Committee on 7 October 1959,

1). Decides that the arrangements for the plebiscite referred to in General Assembly resolution 1350[XIII] shall begin on 30 September 1960, and that the plebiscite shall be concluded not later than March 1961

2). Recommends that the two questions to be put at the plebiscite should be

"(a) Do you wish to achieve independence by joining the independent Federation of Nigeria?

"(b) Do you wish to achieve independence by joining the independent Republic of Cameroun?"

3). Recommends that only persons born in the Southern Cameroons or one of whose parents was born in the Southern Cameroons should vote in the plebiscite;

4). Recommends that the Administering Authority, in consultation with the government of the Southern Cameroons, take steps to implement the separation of the administration of the Southern Cameroons from that of the Federation of Nigeria not later than 1 October 1960.

829th the plenary meeting
16 October 1959.

APPENDIX V

United Nations General Assembly Resolution 1473[XIV] of 12 December 1959:
The future of the Trust Territory of the Cameroons under United Kingdom Administration: organization of a further plebiscite in the northern part of the Territory

The General Assembly,

Recalling its Resolution 1350[XIII] of 13 March 1959, concerning the future of the Trust Territory of the Cameroons under United Kingdom Administration, which recommended that a plebiscite should take place in the Northern Cameroons in November 1959 and requested the United Nations Plebiscite Commissioner to submit to the Trusteeship Council in time for consideration by the General Assembly at its fourteenth session a report on the organization, conduct and result of this plebiscite,

Having examined the report of the United Nations Plebiscite Commissioner and the report of the Trusteeship Council thereon,

Noting from the report of the United Nations Plebiscite Commissioner that the people of the Northern Cameroons have decided by a substantial majority that they are in favor of deciding their future at a later date,

Noting further that the United Nations Plebiscite Commissioner is satisfied that the plebiscite was conducted in a fair and impartial manner,

Noting the statement by the representative of the Administering Authority at the 988th meeting of the Fourth Committee on 5 December 1959 to the effect that urgent action is being taken to introduce reforms in the system of local administration in the Northern Cameroons,

Having heard the petitioner,

Considering that the extremely close date of the election to the Legislative Assembly of the Federation of Nigeria makes it impossible for

the General Assembly to take a decision with regard to the participation
or nonparticipation of the people of the Northern Cameroons in these
elections,

1). Expresses its high appreciation of the work of the United Nations
Plebiscite Commissioner and the United Nations Staff under his
direction.

2). Recommends that the Administering Authority, in pursuance
of Article 76[b] of the Charter of the United Nations and in
consultation with the United Nations Plebiscite Commissioner,
organize under United Nations supervision a further plebiscite
in the Northern Cameroons, the arrangements for which shall
begin on 30 September 1960, and that the plebiscite be conducted
not later than March 1961.

3). Decides that the two questions to be put at this plebiscite should
be:

"(a) Do you wish to achieve independence by joining the independent Republic of Cameroun?

"(b) Do you wish to achieve independence by joining the independent Federation of Nigeria";

4). Recommends that the plebiscite be conducted on the basis of
universal adult suffrage, all those over the age of twenty-one and
ordinarily resident in the Northern Cameroons being qualified
to vote:

5). Requests the United Nations Plebiscite Commissioner to report
to the Trusteeship Council on the organization, conduct and
results of this plebiscite, in order that the Council may transmit
its report to the General Assembly together with any recommendations and observations he considers necessary.

6). Recommends that the necessary measures should be taken
without delay for the further decentralization of governmental
functions and the effective democratization of the system of local
government in the northern part of the Trust Territory.

7). Requests that the Administering Authority should initiate without

delay the separation of the administration of the Northern
Cameroons from that of Nigeria and that this process should be
completed by 1 October 1960.

8). Requests the Administering Authority to report on the process of
separation to the Trusteeship Council at its twenty-sixth session
and requests the Council to submit a report on this matter to the
General Assembly at its fifteenth session.

9). Declares that the participation of the Northern Cameroons in
the elections to the Federal Legislative Assembly should in no
way interfere with or influence the free choice of the people of
the Northern Cameroons in deciding their future in the forthcoming plebiscite.

857th plenary meeting,
12 December 1959.

APPENDIX VI

United Nations General Assembly Resolution 1608 (XV) of 21 April 1961
The future of the Trust Territory of the Cameroons under United Kingdom
Administration

The General Assembly,

Recalling its resolution 1350 (XIII) of 13 March 1959 concerning the future of the Trust Territory of the Cameroons under United Kingdom administration in which the General Assembly recommended, *inter alia*, that the Administering Authority take steps, in consultation with the United Nations Plebiscite Commissioner for the Cameroons under United Kingdom administration, to organize, under the supervision of the United Nations, separate plebiscites in the northern and southern parts of the Cameroons under United Kingdom administration, in order to ascertain the wishes of the inhabitants of the Territory concerning their future, and that the plebiscite in the Northern Cameroons be held about the middle of November 1959 on the basis of two questions set out in paragraph 2 of the said resolution,

Recalling its resolution 1352 (XIV) of 16 October 1959 whereby it decided, *inter alia*, that a plebiscite in the Southern Cameroons would be held between 30 September 1960 and March 1961, on the basis of the two questions set forth in paragraph 2 of the said resolution,

Recalling further its resolution 1473 (XIV) of 12 December 1959 in which the General Assembly, having considered the results of the plebiscite in the northern part of the Cameroons under United Kingdom administration, recommended the organization by the Administering Authority, in consultation with the United Nations Plebiscite Commissioner, of a further plebiscite to be held in the Northern Cameroons under United Nations supervision between 30 September 1960 and March 1961, on the basis of the two questions defined in paragraph 3 of the said resolution,

Having examined the report of the United Nations Plebiscite Commissioner concerning the two plebiscites held in the Northern and the Southern Cameroons in February 1961and the report of the Trusteeship Council thereon,

Having heard the petitioners,

1. *Expresses its high appreciation* of the work of the United Nations Plebiscite Commissioner for the Cameroons under United Kingdom Administration and his staff;

2. *Endorses* the results the results of the plebiscites that:
   (a) The people of the Northern Cameroons have, by a substantial majority, decided to achieve independence by joining the independent Federation of Nigeria;
   (b) The people of the Southern Cameroons have similarly decided to achieve independence by joining the independent Republic of Cameroun;

3. *Considers that* the people of the two parts of the Trust Territory having freely and secretly expressed their wishes with regard to their respective futures in accordance with General Assembly resolutions 1352 (XIV) and 1473 (XIV), the decisions made by them through democratic processes under the supervision of the United Nations should be immediately implemented;

4. *Decides* that the plebiscites having been taken separately with differing results, the Trusteeship Agreement of 13 December 1946 concerning the Cameroons under United Kingdom administration shall be terminated, in accordance with Article 76b of the Charter of the United Nations and in agreement with the Administering Authority, in the following manner:
   (a) With respect to the Northern Cameroons, on 1 June 1961, upon its joining the Federation of Nigeria as a separate province of the Northern Region of Nigeria;
   (b) With respect to the Southern Cameroons, on 1 October 1961, upon its joining the Republic of Cameroun;

5. Invites the Administering Authority, the Government of the Southern Cameroons and the Republic of Cameroun to initiate urgent discussions with a view to finalizing, before 1 October 1961, the

arrangements by which the agreed and declared policies of the parties concerned will be implemented.

994th plenary meeting,
21 April 1961.

Index

condominium 9
Congo 9, 14, 64, 76, 97
Cross River 176

Day of National Mourning 173
decolonization 1, 2, 4, 5, 64, 65, 66, 74,
    79, 80, 81, 83, 84, 85, 106, 169
de Gaulle, Charles 74, 75, 76, 77, 96,
    107, 108, 168, 191
Dibonge, J. K. 25, 26
Dikwa Emirate 21
Dikwa Native Authorities 94
Dixon, J. 52
Dobell, Major General 8
Douala 7, 8, 9, 10, 129, 130, 159, 169,
    176
    Douala Chamber of Commerce 130
Dring, Sir John 42

East Cameroon 125, 129, 131, 132,
    133, 134, 136, 141, 142, 157,
    158, 159, 160, 168
Eastern Region of Nigeria 20, 183, 187
East-West dichotomy 83
economic relations
    Anglo-Cameroon trade 128, 129
    British Overseas Trade Board 129
    Cameroon-Nigeria Trade vi, 130
    Commercial and Economic Cooper-
        ation Agreement 128
    exports 129, 130, 131, 132, 133, 139,
        140
    French markets 131, 132
    imports 129, 130, 131, 134
    industrial plantations 134
Efiom, W.N.O. 47
Ekoi 175, 176
Emir
    of Dikwa 29, 30
Emir of Sokoto 95
Endeley, Dr. E.M.L. 23, 24, 25, 26, 27,
    28, 29, 45, 48, 50, 53, 72, 102,
    103, 150, 188, 189, 203

Enonchong, Henry 156
Equatorial Africa 7, 9, 78, 107, 130
Ethiopia 82
Etoungou, Nko'o 183
European Economic Community xi
exports
    bananas 129, 132, 139, 140, 141, 142
    oil 130, 133, 177
    raw materials 130

Federal Constitution 154, 156, 159
Fernando Po 169
First Northern Cameroons Plebiscite
    v, vii, 40, 43
First World War 1, 3, 8, 15, 18, 73, 175
Foncha, John Ngu 27, 28, 29, 46, 47,
    48, 49, 52, 53, 65, 70, 72, 102,
    103, 104, 126, 143, 149, 150,
    151, 152, 153, 154, 155, 156,
    157, 161, 162, 167, 168, 189, 203
Fonlon, Bernard 160
foreign aid 134
Foumban 125, 126, 152, 155, 156, 160,
    162, 163, 191
Foumban Conference 155, 160, 162
Fourth Committee of the General
    Assembly 65
France 3, 7, 8, 9, 13, 14, 15, 16, 45, 61,
    64, 74, 75, 76, 77, 78, 96, 98, 99,
    101, 104, 105, 106, 107, 108,
    109, 111, 128, 130, 131, 132,
    141, 142, 165, 168, 169, 171,
    173, 183, 189, 191
Franco-African solidarity 75
Franco-British condominium 9
Franco-British Declaration 10, 13, 15,
    73, 193
Franco-British rivalry 140
franc zone 131, 132, 134
Frankel, Joseph 65
French Foreign Ministry 76
French West Indies 132

INDEX

By the same Author

- The Bali Chamba of Cameroon
- The Making of a Fondom
- Foreign Interest in the British Cameroons Plebiscites
- A History of Bali Nyonga